J. M. Coetzee and the Archive

J. M. Coetzee and the Archive

Fiction, Theory, and Autobiography

Edited by
Marc Farrant, Kai Easton and Hermann Wittenberg

BLOOMSBURY ACADEMIC
LONDON • NEW YORK • OXFORD • NEW DELHI • SYDNEY

BLOOMSBURY ACADEMIC
Bloomsbury Publishing Plc
50 Bedford Square, London, WC1B 3DP, UK
1385 Broadway, New York, NY 10018, USA
29 Earlsfort Terrace, Dublin 2, Ireland

BLOOMSBURY, BLOOMSBURY ACADEMIC and the Diana logo are
trademarks of Bloomsbury Publishing Plc

First published in Great Britain 2021
This paperback edition published 2022

Copyright © Marc Farrant, Kai Easton, Hermann Wittenberg and contributors, 2021

Marc Farrant, Kai Easton, Hermann Wittenberg and contributors, 2021 have asserted
their right under the Copyright, Designs and Patents Act, 1988, to be identified as
Authors of this work.

For legal purposes the Acknowledgements on p. xii constitute an extension
of this copyright page.

Cover design: Namkwan Cho
Cover image © Kai Easton

All rights reserved. No part of this publication may be reproduced or
transmitted in any form or by any means, electronic or mechanical,
including photocopying, recording, or any information storage or retrieval
system, without prior permission in writing from the publishers.

Bloomsbury Publishing Plc does not have any control over, or responsibility for, any
third-party websites referred to or in this book. All internet addresses given in this
book were correct at the time of going to press. The author and publisher regret any
inconvenience caused if addresses have changed or sites have ceased to exist, but can
accept no responsibility for any such changes.

A catalogue record for this book is available from the British Library.

A catalog record for this book is available from the Library of Congress.

ISBN: HB: 978-1-3501-6595-3
PB: 978-1-3502-3044-6
ePDF: 978-1-3501-6596-0
eBook: 978-1-3501-6597-7

Typeset by Newgen KnowledgeWorks Pvt. Ltd., Chennai, India

To find out more about our authors and books visit www.bloomsbury.com
and sign up for our newsletters.

Contents

List of Figures vii
List of Tables viii
Notes on Contributors ix
Acknowledgements xii

Introduction: Fiction, theory and autobiography *Kai Easton, Marc Farrant and Hermann Wittenberg* 1

Part One Authorship and autre-biography 15

1 Landmarks: Reading Coetzee's maternal lines *Kai Easton* 17

2 *Summertime* sadness: Coetzee, coordinates and the negation of the archive *Shaun Irlam* 29

3 On the loss of fathers and letters: Reading *Summertime* and *The Childhood of Jesus* alongside Jacques Derrida's *Archive Fever* *Valeria Mosca* 43

Part Two History, politics and the archive 57

4 Writing, politics, position: Coetzee and Gordimer in the archive *Andrew van der Vlies* 59

5 Out of the dark chamber: Violence and desire in the textual history of *Waiting for the Barbarians* *Hermann Wittenberg* 77

Part Three Archival methods: Practice, data, process 93

6 'Humming with fear of sincerity and fabulator': First observations from the Coetzee Corpus and the Coetzee Bot *Peter Johnston* 95

7 Coetzee, the archive and practice research: On reflection *Michael Cawood Green* 117

Part Four On literary objects: Form and style in the archive — 131

8 Archival realism: *Elizabeth Costello*, *Disgrace* and the realm of revision *David Isaacs* — 133

9 In pursuit of style: Coetzee reading Beckett in the archive *Paul Stewart* — 149

Part Five Philosophy and the archive: Between life and truth — 161

10 'The aura of truth': Coetzee's archive, realism and the problem of literary authority *Marc Farrant* — 163

11 Coetzee, biopolitics and the archive of impersonality *Richard A. Barney* — 179

12 Shades of the archive: J. M. Coetzee, the paradox of poetic sovereignty and the lives of literary beings *Russell Samolsky* — 197

Part Six Conversations with Coetzee — 211

13 *Waiting for the Barbarians* and the origins of *Incoming* Richard Mosse — 213

14 Curating Coetzee: From Austin to Adelaide *Jennifer Rutherford* — 219

15 34° South *Kai Easton* — 225

Index — 233

Figures

1.1	Farm, Langkloof	18
1.2	Vera Wehmeyer (front, centre in white dress) and siblings (from left to right: Roland, Winnie, Ellen), *c*.1905	20
1.3	Dark blue photo album, July 1942. 'Street photo'. 'Snap of Mother taken by John, 16 July 1942'. 'In grounds of Rossmere School' (Johannesburg)	22
1.4	'Mr Scott who came from Scotland' and other scenes, from the album, 'Photographs: Ancient and Modern'	23
1.5	'Car', 'Ford', undated farm memoir, Vera Wehmeyer Coetzee	26
2.1	24, Parker Ave, Buffalo, NY	31
6.1	Unique words and text length (correlation of 0.37)	100
6.2	Spareness and text length (correlation of 0.79)	101
6.3	Average sentence length and text length (correlation of −0.72)	101
6.4	Spareness and year (increase of 0.0521 unique words per word per year)	102
6.5	Average sentence length and year (decrease of 0.083 words per year)	102
6.6	Unique words and text length	104
6.7	Unique words and text length, novels between 40,000 and 100,000 words	105
6.8	Spareness and average sentence length	106
14.1	Installing *Traverses: J. M. Coetzee in the World*	220
15.1	Welcome to the Western Cape, Route 62	226
15.2	Entrance to Avontuur	227
15.3	At the gate of Diepkloof	228
15.4	South Africa–Australia T20 International at Newlands	229
15.5	Cape Town Cycle Tour 2020	230
15.6	Kalk Bay fisherman with bicycle	231
15.7	Cape of Good Hope	expect delays	232

Tables

6.1	Corpus data	99
6.2	Sketch difference for woman/man	109
6.3	Sketch difference for black/white	110
6.4	Sketch difference for good/bad	110
6.5	Example values for a simplified instance of the Coetzee Bot process	113

Contributors

Editors

Marc Farrant is a lecturer in English Literature at the University of Amsterdam. He completed his PhD at the University of London, Goldsmiths College, on Samuel Beckett and J. M. Coetzee. He has published widely in academic journals such as *The Journal of Modern Literature*, *Critique: Studies in Contemporary Fiction*, *Samuel Beckett Today/Aujourd'hui*, *The Cambridge Humanities Review* and *Textual Practice*. The archival research for his contribution to this volume was supported by an International Placement fellowship by the UK Arts and Humanities Research Council in 2015.

Kai Easton is Senior Lecturer in English at SOAS University of London. She was one of the first scholars to access Coetzee's archival materials at Houghton Library, Harvard University, in the late 1990s. She is co-curator (with David Attwell) of the international travelling exhibition, *Scenes from the South* (2020), to mark Coetzee's eightieth birthday, in collaboration with Amazwi South African Museum of Literature and the Harry Ransom Center, University of Texas at Austin. She is also engaged in an essay film project, *Roads of France*, on Coetzee's 'poetics of cycling', in collaboration with Rick Barney and John Coetzee. Recent work includes co-editing (with Derek Attridge), *Zoë Wicomb and the Translocal* (2017) and guest curating the exhibition, *Navigating the War*, on the archives of the legendary British navigator and single-handed sailor, Michael Richey. She has previously taught at the universities of Sussex and Rhodes and was an Andrew W. Mellon postdoctoral fellow in English at the University of KwaZulu-Natal. She has twice been awarded research fellowships at the Harry Ransom Center (2014; 2018).

Hermann Wittenberg is Professor of English at the University of the Western Cape, South Africa. He has worked extensively on South African literature, and has published several archival studies on Khoi narratives and on the work of J. M. Coetzee and Alan Paton. His edited books include Paton's *Lost City of the Kalahari* travelogue (2005) and J. M. Coetzee's *Two Screenplays* (2014). He has strong interests in the intersection of literature, film and photography, and has co-curated the *J.M. Coetzee: Photographs from Boyhood* exhibition in the UK, South Africa and Australia (2017–20). A photobook of the same title was published under his editorship in 2020, marking Coetzee's eightieth birthday.

Contributors

Richard A. Barney is Associate Professor of English at the University at Albany, SUNY, and specializes in eighteenth-century philosophy and literature, critical theory and film. His publications include *Plots of Enlightenment: Education and the Novel in Eighteenth-Century England* (1999), and numerous articles and book chapters. Most recently, he has written on J. M. Coetzee in relation to animals and biopolitics for *Textual Practice* (2016), and has co-edited *Systems of Life: Biopolitics, Economics, and Literature on the Cusp of Modernity* (2018).

Michael Cawood Green is Professor in English and Creative Writing at Northumbria University and Fellow of the University of KwaZulu-Natal. He is the author (as Michael Green) of *Novel Histories: Past, Present, and Future in South African Fiction*, and of numerous journal articles and book chapters. He is co-founder and chair of the interdisciplinary Northumbria Practice Research Group and, as Michael Cawood Green, has published three works of historical fiction: *Sinking: A Verse Novella*; *For the Sake of Silence* (awarded the Olive Schreiner Prize for Prose); and, most recently, *The Ghosting of Anne Armstrong* (a practice-led output of a UK Arts and Humanities Research Council Fellowship).

David Isaacs has recently completed a PhD at University College London on revision and twentieth-century authorship entitled 'Second Thoughts: Revision, Anxiety, Ethics', which he is now turning into a book. He is at the beginning stages of a new project: a monograph about the present tense.

Shaun Irlam is Associate Professor in the Department of Comparative Literature at the University at Buffalo, SUNY. His teaching and research interests include eighteenth-century cultural studies in England and France, critical theory, and, especially, postcolonial literature and theory – with emphasis on Caribbean and African literature, including J. M. Coetzee. His publications include *Elations: The Poetics of Enthusiasm in Eighteenth-Century Britain* (1999).

Peter Johnston is Group Manager for English at Cambridge Assessment International Education, a department of the University of Cambridge. He completed his PhD in 2013 at Royal Holloway, University of London, on the resonances between J. M. Coetzee's lifelong engagement with mathematics and his practice as a novelist, critic and poet. In line with his continuing research in the field, Johnston has since published reviews and articles exploring the interface between literature and mathematics, while also acting as co-chair of the Cambridge Refugee Support Committee.

Valeria Mosca recently attained a PhD in Comparative Literature from the University of Genoa. Her work on monological and dialogical tendencies in J. M. Coetzee's fiction also includes the essay 'Ideas and Embodied Souls: J.M. Coetzee's Platonic and Christian Intertexts in *Elizabeth Costello* and *The Childhood of Jesus*' (*European Journal of English Studies*, 2016).

Richard Mosse is an acclaimed Irish conceptual documentary photographer and visual artist. His international exhibition *Incoming* – discussed in his contribution to this volume – was curated at the Barbican Art Gallery, London, in 2017, and has since been shown in France and the United States of America. His film *The Enclave*, made with Trevor Tweeten, was released in 2013; other recent exhibitions include *Beyond Here Lies Nothin'* (Philadelphia, 2018) and *The Castle* (La Coruña, Spain, 2018).

Jennifer Rutherford is Director of the J.M. Coetzee Centre for Creative Practice and Professor of Sociology and Literature in the School of Humanities at the University of Adelaide, Australia. She is the curator of the first exhibition of Coetzee's archives at the University of South Australia in 2014, in tandem with the international conference, *Traverses: J. M. Coetzee in the World*.

Russell Samolsky is Associate Professor of English at the University of California, Santa Barbara. He is author of *Apocalyptic Futures: Marked Bodies and the Violence of the Text in Kafka, Conrad, and Coetzee* (2011) as well as a number of articles and book chapters. The archival research for his contribution to this volume was supported by a Harry Ransom Center fellowship in 2017.

Paul Stewart is Professor of Literature at the University of Nicosia. He is the author of two books on Beckett – *Sex and Aesthetics in Samuel Beckett's Works* (2011) and *Zone of Evaporation: Samuel Beckett's Disjunctions* (2006) – and is the series editor for Samuel Beckett in Company, published by Ibidem Press. His work on Coetzee includes 'Samuel Beckett and J.M. Coetzee: Narrative Power and the Postcolonial' in the collection *Vernacular Worlds, Cosmopolitan Imagination* (2015).

Andrew van der Vlies is Professor of Contemporary Literature and Postcolonial Studies at Queen Mary University of London, and Extraordinary Professor at the University of the Western Cape. He has published widely on South African literatures, print and visual cultures, and is author, most recently, of *Present Imperfect: Contemporary South African Writing* (2017), editor of *Race, Nation, Translation: South African Essays, 1990–2013*, by Zoë Wicomb (2018), and co-editor of *South African Writing in Transition* (2019). He is co-editor of the forthcoming *Bloomsbury Handbook to J. M. Coetzee* and has held a Mellon Foundation Research Fellowship to work on the Coetzee Papers at the Harry Ransom Center in 2015.

Acknowledgements

As editors we would like to acknowledge and thank the many scholars working in the field of J. M. Coetzee's fiction. Their ideas, suggestions, papers and conversations at various conferences and seminars have helped to shape this book. We are especially grateful to Carrol Clarkson for her invaluable feedback. We are also indebted to the publishing staff at Bloomsbury Academic who have guided the process to publication with patience.

Marc Farrant would like to acknowledge the UK Arts and Humanities Research Council for generously supporting the research that contributed to the inception of this book with an International Placement Scheme Fellowship, which enabled him to visit Coetzee's archive, in Austin, Texas, in 2015. Kai Easton would like to thank the Harry Ransom Center for two research fellowships (in 2014; 2018). We express our gratitude to the HRC, the Amazwi South African Museum of Literature and the Research Office at SOAS, who have made this work, and our concurrent exhibition on Coetzee's archives, possible. We would also like to acknowledge the generous support of CHASE (Consortium of the Humanities and the Arts, South-East England) for providing the resources to host a 2017 conference that inspired this book at Senate House in central London. In addition, we are grateful to all the delegates who participated, especially those who travelled from afar, and to J. M. Coetzee for his participation, support and permission to reproduce and quote from archival material.

Hermann Wittenberg acknowledges the research and material support of the National Research Foundation of South Africa, the Research Office of the University of the Western Cape and a Newton Advanced grant awarded by the British Academy.

Introduction: Fiction, theory and autobiography

Kai Easton, Marc Farrant and Hermann Wittenberg

> ... I have been through the letters and diaries. What Coetzee writes there cannot be trusted, not as a factual record – not because he was a liar but because he was a fictioneer.
>
> Coetzee, *Summertime* (2009: 225; italics in original)

The epigraph, taken from J. M. Coetzee's third fictionalized memoir, *Summertime* (2009), speaks to that most ancient of problems: the link between text and reality, art and truth. As the first dedicated collection of essays on the archival questions raised by Coetzee's work, this volume explores and plays with the tensions between his role as a 'fictioneer' and the idea of the archival 'factual record'. The book looks at Coetzee's interest in archival questions as a point of departure, and several contributions in the volume explore the materials from the substantial manuscript collections that have become available with the acquisition of the 'J.M. Coetzee Papers' by the Harry Ransom Center at the University of Texas.[1] This acquired collection, together with Coetzee materials donated over the years to the Amazwi South African Museum of Literature (formerly the National English Literary Museum) in Makhanda (formerly Grahamstown), South Africa, comprise, in their scale and ambition, one of the most comprehensive and rich archival records of any living author, and this book represents a cross-section of scholarly attempts to read these records in relation to the author's published fictions. Not only do these archival collections help to illuminate Coetzee's authorship, but the specificity of the Coetzee archive itself raises wider questions addressed in this book about research and methodology: how do critics, historians, artists and readers approach and utilize manuscript materials, artefacts, photographs and multimedia sources? This book thereby intervenes in contemporary critical debates that are animating the field, including those around notions of critique, historicism, the empirical method and the digital humanities.

Following the historian Antoinette Burton, who defines archives as 'traces of the past collected either intentionally or haphazardly as "evidence"' (2005: 3), several contributions to this book probe how Coetzee's archives provide 'evidence' of authorship or autobiography, of rootedness in facts or actual geographies. What is gained or lost for the reader by looking back from the published work to seeing it stalled or in flow, or the wrestling with words captured at the time in notes or drafts? How do artefacts and objects, correspondence and photographs, ancestral archives – all traces of the past – suggest new ways to think about autobiography: as a dynamic, elusive authorship that feeds into the fiction, even as we read this retrospectively – an afterlife that is contemporaneous with a writing life still very much being lived, with work still being produced at a steady rate? The archive too, like the ever-growing published oeuvre, is not static, but is continuously evolving – shaped not only by institutional interventions but also by Coetzee's own ongoing curatorial management of the records of a 'life in writing', to cite the title of David Attwell's seminal investigation of the Texas collection.

The epigraph to our introductory essay is not arbitrarily chosen, but opens up questions about Coetzee's authorship, and anticipates the growing biographical interest in his writing career. In *Summertime*, Coetzee has wittily tested and entertained his readers by creating a British biographer – just a step ahead of the first actual biography to be written on him by the Afrikaans biographer, John Kannemeyer. We know little about Coetzee's fictional biographer except that his name is Mr Vincent, and he is grappling with the legacy of his subject – the 'late' novelist 'John Coetzee'. What has happened is that Vincent's author, J. M. Coetzee, has cast us forward in time, to that impossible moment when the great author is no longer around, no longer the author of himself, and someone takes over the story of his life, focusing here on the period of the 1970s. One of the intriguing questions which poses itself here is why this timeframe is significant. This is of course the seminal period when Coetzee published his first novels: *Dusklands* (1974) and *In the Heart of the Country* (1977). The fictional Vincent is taking us back to that decade when Coetzee is finding his feet as a writer, before his breakthrough novel *Waiting for the Barbarians* in 1980.

Summertime is an extraordinary final volume of the trilogy that would become *Scenes from Provincial Life,* and its reflections on authorship, archives and origins provide the guiding spirit of this book. By inscribing the archive at the heart of the literary enterprise itself, *Summertime* asks questions about both the archival and the autobiographical enterprise in the making of fiction; it also, of course, asks us to look at this the other way around, posing questions about the fictional nature of the archival and autobiographical enterprise.

1. The archival turn

Coetzee scholarship is only beginning to engage itself with the archival questions generated by the fictions themselves, and by the two substantive manuscript collections in Texas and South Africa. This interest is fairly recent in Coetzee studies, and to properly gauge the major shift that has occurred in criticism, it is important to trace the history of these archival events and the critical turn that they have enabled.

Two key events have had a major impact on Coetzee scholarship with the potential to reshape our understanding of the work and throw new light on an extraordinary literary career. Both are archival events, curiously coinciding temporally at the end of 2011, but unfolding on different continents, and they have shifted Coetzee scholarship into an entirely new direction – a direction in which this book is one of many steps to follow. The first event was J. C. Kannemeyer's completion of his long-awaited biography, which was eventually published posthumously a year later as *J.M. Coetzee: A Life in Writing* (2012). Although not a formally authorized biography, Kannemeyer's monumental work had been supported and facilitated by Coetzee. The book is a landmark event, which places 'Coetzee scholarship on a completely different footing', notes David Attwell, himself a foremost Coetzee scholar (in Kannemeyer 2012). Kannemeyer had been given unprecedented access to Coetzee's archive: private papers, manuscripts, personal and business letters, emails, photographs, collections of press cuttings and reviews, and a substantial volume of unpublished material, including juvenilia. His access to Coetzee's papers was augmented by several hours of recorded interviews with the author. Coetzee, moreover, also gave Kannemeyer his blessing to interview friends, colleagues and acquaintances, many of whom would otherwise have been reluctant to share insights and personal archival material such as correspondence and photographs.

Kannemeyer's biography is significant in two senses. Firstly, Coetzee had for long remained an enigmatic author who shunned publicity, and successfully kept his private life out of the public domain. Coetzee, as is well known, often declined to accept prizes in person, and gave interviews rarely. Kannemeyer's ability to piece together a detailed and candid account of Coetzee's life is thus especially remarkable, given the privacy of his subject. Secondly, the sheer scale of the project makes available a huge amount of significant information that would otherwise not have been readily accessible, making the book the definitive account of Coetzee's life and his writing career. Kannemeyer's biography is itself an archival project, and in his preface he makes his enterprise clear: to illuminate 'the life story of this writer' (2012: 10) rather than focus on biographical details for their own sake. Despite the extensive digging that Kannemeyer undertook into Coetzee's life and archival records, he was not interested in writing a 'psychological study of the man J.M. Coetzee' (2012: 14); thereby acknowledging the limits of the factual record and a material archive to tell us something about the inner life of the artist.

The second major event in Coetzee scholarship – happening in parallel to the Kannemeyer biography project – was the acquisition of the Coetzee papers by the University of Texas's Harry Ransom Center (HRC), publicly announced in October 2011. The HRC reportedly paid $1.5 million for the substantial collection, which included a deal for future materials to be added in time to come (Vertunu 2011). At the core of the collection are the multiple manuscript versions of the thirteen novels, ranging from early handwritten drafts and typescripts to corrected proofs, giving an unprecedented insight into Coetzee's creative process. There is, furthermore, much material that records Coetzee's literary and creative activity, including private diaries (on restricted access), handwritten notes, press clippings and research material. The archive also contains a large volume of correspondence, including incoming and outgoing letters between Coetzee and publishers, editors, academics, writers, filmmakers and scholars. There is also much personal, family and career-related information ranging from early school reports and family photographs to job applications and award certificates. The materials allow researchers to track Coetzee's personal life, creative practice and literary career in fine detail. The archive fills 140 document boxes, 13 oversize boxes and 1 galley file, as well as hundreds of computer disks; and, in view of the sheer volume of materials and the apparent completeness of records up to the date of deposit, it is difficult to overstate their significance for scholarship.

On the face of it, the collection appears to be a record of everything Coetzee ever wrote: from primary school essays to undergraduate research notes and prize-acceptance speeches, and in the crucial novel manuscripts each day's writing is meticulously dated, allowing a fine-grained insight into the development of the narratives. Compared to the papers and archival collections of other authors, which are often characterized by gaps, missing documentation, lack of dating and incomplete records, Coetzee has kept a seemingly complete and detailed record of his own creative career. The extent and scale of the documentation may not be unique on the literary scene, but certainly for no other major modern author, approaching the stature of Coetzee (including the other eight Nobel laureates represented at the HRC), are there comparably extensive archives. The richness of the HRC archive is a consequence of Coetzee's own meticulous archival practice in which nearly every aspect of his literary career has been documented and dated.

The HRC's Coetzee archive was first partially opened to researchers in 2012, giving initial access to a limited number of early manuscript drafts that ranged from the debut novel *Dusklands* to *Boyhood*. But these materials were only available early because of a lesser-known prehistory to the HRC's archive since these comprise manuscripts that Coetzee had deposited previously, first on 31 March 1995, and which were catalogued in boxes and folders at Harvard University's Houghton Library. This date comes from the library's internal file, as transcribed in typed pages of notes taken over a series of visits by Kai Easton between 1998 and 2009 (Easton 2000; 2006). Unlike the acquisition by the HRC in 2011, there was no public announcement that accompanied the arrival of the Coetzee materials at Houghton Library. Since the material was available to researchers for over 15 years, including well after he received a second Booker Prize and a Nobel Prize, it is surprising that so little attention was paid to this archive before its move to Texas. The semi-secret prehistory of Coetzee's archive provokes a consideration of its origins, and even earlier antecedent archives: where were the works written, drafted, published, otherwise housed before they were institutionalized? Where, in other words, do archives 'begin' and 'end', and where might they take us?

The Texas archive, together with the Amazwi collection, opens up new and different paths of scholarship that has for the most part been influenced by the theoretical paradigms of post-structuralism and postcolonial studies. We propose that there are three significant sets of questions that emerge from the archive, which are now likely to impact on the field of Coetzee Studies. Firstly, the archival materials richly illuminate the specific South African context of Coetzee's writings, which are seen to emerge from Coetzee's personal and professional embeddedness even at their most abstract (this is the central thesis behind Attwell's study). Secondly, the academic context that lies at the heart of Coetzee's fictions is made more visible. Coetzee's academic career as a literary scholar not only provided a source of inspiration and ideas, but the university (both as an idea and as institution, specifically the University of Cape Town) is at the centre of Coetzee's political commitments and intellectual engagements. Although in the public imagination Coetzee will always be most well known as a novelist, his more recent publications over the last five years reveal a continuing commitment to non-fiction.

Together with earlier books such as *White Writing: On the Culture of Letters in South Africa* (1988) and *Giving Offense: Essays on Censorship* (1996), there is more recently a strong commitment to non-fiction, and these works draw from his career as a university teacher and researcher. Books such as *The Good Story: Exchanges on Truth, Fiction and Psychotherapy* (2015) and *Late Essays: 2006–2017* (2017) might seem to diverge from the most recent novels, but the archive helps to elucidate their hidden connections and crossovers. In other words, the archive is a means to explore the vital relation between the creative and the critical. Thirdly, the archive now also reveals the rich intersections that arise between Coetzee's novels, and other artistic media and discursive forms. Coetzee's well-known interests in philosophy, history, psychoanalysis and other fields of study are complemented by a critical and creative engagement with music, photography, film and other media. Coetzee's ventures into scriptwriting and opera, and his collaborations with visual artists, choreographers, film directors and theatre producers, allow us to see his authorship extend beyond the prose forms for which he has received public recognition. In these archival records, Coetzee emerges as a more complete artist.

These three propositions, all turning on the inextricability of life and work, largely underpin the first major archival study of the Ransom Center collection: David Attwell's 2015 *J.M. Coetzee and the Life of Writing: Face to Face with Time*. Attwell's expression, 'the life of writing', thus subtly modifies Kannemeyer's 'life in writing', and this modification would seem to cater to the kind of pre-emptive moves that occlude the task of biography in *Summertime*. Whereas *Summertime* makes the biographical ideal of isolating the man beneath the works unattainable, Attwell instead proceeds to isolate the 'the authorship' (2015: 18) rather than the author. The product is a successful compositional biography of the life of the works themselves – an account of the creative process as one thoroughly informed by the writer's life. Attwell thereby painstakingly discloses the 'autobiographical-metafictional' (2015: 145) quality of the oeuvre as a whole. For Attwell, therefore, 'we continue to read biographically, not in order to limit the truth of the work to its biographical sources, but in order to understand how the self is written into the work and then written out, leaving its imprint as a shadowy presence' (2015: 27). Such questions about the uneasy and complex relationship between the fictional and the biographical are brought into focus by the archival records. As Andrew Dean, in a recent essay has argued, the archive may inadvertently draw readers away from the rich and continuing open-endedness of the work itself towards singular interpretations and closure:

> The risk with the archive is that it will move critics away from richly speculative responses to powerful writing, and draw scholars instead into a labyrinth of authorial motivation and biographical resonance. There may be certain intellectual satisfactions with such endeavours, but they ultimately do not respond to what has motivated the scholarship in the first place: the public and private significance of the fictions.
>
> (2020: 232)

This critical and questioning approach to the archive is underpinned by Jacques Derrida's seminal meditation, *Archive Fever* (1996), which begins with an etymological investigation of the twin meanings of the Greek word *arkhē*, both as a 'commencement' and 'commandment'. The first meaning points to the idea of the archive as a place of origin, where things begin – in this case the putative beginnings of Coetzee's fictions and authorial trajectory. The other meaning of the term, 'commandment', points to the troubling idea of the archive as a place of law, command or hermeneutical authority. Derrida's essay questions or deconstructs such limiting notions of origins and ultimate authority. Instead, he regards the archive as 'a place of consignation' (1996: 11), not just as a site where texts are deposited and kept, but also, as one commentator notes, a 'gathering together of signs, *con-sign-ation* ... in which all elements refer to the larger unity of the parts' (Suchak 2018: 62). In this sense then, the archive is not an original place of 'commencement' which marks the place where Coetzee's fictional works supposedly began, nor is it a site of 'commandment' which institutes incontestable, authoritative interpretations of the work. Rather, the archive is a part of a larger body of signs, both published and in manuscript form, which work together, and sometimes against each other, giving us a larger, complex and more interwoven sense of Coetzee's writing.

This volume takes its lead from such a proposition, but extends this argument with readings that both creatively and critically explore Coetzee's work – as in the case of the artist Richard Mosse, where the published work – not the archives – of *Waiting for the Barbarians* has left its imprint on Mosse's own project *Incoming*. Mosse exemplifies the ways in which we might look at questions of authorship and archives more reciprocally. What is the mutual dynamic? How is the archive written *into* and *out of* the final works? If the archive points to the works, how do the works point to the archive?

2. Volatile archives

That Coetzee is a living and working author, and that the archive is, moreover, to a large extent *authored* by him, raises a series of fascinating problems. For example, since Coetzee continues to publish new works, and is likely to contribute manuscript material to the collection in future, this is an open-ended, evolving archive. We also need to consider that some personal materials remain embargoed and may only become available in a distant future, with a possible destabilizing effect on prior scholarship. As Jan Wilm argues in an essay: 'Epistemologically, it can be a complicated endeavour to research archival material by a living writer: the temporal distance traditionally thought to be conducive to rigorous philological analysis is still lacking' (2017: 215). More alarmingly, as Wilm points, the sociological-institutional pressure to swiftly find 'the novel nugget for hermeneutic explanation may easily turn into a race for positivistic extirpation in a climate of growing academic competition and precariousness' (2017: 215). This assessment situates the 'archival turn' in contemporary literary studies, which this book is both concerned with and a part of, as symptomatic of a larger turn towards positivism, and ultimately quantifiable methods.

In the case of Coetzee's dynamic archive, one cannot help but be struck by the irony involved in a positivist approach to excavating knowledge. As Wilm writes, Coetzee's archive constitutes a '*Vorlass*' rather than a '*Nachlass*' (2017: 217) – the standard German designation for the papers and materials one leaves behind *after* death. This unfinished status of the archive is matched by the unfinished status of the oeuvre as a whole, as Coetzee continues to write. This sense of incompletion not only thwarts the epistemophilic impulse of the literary historian, but runs parallel to Coetzee's understanding of writing itself as that which cannot be pinned down to a single origin, context or authority: 'Writing writes us. Writing shows or creates (and we are not always sure we can tell one from the other) what our desire was, a moment ago' (1992: 18). Coetzee's later commentaries on writing can be seen as an extension of the arguments first proposed in his 1969 doctoral thesis, 'The English Fiction of Samuel Beckett: An Essay in Stylistic Analysis'. Coetzee's early unpublished academic work on Beckett (in the fields of structuralist linguistics and quantitative stylistics) sustains an incisive critique of positivism that warns against the reduction of a literary work to any quantifiable or linear foundation of meaning. This challenge to a model of linear causality, of surface and depth, challenges us to refuse the binary opposition between the unruly depth of archive materials juxtaposed with the surface-level polish of the published works. Not only, therefore, might Coetzee's writings problematize conventional archival or historicist methods, but the incompleteness and curated form of the archive itself further stages how the literary demarcates a modality of truth in opposition to what Coetzee terms, in *Doubling the Point*, mere 'truth to fact' (1992: 17). In other words, the archive bears witness to the implicit challenge to the idea that literature might count as 'evidence' at all. The archive, like the works, begs the question: where is the *thing itself*? This opens up a way of conceiving the archive as a work *and* the works as a form of archive.

This possibility of a doubled reading is in keeping with what Coetzee terms 'literary thinking' (2016: 1151); a form of thought that refuses the fallacy of pure objectivity and the reduction of knowledge to binarism, including the binary of surface and depth. Wilm uses the suggestive analogy of a compost heap, a sense of the archive as doubled or mixed up, neither merely a secret depth nor alternative surface: 'the material is always both: rubbish and humus' (222). By avoiding the simplistic hierarchization often involved when approaching archives, this volume proposes to follow in Coetzee's own dialogical footsteps. Derrida perhaps offers a model for such thinking, where he contrasts 'the rigor of the concept' with 'the vagueness or the open imprecision' of the 'impression' (1996: 29). This formulation would seem to be approximate to both Coetzee's sense of literary thinking and to the imperative outlined in *Doubling the Point* to 'evoke/invoke [the] countervoices' (1992: 65) in one's own discourse.

Writing in the *London Review of Books*, Thomas Meaney recounts his experience of visiting the Coetzee archive in Texas and reading through Coetzee's notebooks. He is disappointed: 'They don't lead you to the work; they are scattered chickenfeed for those foolish enough to come pecking in Texas' (2015). There is something ironic about this assessment, as if the archive exists in isolation from the works; an author's archive without an author of its own. The works themselves, and especially *Summertime*, challenge the implicit hierarchy in Meaney's commentary; that the archival materials are a mere substrate to the actually significant published works. As with Coetzee's notion of '*autre*-biography' (1992: 394), which undermines the conventional privileging of life over writing, this volume challenges the conventional privileging of work over archive.

This, of course, means challenging the conventional understanding of the archive: as a deep but static source of empirically verifiable facts and materials that underpins the dynamic surface of the published works. The archive itself is dynamic, not just as a body of texts and materials that change their meaning over time, but also subject to additions, reconstitutions and shifting contextualizations.

3. Theory and method in the archive

It is in light of the complex nature of both Coetzee's oeuvre and his archive that the contributions included in *J. M. Coetzee and the Archive* are inspired by a vein of methodological self-reflection. Indeed, this collection as a whole suggests that Coetzee scholarship is in a state of flux that presents opportunities for new departures. This volume presents the Coetzee archive as a large, interwoven text that comprises a mix of genres and forms, and several of the contributions herein take this as inspiration to offer creative interventions that break the bounds of the conventional academic essay (notably those of Michael Cawood Green and Kai Easton, both outlined in more detail below). Tantalizing questions open up that not only allow us to trace the genealogy of the novels, but also explore their hypertextuality, alternative storylines, development of characters and embryonic novels that were never realized. As a consequence, it seems that the hitherto dominant hermeneutic paradigms in Coetzee scholarship may tilt in energizing ways towards criticism that is more strongly informed by biographical, archival and book historical considerations. This is in sharp contrast to Coetzee's earliest commentators. Indeed, the first academic work published on Coetzee (Teresa Dovey's *The Novels of J.M. Coetzee: Lacanian Allegories*, 1988) focused on his early novels and their relation to psychoanalysis. Since then, literary studies has turned increasingly away from what is perceived, in some quarters, as a 'hermeneutics of suspicion'. Taking this term from the work of Paul Ricoeur, Rita Felski defines this as a 'mode of militant reading' (2015: 1) that deprivileges the work itself in order to lay bare the hidden layers of ideological bias of which the work is seen to be a symptom.

In this current climate of what Felski and Anker term as the 'method wars' (2017: 2), Coetzee's archive is, therefore, perhaps uniquely interesting as a site where current shifts in literary studies are made visible. Notably, this critique of critique runs parallel to Antoinette Burton's critique of positivist historicism. This is somewhat ironic given that, in the literary field, historiography is often set in opposition to critical theory. Yet both are seen as ensnared by a will to identify, whether that means to diagnose the underlying or unconscious condition of the work or to find the biographical Coetzee lurking beneath. This will to identify the forever elusive 'real' authorial identity underneath the work is precisely what Derrida terms 'archive fever', a troubled search for ever-elusive truths and origins that is perhaps more clearly referenced by the original French term *mal d'archive*. For Derrida, this condition of 'archive fever' involves a mad restlessness of 'searching for the archive right where it slips away. It is to run after the archive, even if there's too much of it, right where something in it anarchives itself. It is to have a compulsive, repetitive, and nostalgic desire for the archive, an irrepressible desire to return to the origin, a homesickness, a nostalgia for the return to the most archaic place of absolute commencement' (1996: 91).

As we have suggested above, and as is explored throughout this volume, Coetzee's writings are marked all the time by a resistance to closure and singular truth that redoubles as a resistance to origins. This resistance to closure, which here also marks the resistance to singular biographical origins, implicitly warns against the allegorical enclosure of symptomatic readings, whether historical or archival.

One of the routes out of this conundrum is the re-emergence of interest in methods of empirical investigation, such as genetic criticism (see, for example, Chapter 8 by David Isaacs). Genetic criticism has its roots in structuralist and post-structuralist accounts of textuality which privilege an equality between the work and its *avant-texte* (those materials that precede the finished work, including notes and other documents from the writing process). Despite the protean possibilities for genetic investigations into a hitherto submerged archival realm, there remains a danger that a genetic method risks reinstating a restrictive notion of authorial intention. As Nicola Evans warns: 'genetic criticism can also be construed as resurrecting the authority of the author through its focus on the author's intentions and strategies as these are revealed in the working notes' (2015: 220). By lending an interpretative weight to these materials, perhaps swept away by their novelty, the archival scholar risks undermining the hard-won standard of critical distance from the author. Indeed, Coetzee's archive can be seen to incite a contemporary textual scholarship that draws upon a hierarchy of surface and depth. In Coetzee's larger creative project, where the published novels are akin to the visible part of icebergs, the multiple manuscript versions with their numerous dead-ends, revisions and rewritings reveal a hitherto unknown, submerged fictional world. Such metaphors privilege the notion of archival depth, and are complicit with a tendency in literary studies to valorize, what Burton calls, a 'new kind of sacral character' (2005: 5) of the archive.

More importantly, by affording this submerged realm the truth status of empirical evidence the archival scholar is likely to miss the dynamic potential of attending to this material in its own right; a not insignificant factor given the creative exuberance and acts of self-distancing in many of Coetzee's own notes and drafts. This is reminiscent of what the anthropologist Ann Laura Stoler terms 'reading along the archival grain'. Discussing her research of colonial archives, Stoler notes the tendency to read against the grain of colonial discourse to unearth the ideological biases beneath. Instead, she asserts 'a commitment to a less assured and perhaps more humble stance – to explore the grain with care and read along it first' (2009: 50). This volume is also wary of the ways in which archives can be used to reduce the meaning of a work to a point of origin or a single truth. Instead, we hope to encourage self-reflective, critical and creative engagements with both Coetzee's published fictions and the diverse archives in dispersed collections, which together give us insight into the extraordinary and creative complexity of Coetzee's work. Moving in and out of the manuscripts and books themselves, exploring archival ideas and ancestral archives, thinking visually as well as digitally, the contributors in this volume demonstrate the multiple ways in which to follow in Coetzee's own dialogical footsteps – imprints of which are scattered across the archive.

4. Overview

J. M. Coetzee and the Archive: Fiction, Theory and Autobiography comprises fifteen chapters, arranged in six parts, that address questions of fictionality, authority, autobiography and authorship, and consider how Coetzee's self-archiving of both his manuscripts and his ancestral archives have their fictional counterparts in his published work. We can see traces and correspondences as we look back and forth, deliberately or accidentally, between the materiality of the 'work' (in the Barthesian sense) and the textual tracks of composition. But how do we critically navigate a 'critique of origins' with the 'fever' and fascination of engaging with 'original' materials? Or – if not 'original' materials, with archival questions and biographical questions – with the archive, in a wider sense, as an idea?

The book begins with a 'critique of origins' that is creative in concept. Opening with a visual travelogue through Coetzee's ancestral archives, Kai Easton explores his maternal lines with a series of actual journeys (Chapter 1). The inspiration is an undated farm memoir by Coetzee's mother, Vera Wehmeyer Coetzee. To date, most critical and biographical work has focussed on Coetzee's paternal lines, such as the ones we read in and around *Dusklands* or, later, with reference to the beloved Karoo farm of Voëlfontein that features so strongly in the fictionalized memoirs, and which is now so visually present in the newly discovered images taken by Coetzee in the 1950s – recently exhibited and reproduced in *Photographs from Boyhood*, edited by Hermann Wittenberg (Coetzee 2020). These paternal lines are in fact not very far from his maternal lines. Travelling by mostly gravel road on the R407 from Willowmore, it is some 92 km to Prince Albert.

Part of our interest is in real archives and real places, for these pose questions of the 'truth in autobiography' that has marked Coetzee's work from the beginning. Indeed, paternal lines are investigated in Shaun Irlam's site-inspired reading of the 'origins' of Coetzee's first novel – the *unwritten* story in *Summertime* of the real scene in Buffalo, New York, where, on New Year's Day, 1970, Coetzee wrote that first page of 'The Narrative of Jacobus Coetzee' – a rewriting of an actual eighteenth-century southern African narrative to which J. M. Coetzee is genealogically linked. Chapter 2 by Irlam takes the genesis of *Dusklands* as a moment to think about gaps, omitted scenes: the illuminating archival questions posed not so much by Coetzee's archives in the HRC, but by Coetzee's published fiction *Summertime*, an archive without hierarchies of the real and the fictional. Chapter 3 by Valeria Mosca follows Irlam with a Derridean reading of questions of authorship, fatherhood and authority in *Summertime*, bringing these together with *The Childhood of Jesus* –the first volume of the *Jesus* trilogy that has not yet made its way to the HRC.

Part Two looks at a more dominant decade in the Coetzee canon, when he has developed from the fledgling writer described in the 1970s backdrop of *Summertime* to becoming the most globally recognized English-language South African writer since Nadine Gordimer. Chapters 4 and 5 by Andrew van der Vlies and Hermann Wittenberg, respectively, capture and rethink the impact of 1980s South African history and politics on Coetzee's writing in completely new ways, via meticulously detailed and nuanced readings of the manuscripts and contexts of *Age of Iron* and *Waiting for the Barbarians*. Complementing David Attwell's work, their readings of the archives lead to further questions about state violence and political activism in light of the ethical and moral dilemmas Coetzee was facing as he wrote. There are real-life figures whose lives enter these early manuscripts and notebooks. Van der Vlies pursues a draft of *Age of Iron* in which Mrs Curren is speaking to Florence about this writer from Johannesburg, Nadine Gordimer, while Hermann Wittenberg takes a page from Coetzee's notebook which references Steve Biko. He reads *Waiting for the Barbarians* in the context of South African history in the late 1970s, and in relationship to Coetzee's seminal essay 'Into the Dark Chamber'.

Throughout this volume there is an excavation and re-examination of Coetzee's formative writing, which includes his work as a computer programmer in London in the 1960s, and his doctoral thesis on stylistics and the English fiction of Samuel Beckett when he was a Fulbright scholar at the University of Texas, where his own archives now reside. In Chapter 6, Peter Johnston builds on his own extensive scholarship on Coetzee, and puts his corpus-based research into playful practice by creating a Coetzee Bot – a programme, he says, that 'can be "trained" on specific subsets of Coetzee's writing in order to produce, by means of a stochastic process, sentences that are in some sense characteristically "Coetzeean"' (95). At the core of Chapter 7, by Michael Cawood Green, is the troubling question about what properly counts as 'research', for example, by institutional auditing exercises such as the UK Research Excellence Framework (REF). The unspoken question in Cawood Green's chapter is whether Coetzee's fictional output would have received any substantive recognition in exercises such as the REF. Like Coetzee, Green is a writer-academic, also originally from South Africa, and his contribution mediates the relationship between the creative and the critical by a playful, self-ironizing performance. Both Johnston and Cawood Green offer rigorous and delightful interrogations of archival practice in the making. As Cawood Green notes, 'the archive is an actively produced site of creation and reflection' (126–7).

The question of revision is key to several of the chapters in this volume. Coetzee revises for style, plot, character, form, genre. Characters are abandoned, histories and settings change, the extent to which his work is grounded in the real and the extent to which it engages with questions of realism, evolves too. In Chapter 8 by David Isaacs, the initial inspiration of Coetzee's sentences in *Summertime* leads to an intricate and fascinating genetic reading. Casting a look back at two of the preceding works, *Disgrace* and *Elizabeth Costello*, Isaacs shows how Coetzee 'allows his texts to construct themselves from the doubts, anxieties and obstructions of composition and thus function in such a way as to bring their genetic histories along with them' (134).

The fact that Coetzee's own literary archival research begins with Beckett in Texas offers Paul Stewart and Marc Farrant (Chapters 9 and 10, respectively) another chance to wrestle with questions of authorial control in the archives, and with what Coetzee has himself called, 'the temptations of style' (1992: 43). If Coetzee is trying to get closer to Beckett's 'secret' without trying to get close to Beckett – the author's style, and not the author himself (Beckett won the Nobel Prize in 1969, just a year after Coetzee had completed his thesis on his work and was now teaching at Buffalo) – to what extent does this authorial distancing become compromised by an immersive reading of the author's own notebooks, those material artefacts, bought in France, with incomprehensible scribbles and notes, lists and other markings, combined with the extraordinary work that would become *Watt*, all written during the Second World War, in English, in France, whilst working for the French Resistance?

Stewart and Farrant tease out the philosophical questions that have dominated Coetzee scholarship, particularly since the publication of *Elizabeth Costello* in 2003, in their insightful and eloquent readings of Coetzee and Beckett. Their work is complemented by the chapters of Richard Barney and Russell Samolsky (Chapters 11 and 12, respectively), with further explorations of style, and questions of modernism and impersonality that are so tellingly addressed in Coetzee's own *Youth* (2002). Barney's interest is not material. He is not searching for clues in Coetzee's manuscripts on this occasion, but he is drawing on his extensive work on eighteenth-century archives. In a substantial chapter, he argues for a biopolitical perspective of Coetzee's work, demonstrating that Coetzee's deep engagement with the eighteenth-century archive contains earlier experiments with techniques of conveying impersonality. Samolsky, like several contributors in this volume, is interested in questions of authorial control, and in what Coetzee's self-reflective moments in the archive tell us. His point of departure is a notebook entry from *Life & Times of Michael K* in which Coetzee decides K's mother has to die in Stellenbosch. As Samolsky writes, sometimes Coetzee has to kill characters off – all authors do – to move the story along, or to allow another character to come into their own. Samolsky's interest is in what the notebooks and manuscripts reveal about this tension at the moment of his decision to end a character's life. The archives that track this process, that keep them alive, are, therefore, in a real sense, their afterlives.

We close the book with Part Six, a creative cluster, to bring together 'Conversations with Coetzee': first, as we have already highlighted, Richard Mosse's conference paper which archivally keeps the spontaneity and liveliness of his presentation alive (Chapter 13). Mosse's talk is followed by two forms of curatorial self-reflection. Jennifer Rutherford offers an engaging retrospective account of the first ever exhibition of Coetzee's archives from the HRC which were shown in Adelaide, in November 2014, to mark (a few months early) Coetzee's seventy-fifth birthday (Chapter 14). The exhibition was one of many extraordinary features of an international conference, *Traverses: J. M. Coetzee in the World*. Five years later, in honour of Coetzee's eightieth birthday and inspired by the *Traverses* conference and exhibition, Kai Easton and David Attwell curated the travelling exhibition *Scenes from the South*. A collaboration with Amazwi South African Museum of Literature in Makhanda (formerly Grahamstown) and the Harry Ransom Center at Texas, it is the first exhibition to bring together materials from both collections. Launched on his actual eightieth birthday on 9 February 2020 with a programme of writers and musicians to join in the celebrations, it inspires our closing contribution – *34° South* (Chapter 15). The images here were taken on a journey back from Makhanda to Cape Town, skirting through Coetzee's maternal lines, to that borderline town of Avontuur – a word from Dutch and Afrikaans that translates into English as 'adventure'.

This volume has, of course, its own genealogy and archival 'origins'. Several contributions arose out of a CHASE-funded conference, 'Coetzee & the Archive', convened by Marc Farrant and Kai Easton, held in collaboration with the School of Advanced Study, University of London in October 2017.[2] Through specially commissioned contributions, this book also takes in more recent developments in the archives, and scholarship that concerns itself with the proliferating questions raised by these records and by Coetzee's continually evolving oeuvre.

Notes

1 Hereafter the in-text Harry Ransom Center archival references to the 'Coetzee Papers' are abbreviated in each chapter to 'HRC, CP', followed by the relevant box and folder numbers to allow for easy reference.
2 For material detailing the conference, including video recordings, the reader can turn to these links: https://www.chase.ac.uk/chase-blog1/2018/3/20/coetzee-the-archive-october-5-6th-2017-a-chase-sponsored-international-conference-featuring-jm-coetzee-chasing-the-archives; https://www.chasevle.org.uk/archive-of-training/archive-of-training-2017/chasing-archives/; https://www.chase.ac.uk/chase-blog1/2019/12/2/chasing-the-archive-cartographies-of-the-south.

References

Attwell, D. (2015), *J.M. Coetzee and the Life of Writing: Face to Face with Time*. Oxford: Oxford University Press.
Burton, Antoinette (2005), *Archive Stories: Facts, Fictions, and the Writing of History*. Durham, NC: Duke University Press.
Coetzee, J. M. (1992), *Doubling the Point: Essays and Interviews*, ed. David Attwell. Cambridge, MA: Harvard University Press.
Coetzee, J. M. (2009), *Summertime*. London: Harvill Secker.
Coetzee, J. M. (2016), 'On Literary Thinking', *Textual Practice*, 30 (7): 1151–2.
Coetzee, J. M. (2020), *Photographs from Boyhood*, ed. Hermann Wittenberg. Pretoria: Protea.
Dean, Andrew (2020), 'Lives and Archives'. In: Jarad Zimbler, ed., *The Cambridge Companion to J.M. Coetzee*. Cambridge: Cambridge University Press, 221–33.
Derrida, Jacques (1996), *Archive Fever: A Freudian Impression*, trans. Eric Prenowitz. Chicago: University of Chicago Press.
Easton, Kai (2000), 'Textuality and the Land: Reading "White Writing" and the Fiction of J. M. Coetzee'. PhD thesis, SOAS, University of London.
Easton, Kai (2006), 'Coetzee, the Cape and the Question of History', *Scrutiny2*, 11 (1): 5–21.
Evans, Nicola (2015), 'Inside the Writer's Room, the Artist's Studio and Flaubert's Parrot'. In: Guy Davidson and Nicola Evans, eds, *Literary Careers in the Modern Era*. Houndmills: Palgrave Macmillan, 167–83.
Felski, Rita (2015), *The Limits of Critique*. Chicago: University of Chicago Press.

Felski, Rita, and Elizabeth S. Anker, eds (2017), *Critique & Postcritique*. Durham: Durham University Press.

Kannemeyer, J. C. (2012), *J.M. Coetzee: A Life in Writing*. Melbourne: Scribe Publications.

Meaney, Thomas (2015), 'Coetzee's Diaries', *London Review of Books*, 21 May. Available online: https://www.lrb.co.uk/the-paper/v37/n10/thomas-meaney/short-cuts (accessed 20 February 2020).

Stoler, Ann Laura (2009), *Along the Archival Grain: Epistemic Anxieties and Colonial Common Sense*. Princeton: Princeton University Press.

Suchak, Aakash (2018), 'The Place of Consignation, or Memory and Writing in Derrida's Archive', *Journal of Comparative Literature and Aesthetics*, 41 (1–2) : 55–69.

Vertunu, Jim (2011), 'Texan University Holds JM Coetzee's Past to Ransom', *The Mail and Guardian*, 10 October. Available online: http://mg.co.za/article/2011-10-10-texan-university-holds-jm-coetzees-past-to-ransom (accessed 12 December 2015).

Wilm, Jan (2017), 'The J.M. Coetzee Archive and the Archive in J.M. Coetzee'. In: Patrick Hayes and Jan Wilm, eds, *Beyond the Ancient Quarrel: Literature, Philosophy, and J.M. Coetzee*. Oxford: Oxford University Press, 215–31.

Part One

Authorship and autre-biography

1

Landmarks: Reading Coetzee's maternal lines

Kai Easton

If you do not know where you are, the official agricultural sign for Diepkloof is small and easily missed, but the farm across the road acts as a landmark, with its large white wall and black letters. MEYERSKRAAL.

Meyerskraal is on the left, Diepkloof on the right as you approach from the hamlet of Avontuur near Uniondale in the Western Cape. We are on the R62, on the road west from Joubertina. We are near the Eastern Cape provincial border in the Langkloof and this is where, on 9 February 1904, Vera Hildred Marie Wehmeyer was born.

* * *

Exactly 36 years later, 9 February 1940. On her very own birthday, on a summer's day in Cape Town, Vera gives birth to her first son, John Maxwell Coetzee, at the Mowbray Nursing Home. She has travelled for her confinement all the way from Victoria West in the Great Karoo, where she and Jack (Zacharias) Coetzee first met. She is a schoolteacher, Jack an attorney from the district of Prince Albert. He too was born and raised on a farm. This was in Leeu-Gamka, off today's N1, north of here, in the Koup. The farm was acquired by his father Gert Coetzee (who hailed from the West Coast, from Hopefield and Aurora, inland from Saldanha) in 1916. All over the world, Voëlfontein, the name of this beloved Karoo farm, is now known to readers of *Scenes from Provincial Life* (2011) – the famous trilogy of fictionalized autobiography by the boy, born in 1940 on his mother's birthday, who would become the globally celebrated writer J. M. Coetzee.

* * *

I have seen the green sign for Voëlfontein on the Fraserburg Road: it is nearly a direct line to the farm from the R407, a regional route of some 92 km that connects Prince Albert to Willowmore in the Eastern Cape. This is one of the towns you can easily find today on the N9, where Vera and her schoolmates from Uniondale would sometimes attend or play in sporting events. This is the trans-provincial road (Wes-Kaap/Oos-Kaap) that suddenly comes into focus on my fold-out map. In 2016, I decide to travel with my aunt along the long stretch of gravel road from Willowmore. There are fading bronze signs to nearby destinations, scattered homesteads, some sheep, eventually

Figure 1.1 Farm, Langkloof.
Source: J. M. Coetzee Papers, Box 106.1, Harry Ransom Center.

ostriches. A dog comes running to greet me when I stop for a photograph. The road becomes tarred once you reach Klaarstroom.

The word has been gathering around me. Before I ever actually went there, I had seen this word *Willowmore* in Coetzee's archives. It is in the early drafts of *Age of Iron*, before the novel even had that title. I first read the word *Willowmore* in a place faraway from where these pages were written. From the mid-1990s, Coetzee's literary manuscripts lived at Houghton Library, Harvard University, which I visited between 1998 and 2009. It was only in 2012, after a major acquisition and with the supplement of more than 100 new boxes of additional manuscripts, that they made their way to their new and permanent home – the Harry Ransom Center (HRC) at the University of Texas at Austin, which is also Coetzee's alma mater. He lived here from 1965 to 1968, a doctoral student on a Fulbright scholarship, writing his thesis on Samuel Beckett.

The HRC is right on Guadalupe Street. It is a green and serene setting. Around the entrance, there are succulents landscaped in a square. I stay always on W 35th Street and walk each way, to the HRC and back, no matter the heat. This is through Hemphill Park. There is a creek lining the route. I am in the direction of Hyde Park and Central Market, the scene of Coetzee's essay 'Meat Country' for *Granta* magazine. This is from 1995, a quarter of a century ago, when he was on a return visit to Texas, resident fellow at the Michener Center for Writers, on sabbatical from the University of Cape Town.

When I set off on the road to Willowmore from Cape Town, I am simply curious to follow this word that has taken root in my mind. By chance, at my destination, I find Vera's family name right on my doorstep. My aunt and I are staying in two cottages at the Willowmore Historical Guest House. The address, as it happens, is Wehmeyer Street. At a nearby stop sign, it crosses St John Street.

In my own imagination, the Wehmeyers farmed between Willowmore and Uniondale, and this is where I thought I would find the farm Wolwekraal, a word that is not the same word that I mentioned at the outset: 'Diepkloof'. What has happened? Oude Wolwekraal is said to be the name of Vera Wehmeyer's birthplace. These are the facts I remember from John Kannemeyer's magisterial biography of Coetzee, also in the 2015 critical biography by David Attwell. And then I discover 'Diepkloof' in Stefan Wehmeyer's article in a 2015 issue of the *Cape Librarian*, and he should know because he is related: his grandfather Roland was Vera's brother. He has been kind enough to help me unravel the story further, and tells me that his father, Roland's only son, was raised on this very farm until they moved the family to Stellenbosch. The farm was auctioned off in 1947.

In fiction, we meet the Wehmeyers of Wolwekraal in Dalene Matthee's famous novel, *Fiela se Kind* (1985). I learn that Matthee conceived her novel in the Langkloof, at Belle-Vue, the home of Jimmy Zondagh and his family. Jimmy is a local historian and has recently been featured as 'farmer of the month' in *AgriAbout*, an online South African agricultural magazine. The family network is intricate. The Zondaghs and the Wehmeyers are interrelated, through marriage; settlers in the Cape from Germany, they date back to the eighteenth century.

* * *

Remembering the words of another Roland – '*without adventure, no photograph*' – (Barthes [1981] 2000, 19; italics added), I take the road to Avontuur on my drive back from Makhanda to Cape Town. I have my Leica X. It is 13 February 2020 and I turn off the main road to capture the scene, before stopping in George for the night, after crossing, in the dark, the Outeniqua Mountains. We have just celebrated John Coetzee's eightieth birthday in Makhanda, which used to be Grahamstown, and launched the *Scenes from the South* exhibition at the Amazwi Museum, which in Xhosa means 'voices'. I like this new name for the National English Literary Museum, and I also like this adventurous Dutch name, 'Avontuur' (it seems to follow me everywhere – I have even seen the boat, 'Avontuur IV', in London, on the Thames). On this trip, on the R62, I have crossed from the Eastern Cape to the Western Cape, and there are signs to show for it. I send John three photographs from my dashing visit to his ancestral ground. In exchange, I receive two anecdotes:

> My grandfather Wehmeyer and his neighbour Zondagh used to stand on high points on their respective farms, some kilometres apart, and have shouted conversations. The code was quite abbreviated, according to my mother: one kind of shout meant one thing, another another.
>
> Once, in the 1970s, I wrote off to a Zondagh in Avontuur, sending [a] postal order for R12, and in return received, by rail freight, a 20 kg bag of honeybush tea.
>
> (Coetzee, 24 April 2020; personal email)

How long have the Zondaghs and Wehmeyers lived on this spot, and who else belongs here? Who owns the farm now? How did the grandfather farmer turned road inspector Piet Wehmeyer come to marry Louisa Amalia, the American-born (she is from

Illinois) daughter of Anna and her Polish missionary husband Balthazar du Biel, who first made his way to these southern shores by hitting the hinterland, the borderland of Namaqualand, to work with the man who would become his father-in-law, the Reverend Ferdinand Brecher, whose name is also on a school and also on a street sign in the town of Steinkopf, high up on the N7, just before you reach the Orange River?

I must make this link. This, after all, is the Namaqualand territory we first encounter in Coetzee's first fiction, 'The Narrative of Jacobus Coetzee', in the second half of his 1974 novel, *Dusklands*. This is a fiction, with eighteenth-century archival roots, that is marked by its searing interrogation of colonial history and the complicit expansion of the Coetzees – his paternal lines – in the history of the Cape Colony – north, south, east and west.

* * *

We have read much about his father's family, the Coetzees. Scholars and biographers tend to follow in these fatherly footsteps. But from the routes I have taken, and the scenes that I have seen, this 'father story' is connected – with several twists and turns (the Coetzees and Wehmeyers both lived near mountain passes designed by Thomas Bain on the edges of the Swartberg) – in very real ways with the story of his mother's family. These are geographies that intersect with genealogies: for the marriage of Jack Coetzee and Vera Wehmeyer is not, apparently, the first of the Coetzee-Wehmeyer alliances. According to family historians, if we trace it back, generation by generation, name by name, there is an earlier marriage, descending from the same Gerrit Coetzee, the first generation born in the Colony, son of the progenitor Dirk Coetzee and his wife Sara van

Figure 1.2 Vera Wehmeyer (front, centre in white dress) and siblings (from left to right: Roland, Winnie, Ellen), *c.*1905.
Source: J. M. Coetzee Papers, Box 106_009, Harry Ransom Center.

der Schulp, who arrived from Amsterdam on the ship *Asia* with the Dutch East India Company in 1679. If these records are indeed historically accurate, Jack and Vera share a forefather, but not the same foremother, for Gerrit married twice: first to Susannah Loefke (1703–1751), from whom Jack is descended; then to Anna Johanna van Beulen (1714–1787), from whom Vera is descended, through her father, Piet Wehmeyer.

* * *

Is this how it really all begins?

In my notebook, I write all these names down for the seventh time, trying to work out the different branches of this large family.

> *There is an intermarriage between Catharina Elisabeth Zondagh and Gottlieb Wehmeyer (who also came over with the Dutch East India Company).*
> *They had a daughter, Elisabeth Catherina Wehmeyer who married Gerrit Coetzee (but there are so many of these, it would be easy to mix them up).*
> *This Gerrit is apparently the son of Jacobus Hendrik Coetzee and Susanna Elizabeth Lombard.*
> *Jacobus Hendrik is therefore on Vera's side: the son of the same Gerrit Coetzee (son of Dirk, first generation of the Coetzees in the Cape Colony) and his second wife, Anna van Beulen.*
> *They say, via Leibbrandt [1905: 2], that in 1724:*

Anna van de Caap, Wife of the Burger Jan Jansz van Beulen, mentions that her daughter Anna, 9 years old, is still a slave in the Company's Lodge, asks that she may be manumitted, that she may be better brought up, and offers to give in Exchange a healthy slave, named January of Malabar.

It is this daughter who was freed, and who became Gerrit's second wife.

* * *

If these are initial explorations of Coetzee's 'maternal lines', where do they actually lead us, aside from the fleeting trips I have taken to the Langkloof? Should I not rather be spending my time in the Cape Archives? Where does any of this ephemeral genealogical research on the internet take us when we think about the real thing, the point of origin, the farm itself, where Vera was born, and its traces in her son the Nobel Prizewinner's actual archives at Texas?

The fact is my interest is not only genealogical or geographical or biographical or metaphorical. It is all of these things, but I am using this phrase, in all its connected ways, on a literal level too – in other words, I want to think about maternal and material acts of inscription, lines on the page. Vera Wehmeyer Coetzee has left her own writings about and from this place, which now form part of the public repository of the Coetzee archives at the Harry Ransom Center. As we can see in these once private archives, her presence as a writer and photographer has been captured over and over again in the captions and images of family albums, in her son John Coetzee's own photographs too, from as early as the age of two, in wartime Johannesburg.

Figure 1.3 Dark blue photo album, July 1942, 'Street photo', 'Snap of Mother taken by John, 16 July 1942', 'In grounds of Rossmere School' (Johannesburg).
Source: J. M. Coetzee Papers, Box 106_70, Harry Ransom Center.

It is also thanks to Vera – and we must credit her with co-curating the family archive – that we have so much documentation of John's education: her transcription of his first words and sentences, his reading of maps, his page-turning encounters with Arthur Mee's *Children's Encyclopaedia*, which set the stage for so many later intellectual activities. From as early as the age of eight, he is writing school essays on '*Robinson Crusoe*' and, before long, 'South America'. Thanks to Vera, we have drawings and watercolours, report cards, and notebooks. We have street photographs – sometimes he is wearing a hat – and the images Vera has taken herself with her Kodak Brownie Box camera. It is from Vera that we learn about his earliest years of walking and talking, especially in the blue Exercise Book in which she writes almost daily entries for over a year, before the birth of his younger brother David in Johannesburg on 8 April 1943. There is also the dark blue album with its black pages and white captions. It opens with his birth in 1940 in Cape Town. Since it is dated and captioned geographically, it is a demonstrable record of how the family has to move swiftly in John's first year: first back to Victoria West, then to Warrenton.

His mother documents all of this, including visits back to the Cape Peninsula – his first known trip to the seaside, to Muizenberg, at the age of eleven months; and his first birthday with his mother and Aunt Annie back in Mowbray. We see John and David Coetzee growing up, tree-climbing, sword-fighting, riding bicycles. It is a social history and a family history. All of these pictures are being taken in segregated South Africa before and after the Second World War. Think of the timing: South Africa firmly establishes apartheid as policy, with the victory of D. F. Malan and his Afrikaner Nationalists in 1948, while our aspiring writer John – from an Afrikaans but English-speaking family of Smuts supporters – is a pupil at Rosebank Junior School, spinning off his first sentences, getting glowing reports on his conduct and achievements. He is first in class, 'an outstanding pupil'.

* * *

He loves to page through his mother's albums. …. In her albums he follows her life through the 1920s and 1930s: first the team pictures (hockey, tennis), then the pictures from her tour of Europe.

…

Sometimes they page through the albums together, he and she. She sighs, she says she wishes she could visit Scotland again, see the heather, the bluebells. He thinks: My mother had a life before I was born, and that life still lives in her.

Coetzee, *Scenes from Provincial Life* (2011: 34)

A label is affixed to a red photo book with blue trim on the spine. In blue ballpoint pen over strips of masking tape, his mother has written: 'Photographs: Ancient and Modern'. The Coetzee family photo albums we read about in the epigraph from *Scenes from Provincial Life* are indeed, in real life, as he describes them, and this album is at this point a record of past and present. Multi-authored, both in terms of captions and photographs, we see Vera before she marries; then we see her with Jack and then we see them both with their sons, the next generation. Her family

Figure 1.4 'Mr Scott who came from Scotland' and other scenes, from the album, 'Photographs: Ancient and Modern'.
Source: J. M. Coetzee Papers, Box 106_026, Harry Ransom Center.

photographs and theirs (for the boys also become photographers) begin to merge in these pages. In ink they caption photographs according to their current address – Evremond Road, Milford Road, Avenue Road (where he discovered the music of J. S. Bach), Campground Road (where he began to play Bach on a piano hired by his mother). If you go to Texas yourself, you can see the originals. Some of the pages are in mylar sleeves now – gloves are required and padded velvet holders and special desks.

* * *

...

20 March 1987

If the wagon were to move, if the wheels were to slip and turn, the bed creak, the wagon to roll, you would be left exposed to the sky and the brilliance of the stars, or you would even be crushed by a wheel passing over you, a huge ironshod wheel as tall as yourself. But the wheels are stopped with rocks, the wagon does not roll, you are safe, soon you will be asleep again. You are safe and I am safe. That is how it always is when I say to myself, How did it begin? When I ask, How did it begin? It is always to you I recur, to the little girl under the wagon in the night on the mountain pass, under the wagon that might have begun to roll but did not, that stood firm and still between her and the stars, sheltering her, when it might have failed, and therefore you were, and therefore I am.

HRC, CP, 27. 1: 20-03-1987

Across the top of a blue University of Cape Town exam book, he has written 'Scenes from Provincial Life', in black magic marker. Very soon this writing merges instead with drafts for his sixth novel, *Age of Iron*. Why am I singling it out? It is for this first page, which I have quoted in the extract above – a beautiful first version of a story that is written and rewritten, and that every reader of *Age of Iron* knows through the fictional figure of Mrs Curren.

When he eventually publishes *Boyhood* in 1997, the first volume of what becomes the trilogy *Scenes from Provincial Life*, he is a successful author already. Coetzee knows his audience. He has already won one Booker Prize, for *Life & Times of Michael K* (1983). *Boyhood* opens not in Cape Town but in Reunion Park, Worcester, on 12 Poplar Avenue, where the Coetzee family really did live. Recently, the Breede Valley Municipality has even erected a memorial monument at this address, and has celebrated his eightieth birthday by awarding him the Freedom of the Town.

Kannemeyer speculates that *Age of Iron* borrows from actual stories his mother told them of annual journeys by ox wagon over the mountain pass from Uniondale to Plettenberg Bay: 'We can assume', the biographer writes, 'that this material is biographical' (2012: 444). This would have been the original route, perhaps originally following migratory elephant and antelope tracks. The Prince Alfred's pass, by then long completed, and still the longest accessible original mountain pass in use today, takes you to nearby Knysna. You can approach it on the R339 right from Avontuur, where, as you enter, you will find another large white sign with black lettering, much like the one for Meyerskraal I mentioned when I began this travelogue through Coetzee's ancestral archives. Behind the green sign for Uniondale (the arrow goes to the right) and Knysna (the arrow goes to the left) is this sign, this low wall: MATT ZONDAGH LANDGOED; and below, in smaller lettering: AVONTUUR. You can take a picture of the Zondagh's farm sign on its own, so that it nestles under a distant mountain, almost as if it has always belonged there. This, as we have seen, is one of the landmarks of settlement from Coetzee's mother's own girlhood in the Langkloof on the southernmost tip of Africa, inland from the Indian Ocean.

* * *

because of its being there, the archive becomes something that does away with doubt. ... It is proof that a life truly existed, that something actually happened, an account which can be put together. The final destination of the archive is therefore always situated outside its own materiality, in the story that it makes possible.
Mbembe, 'The Power of the Archive and Its Limits' (2002: 20–1)

Achille Mbembe's contribution to the collection, *Refiguring the Archive* (2002), is a seminal work, and a favourite essay. If he is mostly focussed on state archives and official archives, he nevertheless articulates in this extract the clear link I wish to make to another significant influence: the historian Antoinette Burton, in particular her monograph, *Dwelling in the Archive* (2003), and the edited volume, *Archive Stories* (2006). Together Mbembe and Burton raise questions about archives and architecture, issues of curating, accessibility, censorship, restriction. They bring to light the varying visibility of archives, the dynamic spaces of archival homes.

The Finding Aid at the Harry Ransom Center is publicly available on their website, so that anyone can see the scope of the expansive Coetzee collection. Certain details are provided. For Container 103.4, we have this brief description:

Journal (may contain entries from Zacharias) including loose handwritten correspondence, additional entries, estate documents, and photograph of V. W. Coetzee with baby J. M. Coetzee, 1933–1946.

I order the box of these family papers and take the folder to my desk. I am thinking of Andrew Dean's title, 'Lives and Archives', and where this journey through Coetzee's maternal lines has taken me. In addition to Vera's journal (this is the blue Exercise Book from the 1930s and 1940s, where she records family finances and John's earliest words), there are letters from her grandfather Balthazar du Biel, in English (to his daughter, Vera's Aunt Annie), in German (to his wife Anna). He is writing with a fountain pen in brown ink on white paper, A4. It is Stellenbosch in the early 1920s.

There are further documents in Vera's handwriting, one of which offers a pre-text to the blue Exercise Book. It is a pre-text because it is historical: it is a retrospective account written about a time before the blue Exercise Book. I call it Vera's 'farm memoir', though she has neither signed nor dated it. It is twenty pages long of A5.

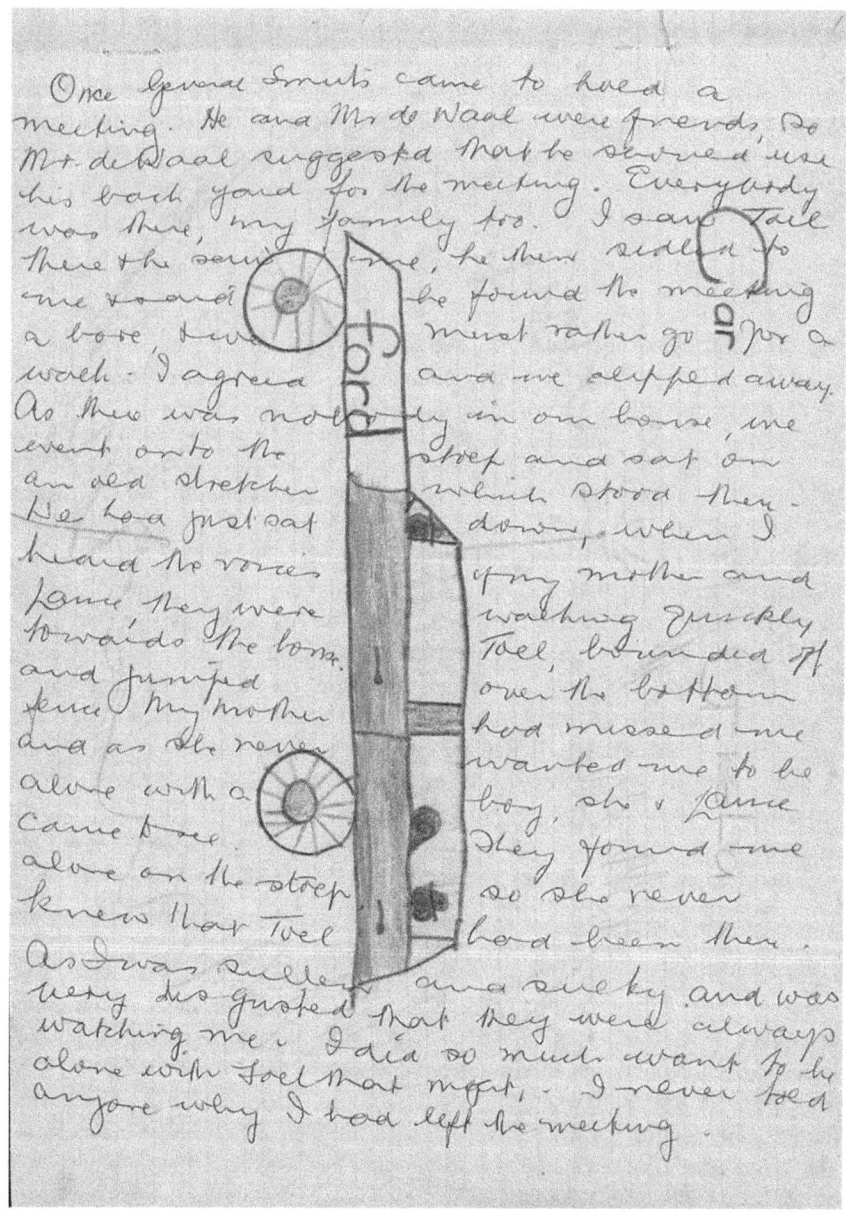

Figure 1.5 'Car', 'Ford', undated farm memoir, Vera Wehmeyer Coetzee.
Source: J. M. Coetzee Papers, Box 103.4, 094, Harry Ransom Center.

I may well be reading it out of sequence (there are no page numbers). It is written in English in blue ball-point pen and has very few corrections. It is beautifully concise.

I remember something her son writes, years later:

> her English is faultless, particularly when she writes. She uses words in their right sense, her grammar is impeccable. She is at home in the language, it is an area where she cannot be shaken. How did it happen? Her father was Piet Wehmeyer, a flat Afrikaans name. In the photograph album, in his collarless shirt and wide-brimmed hat, he looks like any ordinary farmer. In the Uniondale district where they lived there were no English; all the neighbours seem to have been named Zondagh.
>
> (Coetzee 2011: 106)

But what I am reading in this folder does not, to think of another title, have the look of 'fiction in the archives' (see Davis 1990). These are surely Vera's own true words. She does not try to set the scene. There is no title. There is no context or preamble or even reference to the family's surname or the name of the farm itself, and yet there are details: 'Mr McKensie who came for Sundays and was station master at Avontuur'. She records how, on these occasions, her mother Louisa always prepared a roast and served the meal herself, on a starched white linen tablecloth; that the eldest child was responsible for coffee making in the early mornings; that her mother homeschooled five of her six children to Standard V in a cottage converted by 'Mr Scott who came from Scotland, and stayed with us for a long time'; that the siblings (there are six children altogether: three boys and three girls, all with English names) played makeshift tennis and cricket. This is what Antoinette Burton might mean by the phrase: 'to archive the domestic' (2003: 28). She is writing about how women write themselves into history, in descriptions of house and home, even in private papers that have no intended public audience. 'What do we make', she asks, 'of the histories that domestic interiors, once concrete and now perhaps crumbling or disappeared, have the capacity to yield?' (2003: 4).

For we know that Vera has not written this memoir for her son's readers at the Harry Ransom Center in Texas, but this library is now part of her story too. If she offers no sense of the occasion or location of writing, she does provide some key geographical markers. It is thanks to certain sentences that I have come so close to her place of origin. 'Opposite our farm', she writes, 'was the farm Meyerskraal' (which is how this word became my landmark on the R62). 'My mother taught us all excepting Roland who went to the farm school at Wolwekraal 3 miles away' (which is how I came to wonder about the farm boundaries and the true name of the Wehmeyer farm). Uniondale is the nearest town; Avontuur the nearest hamlet; Willowmore, an expedition. She has mapped it all out, but when? For whom has she written?

* * *

The tablet she is writing on has lines, but she is writing against the grain of the lines, and even has to navigate her cursive hand around a child's drawing. The drawing has no name or date either, but these are two interlocking stories – each claiming its own space on the page. The mother is remembering her girlhood in the Langkloof, a rural world of carts and horses, ostriches and sheep-shearing, a visit by General Smuts. The child is not looking back but forward. The child writes the words and draws the picture: 'Car'; 'Ford'. It is a car of many colours. There is a driver; there are passengers.

References

Attwell, David (2015), *J.M. Coetzee and the Life of Writing: Face to Face with Time*. Oxford: Oxford University Press.

Barthes, Roland ([1981] 2000), *Camera Lucida: Reflections on Photography*, trans. Richard Howard. London: Vintage Books.

Burton, Antoinette (2003), *Dwelling in the Archive: Women Writing House, Home and History in Late Colonial India*. Oxford: Oxford University Press.

Burton, Antoinette (ed.) (2006), *Archive Stories: Facts, Fictions and the Writing of History*. Durham, NC: Duke University Press.

Coetzee, J. M. 'J.M. Coetzee Papers'. Austin, TX: Harry Ransom Center.

Coetzee, J. M. (1974), *Dusklands*. Johannesburg: Ravan Press.

Coetzee, J. M. (1983), *Life & Times of Michael K*. London: Secker & Warburg.

Coetzee, J. M. (1990), *Age of Iron*. London: Secker & Warburg.

Coetzee, J. M. (1995), "Meat Country", *Granta* 52 [Food: The Vital Stuff]: 43–52.

Coetzee, J. M. (1997), *Boyhood*. London: Secker & Warburg.

Coetzee, J. M. (2011), *Scenes from Provincial Life*. London: Harvill Secker.

Davis, Natalie Zemon (1990), *Fiction in the Archives: Pardon Tales and Their Tellers in Sixteenth-Century France*. Stanford: Stanford University Press.

Dean, Andrew (2020), 'Lives and Archives'. In: Jarad Zimbler, ed., *The Cambridge Companion to J.M. Coetzee*. Cambridge: Cambridge University Press, 221-33.

Easton, Kai (2020), *Scenes from the South: From the Collections of the Harry Ransom Center and Amazwi South African Museum of Literature to Mark the Occasion of J.M. Coetzee's 80th Birthday*. Makhanda: Amazwi South African Museum of Literature (3-D exhibition tour: https://nationalartsfestival.co.za/show/scenes-from-the-south/; https://www.hrc.utexas.edu/visit-from-home/).

'Farmer of the Month: Jimmy Zondagh', *AgriAbout*, no. 87, 28 July 2020: 6–13. Available online: https://agriabout.com/magazine-editions/ (accessed 27 August 2020).

Kannemeyer, John (2012), *J.M. Coetzee: A Life in Writing*, trans. Michiel Heyns. Johannesburg: Jonathan Ball.

Leibbrandt, H. C. V. (1905), *Precis of the Archives of the Cape of Good Hope: Requesten (Memorials), 1715–1806*, vol. 1. Cape Town: Government Printers.

Matthee, Dalene (1985), *Fiela se Kind*. Cape Town: Tafelberg.

Mbembe, Achille (2002), 'The Power of the Archive and Its Limits'. In: Carolyn Hamilton, Verne Harris, Jane Taylor, Michele Pickover, Graeme Reid and Razia Saleh, eds, *Refiguring the Archive*. Dordrecht: Kluwer Academic, 19–27.

Wehmeyer, Stefan (2015), 'My Amerikaanse oumagrootjie se doodskennisgewing', *Cape Librarian*, 59 (2): 2–3.

2

Summertime sadness: Coetzee, coordinates and the negation of the archive

Shaun Irlam

An 'and' yokes two terms together and asks us to reflect on their conjunction; how do we broach the question before us: *J. M. Coetzee and the Archive*? To begin with, a distinction seems necessary between the archive that Coetzee leaves to posterity and his own, private archive: the reservoirs of memory and imagination from which his works are forged. The former resides at the Harry Ransom Center in Austin, Texas, for example, but should probably also include all the scattered papers, documents, notes, letters, emails, artefacts that Coetzee has dispersed across the globe – constituting a supplemental and largely uncatalogued archive, some of which might one day be gathered in Texas. To this, one might add the places and people whose lives Coetzee has touched: places that perhaps served as inspiration; people, too, whose reminiscences and oral histories would add another stratum to the archive. *Summertime* alludes to this component of the archive, 'if you want the truth you have to … hear from people who knew him directly' (2010: 226).

There is, conversely, Coetzee's own archive to which we only have mediated access: the entire repository of memories, dreams, readings, reveries, experiences and lives that have shaped his life and career, and which are in some oblique and 'anagrammatical' (1990: 173; 1995: 141) fashion inscribed in his works and, perhaps more specifically, in the three volumes composing *Scenes from Provincial Life* (though I decline to privilege these putatively autobiographical works over his '*autre*-biographical' fiction). Coetzee himself has distilled the character of this other archive in his statement that 'all writing is autobiographical' (1992: 391). It is to this latter archive that I turn, and specifically to what Coetzee describes as 'the relation of novels and novel-writing to the time and the place in which we live' (1988: 2).

As we contemplate this question, we must acknowledge the antagonism, even the 'enmity' (1988: 3), between the terms 'Coetzee' and 'Archive'; indeed, these terms might serve as translations for 'fiction' and 'testimony', or, in terms offered by *Summertime*, the opposition between 'romance' and 'truth' (2010: 185).[1] The ampersand used in the original title for this volume yokes them together like a knot, but they are not happy campers – more like Costello and Rayment in *Slow Man* – for the writer, or rather, 'fictioneer' (2010: 225), designated as *Coetzee*, has consistently insisted that 'the relation between history and fiction is … a rivalrous one' (Coetzee and Scott 1997: 101; 1988: 3).

Disdain for the archive begins as early as the 'Preface to the Narrative of Jacobus Coetzee', with its spurious 'thanks ... to the staff of the South African National Archives' (1974: 59). The entire Jacobus *Narrative* is a satiric assault on history and the pieties (1974: 115) of the archive and, conversely, an oblique 'defense of poesy'. Moreover, of the archive, the narrator concludes, 'whether I am alive or dead, whether I ever lived or never was born, has never been of any real concern to me. I have other things to think about' (1974: 114). Already audible here is the impossible, transgressive predicate uttered by Poe's M. Valdemar, 'I am dead', drawing a bright line between literary statement and historical truth, between *Dichtung* and *Wahrheit* (Goethe).[2] This diffidence towards the archive and 'facts of life' marks Coetzee's entire literary career.

The archive thus confronts us with a question: what is its allure – this repository for all the detritus, the *disjecta membra* of everything absorbed, transfigured, sublimated into the published texts? What do we – readers, scholars, literary pilgrims, hagiographers, scavenger hunters – hope to find in the places the author has lived, visited, traversed, and in the notes, drafts and fragments from which their finished works emerged? Literary tourism and archival scholarship take their cue, no doubt, from religious pilgrimage and from reliquaries. Senor C.'s own literary pilgrimage around Provence on the trail of Ezra Pound offers a cautionary tale here:

> Pound seems to have believed that he could not properly appreciate troubadour poetry until he had ... seen the landscapes familiar to his poets. On the face of it this seems reasonable. ... Following in the tracks of Pound and his poets, I cycled some of those same roads. ... What I achieved by doing so I am not sure ... neither of us seemed ... able to demonstrate ... why or how that mattered. To me all that was extraordinary about seeing Roquefixade ... was to find out how ordinary Roquefixade was: just another point on the great globe. It gave me no shivers.
> (Coetzee 2008: 141–2)

Lastly, *Summertime*, with its 'posthumous' recollections of Coetzee, amplifying Valdemar's predicate, 'I am dead', and his comment that 'I wasn't destined for ... [t]he fate of being a rich and successful writer' (2010: 149) – both assertions belied, among many others in the novel, by historical facts – offers us a sustained satire on the authority of the archive; when Julia ferrets through Coetzee's possessions in his bedroom, she asks, 'What was I looking for? I didn't know. For something I would recognize only when I found it. But it was not there' (2010: 80). Moreover, the archivist, embodied by the inquisitive Mr. Vincent, is tantalized with artefacts lost, artefacts that belong to the 'full story of his letters' (2010: 190), when Adriana Nascimento reveals that 'He wrote many times' (2010: 171) but adds, 'I don't have any of his letters. I did not keep them' (2010: 170).

With these provisos behind us, let me briefly adopt the guise of archivist to open a chapter from Coetzee's life that has received no coverage in his own *Scenes from Provincial Life*. While his years in Austin, Texas are memorialized in several essays, a remarkable silence surrounds his four years with the English department at the State University in Buffalo, New York. This silence is all the more surprising perhaps, given that this is where John's public writing career was spawned, and given that a single act of political protest in Buffalo, described as 'a turning point in his life' (2010: 227; cf. 1992: 338), forced his return to South Africa.

Coetzee has said in interviews that he began *Dusklands* as a New Year's resolution on 1 January 1970 at 24 Parker Ave, Buffalo, NY, after years of flirting with poetry. He added in conversations with Attwell that he donned overcoat and boots and descended into the unheated basement of his Parker Avenue residence to begin writing.

Figure 2.1 offers us the rather prosaic manger in which *Dusklands* was born; it seems hard to believe such rich fruit germinated inside such an unpromising-looking rind. The house today appears to be a multiple occupancy rental unit and is in quite poor shape. The surrounding neighbourhood, sandwiched on a very short block behind a subway station, and between two busy intersections, is also rather shabby. Most notably, this neighbourhood marks the frontier between black and white in Buffalo, still a deeply segregated city today. This racial locus no doubt resonated deeply with Coetzee as he projected himself back into the origins of racialized conquest in southern Africa.

There is something quite unique about the gestation of Coetzee's literary career; how often, after all, are we able to assign such precise spatio-temporal coordinates to the beginning of a writer's career? What is most notable, however, is that the very

Figure 2.1 24 Parker Ave, Buffalo, NY.
Source: Photograph by Shaun Irlam.

precision of this spatio-temporal moment seems also eerily and *negatively* consolidated by the imagination that then emancipates itself so scrupulously from *this* time and *this* place in order to transport itself from a frigid Buffalo winter to the dry, arid heat of Namaqualand and to float across the centuries from the 1970s to the 1760s. It is as if, by repeatedly marking it so precisely in interviews, Coetzee urges us to compare Buffalo with the envisioned world of eighteenth-century Namaqualand that it leaves behind; against the backdrop of Buffalo, so thoroughly purged from the literary space of *Dusklands*, the narrative, the milieu of *Dusklands*, like that of *Waiting for the Barbarians* after it (1992: 143), is a tour de force of *spatial negation*. It is the act of 'envisioning' or, in Keats's phrase, *negative capability*, that sets the aesthetic achievement in a dialectical relationship to the quotidian and quiddity that it simultaneously annuls. Barton articulates this capability most precisely in *Foe*; it is 'the knack of seeing waves when there are fields before your eyes, and of feeling the tropic sun when it is cold; and … the words with which to capture the vision' (1986: 52).

The genesis of *Dusklands* illustrates how vigorously writing wrests itself free from any determinate time, place, origin and context, even from the historical life of its author, to enter that strange immortality called Literature. Long ago, Roland Barthes commented that 'writing is the destruction of every voice, of every point of origin … the negative where all identity is lost, starting with every identity of the body writing … the author enters into his own death, writing begins' (1977: 142). Similarly, Maurice Blanchot, drawing from Hegel (a tutelary presence in *Dusklands*), writes: 'The meaning of speech … requires that before any word is spoken, there must be a sort of immense hecatomb, a preliminary flood plunging all of creation into a total sea. God had created living things, but man had to annihilate them' (1995: 323). Speaking of his own career, Coetzee echoes both, 'I knew that once I had begun, I would have to go through with the thing to the end. Like an execution' (1992: 19).

This *inverse* relation to all the coordinates of autobiography, history, geopolitical specificity, everything that might properly belong in the archive, is precisely what constitutes the singularity of literature and the singular fecklessness of the 'fictioneer'. It is this 'negative capability' (2003: 200), or in the idiom of *Summertime*, '*meegevoel*, feeling-with' (2010: 97) that at once captures both the magnitude of the writer's historical burden as well as the vigour of his imagination. Writers engage in a process of imaginatively fashioning a means to slip the specific coordinates by which they find themselves bound. This, then, is the first negation of the archive, but it also, of course, becomes an argument for the continuing value of the archive: the deposits in the archive allow us to measure how thoroughly the creative work has sublimated or transcended its mundane origins, providing, as John says of manual labour in *Summertime*, 'immortality of a kind' (2010: 7). Inherently, the act of writing, before it becomes anything else, is an act of negation and sublimation. 'Story' displaces 'life', writing steps out of mundanity and 'flesh and blood experiences' (2002: 24), and rises, fire-washed, into the empyrean realm of Meaning – 'subjected to the transfiguring fire of art' (2002: 25), shabby rural windmills become giants and dragons.

Among the best illustrations of this painstaking, Hegelian process of negation and sublimation in Coetzee's work might be found in the pages of *The Master of Petersburg*, a sustained allegory on the metamorphosis of personal experience into art. The work of mourning – the loss of Pavel – germinates the 'Work-of-mourning', as its displaced, allegorical double. The negation of innocence and the betrayal of loss is monumentalized in the monstrous 'marmoreal coldness' (1995: 241) of Stavrogin; Stavrogin becomes the embodiment of this act of coldness that is writing. I describe this as allegory, but the novel's own vocabulary is *perversion* and *betrayal*: the tropic diversion or conversion of private and intimate experience into publication. However, this tale of transformation and the engendering of Stravogin as an 'anagram' of Fyodor's grief, 'he will give a home to any word ... if there is a chance it is an anagram for Pavel' (1995: 141), is only half the story. This story of allegoresis – the death of Pavel feeding the life of Stavrogin – is in turn an allegory for another story of loss. Coetzee's novel takes the writer's own deep, personal loss of his son, Nicolas, who had indeed fallen to his death in 1989, and transmutes it into a novel about the grief (and the eventual sublimation of that grief in writing) of Dostoevsky over the fictional death of his stepson, Pavel Isaev.

This narrative of the transmutation, or 'betrayal' of grief into literature through an allegory of grief betrayed for literature, yields a mode of narration that the novel itself describes, 'every word double ... Split writing, from a split heart' (1995: 219; cf. 'double meaning', 148). The issues I have explored so far all pertain to what constitutes an archaic act of negation/transformation that is embedded in the very act of writing. However, if this primary negation is a necessary general condition of any writing, we must take stock of a *second* order of negation in Coetzee's work that emerges as an enduring thematic exigency.

* * *

I do not know whether this text belongs to the space of literature ... whether it is a fiction or a testimony.

Derrida, *Demeure* (2000: 26)

The shedding of the archive is more urgent and more explicitly thematized for Coetzee. It becomes an announced theme throughout his work and most notably in *Scenes from Provincial Life*, which dwells unwaveringly on the scourge of the past *even as it memorializes it*. Indeed, Coetzee remarks, 'We ... must look at the past with a cruel enough eye to see what it was that made that joy and innocence possible' (1992: 29). As I wish to suggest, a double, oscillating movement of remembering – dismembering places the past under erasure and constitutes the singular, idiomatic melancholy of *Scenes*, their *Summertime* sadness.

History – South Africa's history – the stuff of Coetzee's archive, is a perpetual source of shame, loathing, revulsion, 'horror upon horror, atrocity upon atrocity, without relief' (2002: 100), and there is perhaps here a broader meditation on the siren song of a colonial past, to yield to whose call is a path to destruction. How should one acknowledge the formative, mourned experience of a childhood under colonialism, while at the same time repudiating it, not becoming empire's accomplice? Coetzee's work reveals an anguished ambivalence towards South Africa, a land both loved and abhorred.

In Jerusalem in 1987, Coetzee proposed that 'South African literature is a literature in bondage. ... It is exactly the kind of literature you would expect people to write from a prison' (1992: 98). Adriana Nascimento later echoes this trope in *Summertime*, 'we wanted to be released, all of us' (2010: 181). If *bondage* is the operative metaphor here – and its bonds take many forms across his works (1992: 63) – then Coetzee's writing career might be approached as a 'willed act of the imagination' (1992: 98) to emancipate itself from the '*crudity* of life in South Africa' (1992: 99). Elaborating this image of bondage, Coetzee comments to Attwell, 'I am someone who has intimations of freedom (as every chained prisoner has)' (1992: 341).

Let us retrace our steps along the road to Roquefixade: the experience that left the narrator with 'no shivers'. One reviewer wrote of Coetzee's first memoir, '*Boyhood* is full of shuddering' (Cooper 1997). The shudder, 'visceral loathing' (2010: 252), is the visceral correlative of negation and *shedding* and takes so many different forms in Coetzee's work. Coetzee has already taught us how to read these signs of national shuddering that are endemic to South Africa. He spoke in precisely these terms in his 1974 essay on Alex La Guma, 'Each of his novels exposes us to a long-sustained shudder of revulsion' (1992: 359). *Boyhood* and *Youth* likewise enact precisely this long-sustained shudder, 'the testament of one man's horror of a degraded world' (1992: 360). In *Boyhood*, he establishes that young John is 'the product of a damaged childhood' (2010: 252; 1992: 392–3), the antithesis of a happy, well-formed, 'Kuyperian family ... within a community, within a homeland' (2010: 254); 'shuddering' seems to be the distinguishing formal gesture governing *Boyhood*.

One moment in *Boyhood* might stand as a specimen for many others. The memoir narrates the 'self' as a principle of refusal and disidentification; it is, as Coetzee put it to Attwell, 'trying to find a capsule in which he can live, a capsule in which he need not breathe the air of the world' (1992: 393). Little John's attitude towards etiquette becomes an organizing metaphor for his attitude towards socialization in general and, later, towards literary conventions in particular, 'He flees polite talk because of its formulas. ... Yet finally he is not ashamed of his wildness ... he begins to *mock* the commonplaces of politeness ... the life he would face if his father ran the household, a life of dull, stupid formulas, of being like everyone else' (1997: 78–9). From the formulas that script the quotidian horrors of South Africa, the boy retreats into a secret, hidden life, negating the primordial negative gesture embodied in apartheid itself, its systemic 'denial of an unacknowledgeable desire to embrace Africa' (1992: 97); he begins to retreat from his parochial life, segregating himself from segregation as a prophylactic precaution.

If the defining negative gesture of *Boyhood* is the shudder, and the corollary retreat into a secret, inner life where he can construct a Russian – and even Ashkenazy – childhood for himself instead (he reports a loyalty to the Russians and is misrecognized and persecuted by bullies as a Jew (1997: 24)), then the organizing gesture of *Youth* is renunciation: he commends himself for 'having shaken the dust of ... South Africa from his feet' (2002: 137).

In Greek legend, the wrestler, Antaeus draws his strength from contact with his natal earth. In Coetzee's work we find instead the figure of an *anti-Antaeus*: poetic power derives from 'shaking the dust of the country from his feet' (1992: 96, 393). He persuades himself that true artistic accomplishment can only be achieved in the metropolises of the world: London, Paris, Vienna (2002: 41). What began as a shudder in *Boyhood* becomes a rage of repudiation in *Youth*, 'he departs South Africa, very much in the spirit of shaking the dust of the country from his feet' (1992: 393).

It is no doubt a truism that the sympathetic imagination must negate and transcend its own coordinates to inhabit the worlds of others; this is what I take Keats to mean by 'negative capability'. Fiction, *fictioneering*, begins with a willed negation of the autobiographical, archival self in order to achieve that *meegevoel* (2010: 97) which permits us to 'think ourselves into the being of another' (2003: 80). However, as much as it is driven by a desire to shed one's own coordinates to enter those of others, as we have begun to suspect, this impulse is equally motivated by a shuddering from history, a wish to emancipate oneself from a history too painful to face. 'He would prefer to leave his South African self behind as he has left South Africa itself behind. South Africa was a bad start, a handicap ... he has, more or less, escaped' (2002: 62). These sentiments are furthermore carried through to a repudiation of the South African literary archive (as *Summertime* will later attest), intimated when Magda concludes *In the Heart of the Country*, 'There are poems ... about the heart that aches for Verlore Vlakte, about the melancholy of the sunset over the koppies. ... They are poems I could write myself ... hymns I could have written but did not because (I thought) it was too easy' (1978: 138). These sentiments towards the mother country are to some degree personified in the mother who attempts to hold him to his past, to the archive he wants to abandon, 'Will his mother not understand that when he departed Cape Town he cut all bonds with his past ... the process of turning himself into a different person ... will be carried through remorselessly until all memory of the family and the country he left behind is extinguished?' (2002: 98). It is an image of holocaust, echoing Blanchot's image of the hecatomb: '*burnt*. The perfective, signifying an action carried through to its conclusion' (1999: 71). Similarly, 'South Africa is like an albatross around his neck. He wants it removed ... so that he can begin to breathe' (2002: 101; cf. 1992: 393). In conjunction with the imagery of bondage, the idiom of asphyxiation compounds the vision of South Africa as a horror that must be disowned, discarded, denounced, 'South Africa is a wound within him' (2002: 116). Yet, it is also a wound that he continually scratches to ensure that he can still shudder as a form of atonement; thus, in *Youth*, he reads the reports in the *Manchester Guardian* 'with dread' because 'the *Manchester Guardian* can be relied on not to miss anything that will make the soul cringe' (2002: 101). Similarly, back in Cape Town, he will later read the local *Sunday Times*; he 'reads the reports and feels soiled' (2010: 4). We have travelled very far from William Cowper's 'loophole of retreat' in his 1785 poem, *The Task*.[3]

So, the defining postures of *Scenes from Provincial Life* – these works that consolidate the portrait of the artist as a young man – are remorselessly valedictory. However, if the first two volumes of *Scenes* narrate an adventure of repudiation, *Summertime* records the return of the prodigal in 'some disgrace' (2010: 89). The preceding project of self-fashioning, 'Cut yourself free of what you love and hope the wound heals' (2010: 132, 134), has ended ignominiously and so the narrator must craft a new relationship with his homeland, refracted through all the frames and prisms of *Summertime*.

What structurally sets *Summertime* apart from its two 'autobiographical' predecessors is the 'book within a book' conceit, which yields the undecidable distinction between author (Coetzee? Vincent?) and character (Coetzee? Vincent?) and the unstable, playful tension around the state of the text itself: Coetzee's complete, published novel (identified as 'Fiction' on the cover and title-page), or Vincent's incomplete, unpublished manuscript; is Vincent framing Coetzee in his biography, or is Coetzee framing Vincent as a hapless biographer? This unstable, oscillating difference, which has been a meta-fictional dimension in Coetzee's work since its inception, has received renewed attention as the phenomenon of metalepsis. The concept of metalepsis, drawn from Gerard Genette's work on narrative discourse, has recently been applied to Coetzee's work by Alexandra Effe to think about all the different ways his novels resourcefully blur and trouble the boundaries between world and storyworld – what in theater parlance might be called 'breaking the fourth wall'. Genette writes of the 'sacred frontier between two worlds, the world in which one tells, the world which one tells' (1980: 236); it is this frontier that Coetzee's works, and *Summertime* among them, consistently and creatively transgress.

A modal shift occurs in this 'posthumous biography', precipitated by the fact that the protagonist has been forced home. The new predicament is brutally posed in the opening pages of *Summertime*; the dust of South Africa, shed in *Youth*, has become a clinging soil: 'So this is what he has come back to! Yet where in the world can one hide where one will not feel soiled? … how to escape the filth' (2010: 4). *Summertime* thus poses a different moral problem and a different aesthetic solution from its predecessors in *Scenes*: the challenge of living with, living on, surviving in apartheid South Africa.

As if literalizing Barthes in 'The Death of the Author', the author is himself negated in *Summertime*; he adopts the other premiss articulated in *Youth*, 'He would prefer to leave his South African self behind' (2002: 62). The governing conceit of *Summertime* is, of course, that Coetzee is already dead, now remembered by former lovers, acquaintances, colleagues. The aesthetic challenge is to negotiate some reconciliation between the returning exile, his natal earth and the loathing he continues to feel, 'This place … wrenched my heart when I was a child and I have never been right since' (2002: 97; cf. 1997: 9; 1992: 392–3). Let us first note the reiteration of the negative gesture: all the interviewees bar Margot (and arguably, even she) have, in one fashion or another, repudiated South Africa, 'spit on this atrocious earth of South Africa' (2010: 179) and the interview with Martin renews the defining theses, 'toward South Africa … we cultivated a certain provisionality in our feelings … since sooner or later our ties to it would have to be cut' (2002: 211).

One place to open this question is in the second interview from *Summertime* –the conversation with cousin, Margot Jonker. The episode is deliberately in the elegiac, *ubi sunt*? tradition from Latin literature; however, the elegiac narrative is formally bracketed and qualified to corrosively *dismember* this remembering:

> In the old days there would be huge gatherings on the family farm. … But by now, … those family gatherings are sadly diminished. Gerrit Coetzee is long in the grave. … The firstborn has already departed this life. … Among the survivors the joking has grown more subdued, the reminiscing sadder. … As for the hunting parties, there are no more of those … there is nothing left in the veld. …. She alone [Margot] she suspects, looks back to the old days with nostalgia.
>
> (2010: 87–9)

The tenor of the passage is unmistakably mournful, the 'gatherings ... sadly diminished', the 'reminiscing sadder', but something else is happening here as well. Nostalgic sentiment is filtered through layers of framing that refract and dismember these memories even as they are assembled. As already noted, it is framed by the postulate of the author's demise (mischievously belied by the fact that Coetzee is still very much alive), as well as by the satirical parody (paradoxically, metaleptically, substituting for an unpublished 'third memoir, the one that never saw the light of day' (2010: 205)) of the genre of literary biography. Moreover, the wistful sentiments expressed are imputed to Margot, 'she alone ... looks back ... with nostalgia'; 'she is hankering for the past' (2010: 140) while the formal playfulness of the text sports with them. These reminiscences are also filtered through the sustained struggle between Margot and Mr. Vincent over his redaction of their earlier interview, problematizing the archival veracity of Vincent's transcription and inserting yet another textual layer between Margot's testimony and the reader's reception. Finally, our attention is deflected by Vincent's broken promises ('as you promised' (2010: 152), 'I will tell you one thing ... you must not repeat in your book' (2010: 172)), to the extent that these drafts disclose details Margot had explicitly requested he suppress. The narrative repeatedly underscores the gaps and inconsistencies between the constative and performative dimensions of the text, epitomized by M. Valdemar's statement, 'I am dead'. *Summertime* is, of course, built around that impossible statement.

The complex, superimposed framing apparatus brackets, displaces and mitigates the underlying melancholy and nostalgia as well as parodies the archive's earnest preoccupation with drafts and revisions (2010: 205). Indeed, the earnestness of melancholic nostalgia (*weemoed* (2010: 120)), paired with the quixotic scheme of relocating to the Karoo to pursue poetry, becomes an explicit focus of fun and derision, when the 'barefoot children' (2010: 104) of Merweville are imagined laughing at the laureate of Leeu-Gamka, '*Op sy ou ramkiekie maak oom gedigte*' (2010: 128).

The solemn, serious aspirations of the poet-lover are also persistently negated through comedy, satire and '[Laughter]' (2010: 200), as when poetic metaphor meets reality and gutters away into the paler fire of bathos. For example, 'Coetzee', the 'examination coach', outlines his teaching philosophy as one of mutual conflagration, 'The true student burns to know... the teacher ... responds to it by burning with an intenser light' (2010: 163, 187). As Mrs. Nascimento later watches Coetzee's picnic fire die in the rain on a winter afternoon, she smirks, 'Maria Regina should see what her hero was like in real life, this poet who could not even make a fire' (2010: 168). She subsequently speculates about Dutch Protestant courtship rituals dissipated in writing, 'without fire' (2010: 172, 196). In the vein of Pope in *Peri Bathous*, during the interview with Adriana, *Summertime* becomes a satire on the poetics of the sublime; Coetzee's reflections on Schubert and the sublime turn to bathos in Adriana's reading, 'nonsense, worse than nonsense' (2010: 175).

Summertime provides ample encouragement to regard it as a comic work; Sophie Denoël's characterization of her relationship with Coetzee as 'comical in its essence. Comico-sentimental. Based on a comic premise' (2010: 241) is a fitting description of all the relationships with women described in *Summertime*. Julia likewise comments: 'Principles are the stuff of comedy ... John Coetzee was actually quite funny. A figure of comedy. Dour comedy' (2010: 63); echoing Julia's remarks, when Margot realizes she is stranded with John because of his principle that 'white folk should do their own car repairs', she reflects, 'How comical' (2010: 111). Martin similarly remarks of the late settler's predicament, 'I did not regard our fate as tragic. ... If anything, it was comic' (2010: 210).

Summertime even hints that it is all an elaborate joke at Mr. Vincent's expense; the interview with Julia constantly reminds the reader how much is withheld, how much is Shandyesque digression about herself, how much she toys with her interlocutor, even while teasing him with 'frank talk' (2010: 25). Adriana likewise leaves Vincent to muse ruefully on the possibility that some sublime, transformative Word that would clinch this portrait of the artist has been forever lost, '*What if the letter you did not read contained the words that would have moved you or even changed your feelings about him?*' (2010: 193). He also reflects that, whatever the gaps, silences and shortcomings in the archives, it remains the only resource he possesses for accessing the truth of 'Coetzee'; when Adriana questions Vincent's cautious speculations about 'Coetzee's' demeanour towards her, 'How do you know that?', Vincent replies, '*From the record he left behind*' (2010: 196). The negation of the poetic hero, a corollary virility, and the poetic vocation all thread together through her interview.

In *Scenes*, then, Coetzee crafts an idiom of remembering – dismembering that at once summons up the past, yet scrupulously eschews any nostalgia or mourning, striving instead to sustain a poetic voice suspended between embrace, laughter and shudder, an idiom that is 'grimly amusing' (2010: 110). Indeed, if Adriana could be an inspiration for Susan Barton in *Foe* (2010: 200–1), then she also becomes a metaphor, a proxy for the narrator of *Scenes* and the 'cruel eye', simultaneously attracted and appalled by the object of love: '*Never again will a woman look with love on this mutilated face ... so let me at least look, without flinching*' (2010: 179). As the 'Jerusalem Prize speech' reminds us, South Africa resembles the mutilated face of the beloved, a milieu of 'the deformed and stunted' (1992: 98), impossible to love unconditionally, but impossible to discard so that one might 'be away, free of him. ... How I longed for it all to end, this life, this death, this living death!' (2010: 181). *Scenes* articulates a 'summertime sadness', a valedictory voice that nevertheless refuses to sentimentalize what is lost – cloaking itself instead in self-deprecation, irony and self-satire; in antithesis of Flaubert, it narrates the author's 'unsentimental education'. Satire becomes the new medium of negation, no longer the angry, vehement repudiations of *Boyhood* and *Youth* but rather a mode of discourse that holds the referent (here the deceased 'Coetzee') at a distance through irony and mockery as an object of dark comedy. What replaces, displaces country and community as the target of negation in the previous two *Scenes* is a much more intimate domicile: the author himself, the awkwardness of his embodiment, the clumsiness of his social demeanour. The 'memoir' is an excoriating critique of the 'deceased' Coetzee's failings as lover, as companion, as son, as man, as human being, 'he was not human, not fully human' (2010: 83; cf. 2010: 199); or in the words of his harshest critic, Adriana, 'He was nothing and his words were nothing ... to me he really was a fool' (2010: 193). She adds, 'He was a little man, an unimportant little man' (2010: 195).

'Summertime sadness' is the voice of *Summertime* that marks and retains the traces of nostalgia through its negation, that says of the past and, specifically, of the past anchored melancholically to a *nostos*: 'These are poems I could have written myself, but did not, because, I thought, it was too easy' (1978: 138). This is the singularity of Coetzee's 'summertime sadness' – that was does not embrace a maudlin, autumnal melancholy, but rather, that it summons, frames, holds up the archives of memory to scrutiny and to mirth, yet eschews their siren song: 'It was granted to spend their childhood summers in a sacred space. That glory can never be regained: best not to haunt the old sites and come away from them mourning what is forever gone' (2010: 134).

Margot is again permitted to be the voice of sentiment and melancholy that the aspirant poet feels compelled to repudiate, 'Whose idea was it to lay down roads and railway lines ... bring people in and then bind them to this place, bind them with rivets through the heart, so that they cannot get away? *Better to cut yourself free and hope the wound heals*' (2010: 140). To the question she asks next, 'How do you cut through rivets like that?' (2010: 140), the answer is perhaps contained in the extraordinarily complex speech act that is *Summertime*, this layered, legion, precarious utterance that is 'summertime sadness'. Margot's reflections provide a cautionary preface to an elegy that genuinely wrenches her heart, reminding us that these forsaken reaches of the Karoo are 'Nietverloren' as long as she is there to remember them:

> Meyerowitz ... has been here longer than she can remember. Babes in the Woods used to be Jan Harmse Slagter. Cosmos Café used to be Cosmos Milk Bar. Foschini Modes used to be Winterberg Algemene Handelaars. All this change, all this busyness! O *droewige land!* O sorrowful land!
>
> (2010: 141)

In this refracted manner, mediated through the memories of Margot and the revisions of Vincent, *Summertime* restores the authorial archive to the reader – the memory of a receding childhood lived among these dwindling scenes of provincial life.

This 'cruel eye', this stoic 'unflinchingness' (1992: 29), long turned against the archive and against the corrupted natal coordinates of space and time, seems finally, after a life and career of atonement, to bend towards a kind of reconciliation. In his 2016 inaugural address to the recently launched *Literatures of the South* seminar at the Universidad Nacional de San Martín in Buenos Aires, Coetzee commented, 'There is only one South. ... In this South the winds blow in a certain way and the leaves fall in a certain way and the sun beats down in a certain way that is instantly recognisable from one part of the South to another' (quoted in Halford 2016). The phrase 'in a certain way' is the anthem of the idiomatic, the vernacular.[4]

The emergence of this broad, transnational 'South' marks a sublimation of parochial South Africa, now one of several constituent terms – those 'scenes of provincial life' that were formerly repudiated. Nevertheless, the southern trade winds that 'blow in a certain way', familiar to any summertime inhabitant of the southern Cape as the idiomatic south-easter that so ceaselessly scours the region, yield a fitting figure for the double movement of negation/sublimation in Coetzee's *Scenes of Provincial Life* while at the same time evoking a signature summertime sadness. It seems we are not quite done with the siren song of melancholy, of *weemoed* and the mournful winds that bear it. To circle back to where we began, the agonistic relationship I have articulated between Coetzee and the archive might be distilled in this striking image that concludes

Summertime, as the young artist strides forth to confront the prevailing *Geist* or spirit of the times. Lest we underestimate the full import of these isobars of *accidie*, another southern poet provides the pertinent details:

> It can come in several forms, no matter where you live. Particularly in this city, Cape Town, it is November that usually brings the worst of it ... overnight these winds have swung around from north to south to begin their summer-long blowing. These southeasters ... air-blast the city ... until they seem less a part of local weather ... and more nature's way of having a nervous breakdown. They can blow until they shift the day slightly off-centre, become something metaphysical, enlarging nothingness. They bring with them the perennial refuse, the newsprint that wraps itself around lamp-posts and is torn to shreds by its paroxysms of vain flapping. Under this gritty scouring all surfaces become more surface-like, dry ... raspingly abrasive ... the curl of leaves grows bruised, wind-bitten. ... All too soon along the many sections of unpaved ... pavement, scabs of dead, grey sand appear. .... On the mountain flanks pits of gravel, like sores, open up and erode in smudges of orange dust. From other patches of raw earth and construction sites beside major roads, an incessant stream of runaway dust and builder's sand skids across the tar. This wind diminishes everything. ... It brings with it that feeling.
>
> (Watson 1990: 173)[5]

What Watson evokes here is his 'version of melancholy' (1990: 177). These southern trades that return each summer bear a seasonal affective disorder, a vernacular *weemoed*. This austral melancholy against which the aspiring author vigorously strives, the prevailing affect induced by the sorry history of South Africa, brings us by a different tack to the spectre of summertime sadness once more.

As his father lies dying in hospital, the closing pages of *Summertime* offer us a final fragment from the author's *Notebooks* (therefore, ostensibly his own words now, not those who remember him), 'the south-easter is howling, whipping up trash from the gutters. He walks fast, conscious of the vigour of his limbs, the steadiness of his heartbeat' (2010: 263).[6] It is a last glimpse of the 'filth' (2010: 4), 'the perennial refuse' to which John Coetzee had returned in 1972, yet, here, pushing against that parochial, idiomatic, idiot wind 'enlarging nothingness', pushing against the 'trash from the gutters', no longer seeking 'a capsule in which he need not breathe the air of the world' (1992: 393), but rather, refusing the refuse, negating this degraded, quotidian world in which he finds himself immersed, the narrator discovers a visceral vigour and a steadily beating heart in which to forge the uncreated conscience of his people. It is as much an image of the political climate of the times, the life and times of apartheid rampant, as it is an image of the author's struggle against history, against the archive, against all the burdens of the past: literary, cultural, political, historical. We remember that Benjamin's angel of history is blown from Paradise backwards into the future while a growing trail of debris accumulates at his feet (1982: 259); here the author, striving to reach, through his art, a space of redemption, a paradise of sorts, flies in the face of that wind – and all the detritus it carries with it – repudiating it, trying to deflect its passage and define its path differently, turning aside the vanes of the archive.

Notes

1. See Jacques Derrida's extended reflection on the relationship between 'fiction' and 'testimony' or, borrowing from Goethe, *Dichtung* and *Wahrheit* in *Demeure* (Derrida 2000).
2. I refer here to Edgar Allan Poe's story, 'The Facts in the Case of M. Valdemar' and the protagonist's impossible statement which has attracted much commentary from literary scholars. Derrida has commented on this statement in more than one place, most notably in *The Structuralist Controversy* (1972: 155–6). See also Derrida (1973: 96–7).
3. In his extended 1785 poem, *The Task*, William Cowper famously wrote of reading the news, 'This folio of four pages':

   > 'T IS pleasant, through the loopholes of retreat,
   > To peep at such a world; to see the stir
   > Of the great Babel, and not feel the crowd;
   > To hear the roar she sends through all her gates,
   > At a safe distance, where the dying sound
   > Falls a soft murmur on the uninjured ear.
   > Thus sitting and surveying thus at ease
   > The globe and its concerns, I seem advanced
   > To some secure and more than mortal height,
   > That liberates and exempts me from them all.
   > (*The Task*, IV, 50, 88–98)

4. See Benítez-Rojo 1992. In *The Repeating Island*, Benítez-Rojo develops this phrase, 'in a certain way', as the signature of the Caribbean archipelago. This 'certain way' in which the Caribbean discloses itself frequently takes the form of syncretism, a concept which may well be productively applied in constructing the singularity of the South too.
5. To fill out this particular signature of the South, one might also adduce Ingrid de Kok's recent poem, 'Cape South-Easter' (2020: 45).
6. This wind of ill omen, against which one must strive, uncannily echoing but inverting an episode in Paul Valéry's dialogue, *Eupalinos, or the Architect*, allows Valéry's text to offer further guidance to reading the dialectical structure of the writer in the wind and brings us again to the shores of Africa; Valéry writes, 'I was walking along the very edge of the sea ... overflowing with life. ... The air ... pressing against my face and limbs, confronted me – an impalpable hero that I must vanquish in order to advance. And this resistance, ever overcome, made of me, too, an imaginary hero, victorious over the wind, and rich in energies that were ever reborn, ever equal to the power of the invisible adversary. ... This is just what youth is. I watched ... those mighty shapes ... charioting ... their relentless energy from Africa' (1956: 111–12).

References

Barthes, Roland (1977), 'The Death of the Author'. In: Stephen Heath, trans., *Image-Music-Text*. London: Fontana/Collins.

Benítez-Rojo, Antonio (1992), *The Repeating Island: The Caribbean and the Postmodern Perspective*, trans. James E. Maraniss. Charlotte, NC: Duke University Press.

Benjamin, Walter (1982), 'Theses on the Philosophy of History'. In: Harry Zohn, trans., *Illuminations*. London: Fontana.
Blanchot, Maurice (1995), *The Work of Fire*, trans. Charlotte Mandell. Stanford: Stanford University Press.
Coetzee, J. M. (1974), *Dusklands*. Johannesburg: Ravan Press.
Coetzee, J. M. (1978), *In the Heart of the Country*. Johannesburg: Ravan Press.
Coetzee, J. M. (1981), *Waiting for the Barbarians*. Johannesburg: Ravan Press.
Coetzee, J. M. (1986), *Foe*. Johannesburg: Ravan Press.
Coetzee, J. M. (1988), 'The Novel Today', *Upstream: A Magazine of the Arts*, 6 (1): 2–5.
Coetzee, J. M. (1990), *Age of Iron*. New York: Random House.
Coetzee, J. M. (1992), *Doubling the Point: Essays and Interviews*. Cambridge: Harvard University Press.
Coetzee, J. M. (1995), *The Master of Petersburg*. New York: Penguin.
Coetzee, J. M. (1997), *Boyhood: Scenes from Provincial Life*. New York: Penguin.
Coetzee, J. M. (1999), *Disgrace*. New York: Penguin.
Coetzee, J. M. (2002), *Youth*. London: Secker & Warburg.
Coetzee, J. M. (2003), *Elizabeth Costello: Eight Lessons*. London: Secker & Warburg.
Coetzee, J. M. (2006), *Slow Man*. New York: Penguin.
Coetzee, J. M. (2008), *Diary of a Bad Year*. New York: Penguin.
Coetzee, J. M. (2010), *Summertime*. New York: Penguin.
Coetzee, J. M. (2011), *Scenes from Provincial Life*. London: Harvill Secker.
Coetzee, J. M., and Joanna Scott (1997), 'Voice and Trajectory: An Interview with J.M. Coetzee', *Salmagundi*, 114/115: 82–102.
Cooper, Rand Richards (1997), 'Portrait of the Writer as an Afrikaner', *New York Times Book Review*, 2 November. Available online: http://movies2.nytimes.com/books/97/11/02/reviews/971102.02coopert.html (accessed 3 March 2020).
Cowper, William (1994), *The Task and Selected Other Poems*, ed. James Sambrook. London: Longman.
De Kok, Ingrid (2020), 'Cape South-Easter', in *A Book of Friends: In Honor of J.M. Coetzee on His 80th Birthday*, ed. Dorothy Driver. Makhanda: Amazwi South African Museum of Literature.
Derrida, Jacques (1973), *Speech and Phenomena and Other Essays*, trans. David B. Allison. Evanston, IL: Northwestern University Press.
Derrida, Jacques (2000), *Demeure: Fiction and Testimony*, trans. Elizabeth Rottenburg. Stanford: Stanford University Press.
Effe, Alexandra (2017a), 'Coetzee's *Summertime* as a Metaleptic Conversation', *Journal of Narrative Theory*, 47 (2): 252–75.
Effe, Alexandra (2017b), *J.M. Coetzee and the Ethics of Narrative Transgression: A Reconsideration of Metalepsis*. London: Palgrave Macmillan.
Genette, Gerard (1980), *Narrative Discourse: An Essay in Method*, trans. Jane E. Lewin. Ithaca, NY: Cornell University Press.
Halford, James (2016), 'Reading Three Great Southern Lands: From the Outback to the Pampa and the Karoo', *The Conversation*, 11 June 2016. Available online: http://theconversation.com/reading-three-great-southern-lands-from-the-outback-to-the-pampa-and-the-karoo-60372 (accessed 1 June 2020).
Macksey, Richard and Eugenio Donato (1972), *The Structuralist Controversy: The Languages of Criticism and the Sciences of Man*. Baltimore: Johns Hopkins University Press.
Valéry, Paul (1956), *Dialogues*, trans. William McCausland Stewart. Princeton: Princeton University Press.
Watson, Stephen (1990), *Selected Essays 1980–1990*. Cape Town: Carrefour Press.

3

On the loss of fathers and letters: Reading *Summertime* and *The Childhood of Jesus* alongside Jacques Derrida's *Archive Fever*

Valeria Mosca

Personal, historical and archival memory are pivotal themes in J. M. Coetzee's literary production since its very beginning. David Attwell defined Coetzee's first novel, *Dusklands*, as a 'linking of self and history on a grand, world-historical scale' (2015: 52); much of his subsequent fiction may well be described in similar terms. Autobiographical tendencies merge in Coetzee's oeuvre with authentic historical sources and fictive archival documents, while narratives unfold against the backdrop of a deep engagement with philosophy and critical theory. My essay will explore the intertwinement of fictional representations and philosophical theories of archival memory in two of Coetzee's late works, *Summertime* (2009) – his third fictionalized memoir – and the novel *The Childhood of Jesus* (2013), with a Derridean theoretical framework.

Coetzee's engagement with critical theory is generally recognized as one of the main traits that mark the distinctiveness of his voice.[1] The relationship between his fiction and philosophical discourse regularly receives in-depth critical scrutiny, such as cannot be summed up in a few introductory remarks. This impossibility is especially obvious in the context of this study, as the kinship between Jacques Derrida's elaborate and multifarious work and Coetzee's literary production is a theoretical milestone of its own. Outlining it is a task best left to the words of an authoritative voice in both Coetzee and Derrida studies: in his 2010 monograph *Reading and Responsibility: Deconstruction's Traces*, Derek Attridge writes that 'Coetzee and Derrida are animated by some of the same concerns and haunted by some of the same fears' (42). While 'Coetzee's novels are by no means "illustrations" or "exemplifications" of Derrida's thinking' (42), turning to Coetzee's writings after acquainting oneself with Derrida's 'discussion of ethics, hospitality, and the future as *arrivant*, is to experience the fraught encounter with the other in a way that both confirms and tests the philosophical account one has been absorbing' (43).

Critical opinions on Coetzee's relationship with philosophy are copious and diverse. His works and characters have variously been defined as masks worn by the author not to state his opinions openly,[2] allegorical embodiments of abstract theories,[3] or philosophical debates staged in fiction.[4] However, critical analyses such as Attridge's – accounts which set out to investigate the ever-elusive specificity of Coetzee's literary voice and the way it both validates and challenges theoretical discourses – have gained prominent consensus in the community of Coetzee scholars and were substantiated further in David Attwell's *J.M. Coetzee and the Life of Writing* (2015).[5] Attwell's archive-based study also rejects the 'widely held assumption' that Coetzee's novels are 'spun from quotations drawn from literary theory' (20). Archival evidence from the Harry Ransom Center indeed proves that Coetzee, while obviously deeply aware of critical theory, crafts his fictions out of deep personal impulses, only to bring in references to theorists and philosophers after completing his first drafts.[6]

Based on these premises, I set out to give a Derridean reading of *Summertime* and *The Childhood of Jesus* and, more specifically, to unearth their engagement with Derrida's *Archive Fever* (1995). I will dwell on the relationships between characters, their memories and material evidence from their pasts, arguing that such relationships shape both narratives, and that new aspects of Coetzee's depiction of personal and historical memory will emerge from a Derridean framing.

1. Meaningful contrapositions: *Summertime* and *The Childhood of Jesus*

Discussing *Summertime* is almost mandatory in the context of a reflection on Coetzee and the archive. The 2009 book is the third and most experimental instalment in Coetzee's pseudo-autobiographical trilogy; the portrayal it offers of the Coetzee *persona* is entirely constructed upon a rich apparatus of fictive documents, notes and interviews. The whole narrative is framed by an opening and a closing section, both titled 'Notebooks' and made up of fragments and notes from an unfinished autobiographical project. The focalizer in these third-person, present-tense narrative sections is the same fictionalized Coetzee we find in the other autobiographical volumes, *Boyhood* and *Youth*; the style, however, is much more fragmentary. Narrative segments alternate with instructions and reminders written in italics by the fictional author of the autobiography, who seems to be jotting down notes on how to best develop his drafts. Aside from the opening and closing 'Notebooks', five chapters make up the bulk of the book. Each of them is an interview. The interviewer is a rather inconspicuous character; we know nothing about him but his name – Mr Vincent – and the fact that he is an unauthorized biographer trying to write a book about a deceased, world-famous author named John Coetzee. To do so, he has selected and approached five people from the dead author's life – all of whom seem to disappoint his expectations, question his objectivity, and undermine the legitimacy of his biographical enterprise, techniques and sources.

Compared to *Summertime*, *The Childhood of Jesus* has a more obscure connection with archival memory. The link I posit between the two works is, perhaps, equally obscure. The reasons behind this selection of works will emerge as my argument unfolds and their connections with *Archive Fever* are traced. To that end, however, it may be useful to dwell upon a few meaningful similarities and discrepancies between the two works of fiction before starting a comparative close reading alongside Derrida's work. The most obvious comparison is between the different depictions of archival memory and materiality; however, I will endeavour to show that other contrasts between the two books are equally significant in a discussion on memory.

The most immediate analogy between *Summertime* and *The Childhood of Jesus* lies in the fact that both books revolve around father-son relationships.[7] *Summertime* purports to reconstruct the first few years of Coetzee's life after he moved back to South Africa from the United States in 1971. However, as David Attwell remarks in *J.M. Coetzee and the Life of Writing*, many events are manipulated so that two distinct periods of time merge into one (2015: 180–1). When Coetzee left the United States, he was still married to Philippa Jubber, and his parents were still alive. His divorce happened in 1980, nine years after his return to South Africa, whereas his mother died in 1985. Yet, no mention of his marriage, his children or his mother is ever made in *Summertime*, where John is depicted as a single man living with his widower father.[8] At the beginning of the book he is struggling to come to terms with everything he has come back to: apartheid South Africa in its more violent phase, of course, but also his family ties. John's father features prominently in the book, and so do John's reflections on the relationship between the two of them, their shared past and the roles they play or should play in each other's life. The incommunicability between father and son is highlighted by many different factors, including their different relationships with memory and archival materiality. John is depicted in two stages of his life: as a famous author dealing with a massive autobiographical project in the 'Notebooks', and, in the interview sections, as a young writer shaping *Dusklands* as a personal and historical narrative. Both situations obviously imply an exploration of personal identity that is at least in part based on memory and archival documents. Conversely, John's father 'does not talk about himself, does not keep a diary or write letters' (Coetzee 2009: 251). His personality is indecipherable to John. The only mortifying glimpse the son ever gets of the father's inner life does not come from direct communication, but rather from a written source that stands in stark contrast with John's intellectualized approach to self-writing: a multiple-choice quiz in a lifestyle magazine which the father filled in and then left lying around.

The Childhood of Jesus presents us with a reverse perspective on the father-son relationship, even though the parental figure is equivocal at best. The main character and focalizer is Simón, a middle-aged man. The plot follows his quest to find the mother of a young boy, David, who lives and travels with him and whom Simón repeatedly describes with a somewhat enigmatic sentence: '[he is] not my grandson, not my son, but I am responsible for him'.[9] Explanations about Simón's pseudo-parental status are never asked nor given. Questions about the nature of his responsibility for (and authority over) David accompany the readers throughout the book and find no resolution in its ending.

The Childhood of Jesus begins when the father-son duo enters a town named Novilla. The unclear nature of Simón's relation to David is not cause for concern to any of its inhabitants; in fact, Novillians appear to be incapable of any kind of bewilderment.

We soon learn that they conduct austere lives, entirely regulated by rationality and matter-of-factness, and that even their closest relationships are conducted with cold and impersonal benevolence. Readers, however, are never clued in to whichever knowledge the characters may have about their Kafkaesque place of residence and the laws that regulate it. Everyone who enters Novilla, including Simón and David, has been 'washed clean' of his or her memories and assigned a new name and age. Official documents are kept by the authorities in the form of passports and records of job opportunities; historical archives, however, do not exist in Novilla. The absence of memories is also an absence of written or material evidence from the past. No sense of collective or personal history seems to exist and, since the characters have no recollection of their own mother tongues, communication only happens in a clumsy Spanish that is everyone's second language.

A book like *The Childhood of Jesus*, whose setting has variously been described by critics as 'unfathomable', 'Kafkaesque' and 'dystopic' (respectively, Farago 2013: online; Oates 2013: online; and Bellin 2013: online), obviously stands in stark contrast with the 'faked realism' of *Summertime*, a work deeply rooted in the very specific social and historical context of apartheid South Africa. Moreover, *Summertime* features a series of characters who are acutely aware of their linguistic capabilities and shortcomings: the book comprises fictional conversations between a British biographer and first-language speakers of German, Afrikaans, Portuguese and French, none of whom fails to bring up various issues connected to using words properly, having to speak a second language or needing a translator.[10] Conversely, 'all human relations' in *The Childhood of Jesus* 'have to be conducted in beginner's Spanish' (2013: 106). While most characters do acknowledge this predicament, they entirely lack the linguistic and metalinguistic tools to either overcome it or discuss it. What is more, aside from Simón's occasional bouts of frustration, they accept their linguistic limitation with the usual tepid serenity.

Clearly, it is not just the difference in setting and the characters' relationship with language that marks the contrast between *Summertime* and *The Childhood of Jesus*. However, I will endeavour to show now that these particular discrepancies between the two books are not randomly different, but rather meaningfully antipodal to one another, and that such an opposition is not merely framed by, but also offers a fundamental insight into the idea of archive in Coetzee's entire body of work. *Summertime* and *The Childhood of Jesus* are shaped by the characters' relationships to their past – or lack thereof. While the latter narrative is populated by characters who cannot remember their own stories and origins, the former is constructed upon a well-documented biographical enterprise. Moreover, both books depict a *post-mortem* situation – a supposedly favourable perspective from which to start the historicization of memories. The events in *Summertime* take place after the fictional J. M. Coetzee is dead: it is only then that those who have known and outlived him are sought after by an unauthorized biographer. Everything is characteristically murkier in *The Childhood of Jesus*: even though no direct mention of death is ever made, its characters refer repeatedly and unambiguously to those 'previous lives' they cannot remember but know for a fact they lived.[11] As a result, the whole narrative is permeated by an indefinite feeling of *after-ness*.[12]

2. Archival ambivalence

Jacques Derrida's *Archive Fever: A Freudian Impression* is particularly relevant to questions of memory posed by both of Coetzee's late novels. However, it also sheds light on the other, seemingly less conspicuous issues mentioned so far: language, setting, the post-mortem condition and father–son relationships.

Derrida's essay was originally a speech given at a 1994 international conference. The event, entitled *Memory: The Question of Archives*, was held under the auspice of the *Société Internationale d'Histoire de la Psychiatrie et de la Psychanalyse* at the Freud Archives in London – significantly, Freud's last place of residence, later turned into a museum. In customary deconstructive fashion, *Archive Fever* aims at unearthing the coexistent, aporetic meanings that the concept of archive spans and implies. Characteristically, Derrida begins his discussion by focusing on etymology and opens his speech by questioning 'so familiar a word' as *archive*, which 'names at once the *commencement* and the *commandament*' (9). We see right away that two principles are at stake at the same time: a physical, historical or ontological one (*arkhé*, the beginning) and a nomological one (law and authority). As Derrida goes on to explain, *arkhé* comes from *arkheion*, a residence for superior magistrates in ancient Greece. Those magistrates, the *archons*, were officially in charge of making, interpreting and publicly representing the law. On account of such authority, official documents were filed in their houses. It is with such domiciliation, Derrida remarks, that the archive began, while also becoming public and hidden at the same time (10): it inhabited a place of privilege and power that was visible to all, but it was also located in the private residences of those few men who were allowed to give their interpretations on it. As a result, the archive became a place in the public imagination that held exclusive hermeneutic rights on itself; because of both these conditions, as well as safety measures, it was not easily accessible.

The ambivalence that makes the archive simultaneously public and inaccessible is the focus of the first part of Derrida's essay. According to Leonard Lawlor, Derrida sets out to prove that that 'an archive ... consists in both a fever to safeguard information within for one person and a fever to expose information to the outside for others' (1998: 797). Such ambivalence is obviously not new for those who are familiar with Coetzee's public *persona* and autobiographical writing. Coetzee is a famously difficult interviewee who refuses to share personal opinions and never dwells on past experiences;[13] yet, the Texas archive is remarkably open and accessible, giving insight into intimate personal details. Even more significantly, Coetzee's narrative strategies in his pseudo-autobiographical trilogy estrange himself from his life while simultaneously exposing it to others. Such techniques have often puzzled critics because of their ambiguity. Although a confessional tone clearly permeates *Boyhood* and *Youth*, the main character does not give an account of his past from the privileged position of old age and, possibly, wisdom – in fact, he only appears in his life story as the focalizer of a third-person, present-tense narration.[14] This stylistic choice, in addition to Coetzee's refusal to comment on the critical disputes that have developed over his own works, has made it very difficult to determine whether those books should be labelled as autobiography or fiction.[15]

The narrative techniques in *Boyhood* and *Youth* are the same ones we find in *Summertime*'s 'Notebooks'; the sense of estrangement, however, grows and peaks in its middle sections. As we know, those chapters feature fictional interviews between a critic who wants to write an unauthorized biography of the fictional Coetzee, described as a deceased South African author and Nobel Prize winner, and some characters whose identities can be traced back – more or less loosely – to real-life acquaintances, family members or lovers of the real-life Coetzee.[16] The resulting sense of uncertainty as to *Summertime*'s documentary significance is pervasive, and it escalates even further after we learn that the interviews as we read them are presented to us after various stages of translation and editing on the curator's part.

During an interview, Mr Vincent himself voices his concerns about the reliability of documentary material in a biographical study on John Coetzee:

> What Coetzee writes there cannot be trusted, not as a factual record – not because he was a liar but because he was a fictioneer. In his letters he is making up a fiction of himself for his correspondents; in his diaries he is doing much the same for his own eyes, or perhaps for posterity. As documents they are valuable, of course; but if you want the truth you have to go behind the fictions they elaborate.
>
> (Coetzee 2009: 225–6)

Some real-life critics have expressed entirely similar views, and they have pointed out that *Summertime* blurs the line between the factual and the fictional so irrevocably as to make it impossible to write Coetzee's biography, unless of course elements of self-consciousness are ingrained in its fabric.[17] This very phenomenon – the commentary on the archive becoming part of the archive itself, thereby changing its nature – was discussed in remarkably similar terms by Derrida, who described it as a by-product of the 'archival fever' to both safeguard and expose. Derrida articulates this argument in the context of a discussion on Yosef Yerushalmi's analysis of Sigmund Freud's *Moses* (*Freud's Moses: Judaism Terminable and Interminable*, 1991). Yerushalmi, renowned historian of Jewish culture, uses both historical and philological analysis to offer his interpretation of *Moses*. Although he 'uses the conventions of scholarly objectivity', some reviewers argue that 'Yerushalmi's presentation of Freud is decidedly interpretative' (see Kepnes 1996: 193). Indeed, the book closes with a fictional section entitled 'Monologue with Sigmund Freud', where the scholar becomes a character in his own (supposedly theoretical) book and addresses directly the object of his study. Derrida describes these final pages as a *coupe de théâtre*: 'it is the moment where Professor Yerushalmi, with the incontestable authority of the scholar, but in an apparently more filial position, addresses himself or rather pretends to address himself to Professor Freud, in truth to Freud's ghost' (1994: 29). Derrida notes that the 'Monologue' departs from the scholarly norms that dominate the whole book: it is a fictional piece, an address to a dead person who is called to reply, but cannot do so for obvious reasons and is therefore only able to acquiesce. Still, the piece is contained within the book, and its ambiguous closing sentences – the statement that Yerushalmi's questions about Judaism are probably destined to stay unanswered, at least until 'much future work has been done' (Yerushalmi 1991: 100) – 'retrospectively determines what precedes it, ... marking it indeed with an essential indecision, namely the umbilical opening of the future' (Derrida 1994: 30).

The analogy between Yerushalmi's work and *Summertime* is easily seen: both books feature their authors as characters who are in conflicted relationships with their father figures and, most importantly, both use fiction and fictionalization in such a way that it becomes impossible to clearly distinguish between documentary, scientific material and the commentary it inspires. The similarity is so poignant that Derrida's comment on Freud's *Moses* can fittingly apply to *Summertime* as well: 'another archive effect. In its very fiction, this apostrophe ['Monologue with Sigmund Freud'] enriches the corpus that it claims to treat but that it enlarges and of which in truth it is henceforth a part' (1994: 29). In light of this, *Summertime* appears as another example of archival ambivalence: a commentary on Coetzee's life and works that is also *part of* his life and works – an element that is both internal and external to the archive and that redefines its nature while trying to comment on it.[18]

Summertime presents us with an abundance of semi-fictional documentary, archival material. Therefore, sketching its connection to *Archive Fever* is a relatively straightforward task. Conversely, *The Childhood of Jesus* is construed precisely on the lack of a past for the characters to document. People in Novilla do share a common substratum of assumptions about the world; such substratum, however, is stripped down to a bare minimum, as they lack not only a *shared* mother tongue, but rather a mother tongue *per se*. Many documents such as proofs of residence, or passports, are mentioned in the book. However, none of them provides insight into past events. Only one exception exists, and it is mentioned in the book in a surprisingly inconspicuous manner: a lost letter, which David claims (but cannot prove) he has received as guidance for his new life. We learn early on in the book that Simón feels it is his duty to find David's lost mother; indeed, he feels that is 'the chief task' (Coetzee 2013: 18). Why that may be, however, we do not know – and we are equally uncertain as to why Simón thinks he and David will be able to recognize the mother when they see her, even though neither one of them remembers her name and what she looks like. In the fourth chapter readers become privy to a little more information. Simón and David have gone out to a picnic with Ana, a mysterious young woman who works as an employee at a non-specified institution in Novilla. When Ana questions David about his lost mother, Simón explains that

> [David] doesn't know her by name. ... He had a letter with him when he boarded the boat, but it was lost. ... The letter was in a pouch ... which was hanging around his neck on a string. The string broke and the letter was lost. There was a hunt for it all over the ship. That was how David and I met. But the letter was never found.
> (Coetzee 2013: 28)

Surprisingly, Ana does not show any kind of interest in this explanation, nor does she seem sorry for David. In fact, she goes on questioning the child as if the letter were never mentioned, and neither she nor Simón bring up the subject again.

A lost letter containing details of the main character's forgotten past may well be a major plot element in a work of fiction. It is not so in *The Childhood of Jesus*. It is only after many chapters – after a woman named Inés has taken on a motherly role in David's life, and after Simón has adjusted to having her in his – that the letter is discussed again. In the final part of the book, David is attending sessions with the school psychologist, as concerns have arisen about his highly peculiar learning style and outlandish behaviour. When the psychologist meets with Inés and Simón, she reports that David has been talking about his origins:

> 'There is the matter of a certain letter. He speaks of a letter containing the names of his true parents. He says you, señor, know about the letter. Is that true?'
> 'A letter from whom?'
> 'He says he had the letter with him when he arrived on the boat.'
> 'Aha, *that* letter! No, you are mistaken, the letter was lost before we came ashore. It was lost during the voyage. I never saw it. It was because he had lost the letter that I took on the responsibility of helping him find his mother. Otherwise he would have been hopeless'.
>
> (Coetzee 2013: 209)

There is no more discussion of the letter: at first, Simón does not even seem to remember it and, even when he does, both he and the psychologist deem it unnecessary to explore the matter further. The lost letter is, indeed, lost; it may look like a crucial plot detail in the readers' eyes, but it is barely mentioned in the book – and when it is, characters react dismissively. Its absence, however, permeates the narrative, and poignantly enlightens the antithetical stance of *Summertime* and *The Childhood of Jesus* with respect to archival memory. The former book shows us an ever-growing bulk of notions and perspectives, all of them regarding the single individuality of John Coetzee; in the latter, even the focalizer – Simón – is alien to himself, and readers are constantly reminded of an ever-present, but nonetheless inaccessible, body of information: the lost letter, of course, but also the characters' memories. Reading the two books comparatively forces us to focus on the relationship between the inside of a hypertrophic, ever-growing, self-modifying archive and the outside of an inaccessible one. Such a relationship is also an extremely meaningful part of Derrida's argument, and in the last part of my analysis I wish to focus on its implications.

3. The ghost of the father

'There is no archive without a place of consignation, without a technique of repetition, and without a certain exteriority. No archive without outside,' Derrida writes (1995: 14), only to point out shortly afterwards that

> If there is no archive without consignation in an external place which assures the possibility of memorization, of repetition, of reproduction, or of reimpression, then we must also remember that repetition itself, the logic of repetition, indeed the repetition compulsion, remains, according to Freud, indissociable from the death drive. And thus from destruction. (14)

This concept is expanded and explained further when Derrida discusses the French word *memoire* and its polysemy (18). *Memoires* (masculine plural) suggests the idea of autobiography: something that comes from the inside of an alive *who*; *memoire* (masculine singular) reminds him of a memorandum, a fictional artifice, an inanimate *what* that functions as a 'prosthesis of the inside' (18). Finally, *memoire* (feminine singular) is an absolute faculty that does not account for the past and does not produce anticipations of the future. As a consequence, Derrida describes the archive in terms of *hypomnesis* rather than of *anamnesis* (18): it may make living memory possible, but, being a prosthetic artificial device, it also tinges it with the image of death.

Several critics have commented on the multiple intimations of death in Coetzee's work, with Chris Danta going as far as to describe him as a 'theorist of the afterlife' (2009: 1). As both Danta (2018: 3) and Jan Wilm aptly state, however, death is never 'unambiguously narrated' in Coetzee's fiction (Wilm 2016: 196): sometimes it is a looming perspective, anticipated but still not yet occurring (*Age of Iron*, *Diary of a Bad Year*); on other occasions, death has already happened off-stage and it stands as a somewhat mysterious premise to the whole narration.[19] Clearly, both *Summertime* and *The Childhood of Jesus* belong to the latter category, and the idea of mortality that permeates both works is easily framed in a Derridean perspective. *Summertime* presents us with *memoires* (masculine singular) of living characters who are building an archive on the now-dead, spectral, inanimate *what* that John Coetzee has become: the subject of a biography, the deceased and external prosthesis of other people's memories. In *The Childhood of Jesus*, on the other hand, such prosthesis is inaccessible, and the absolute faculty of memory – of *hypomnesis* – becomes an uncanny and useless feature of an afterlife world where it cannot be exercised on any object.

The uselessness of the *hypomnesis* is seen clearly in the quest for David's mother. Her name was written in a letter, now lost; David has no memory of the way she looked like. Nevertheless, Simón is sure that he and David will be able to recognize her as soon as they see her, and, indeed, he experiences a flicker of recognition when Inés appears for the first time: 'something stirs inside him. Who is this woman? Her smile, her voice, her bearing – there is something obscurely familiar about her' (Coetzee 2013: 69). However, David does not share his feelings: he does not recognize Inés and, even though Simón pushes him, the only thing the boy can do is shake his head (71). Inés herself shares David's puzzlement. She does not remember the boy either, and she seems confused when Simón suggests that she act as his mother. She mentions adoption, but Simón replies that she should not adopt him, but rather 'be his mother, his full mother' (75). Ultimately, Simón cannot appeal to Inés's feelings or her rationality, and much less to her distant memories of a supposedly lost son. It is only when he presents motherhood as a matter of faith and unconditional belief that Inés welcomes the role he so desperately wants her to take on: 'Please believe me – please take it on faith – this is not a simple matter. ... Yet I promise you, if you will simply say Yes, without forethought, without afterthought, all will become clear to you, clear as day, or so I believe' (75).

Derrida begins his essay on the archive with a discussion on its ambivalent meaning, and he goes on to discuss its link to destruction and the death drive; both these concepts are linked to the idea of documentary memories in Coetzee's narratives.

The closing section of *Archive Fever*, however, sheds light on the other major analogy between *Summertime* and *The Childhood of Jesus*, namely the depiction of father-son relationships.

Derrida's closing argument is a discussion on the nomological aspect that is enclosed in the concept of the archive – on the patriarchal authority that is associated with the archival one. Since *Archive Fever* was first delivered as a speech in Sigmund Freud's London residence-turned-museum, it was easy for Derrida to make a point about a pivotal theme in his philosophical production – that of hospitality. It is well known that, in the Derridean logic of hospitality, the host becomes a guest in his own house: a spectral presence who is supposed to disappear in order to make his guests feel at home. Freud is the host to all the life-and-blood participants in the event: the father of the family, the head of the household and the person in charge of his guests' well-being. On the other hand, in light of previous remarks, it is not difficult to imagine why Freud – the dead object of archival attention – is seen as a spectral participant in the conference. Once again, the two sides of this contradictory depiction of the spectre of the father are to be found in Coetzee's novels.

In *Summertime* an all-too-present father haunts J. M. Coetzee, an adult but still a child, and still a guest in his paternal home. In David Attwell's words, the book is the conclusion of a three-book long phase of a son hating the father, a story where the latter's death is less important than the former's maturation (2015: 177–8). Indeed, a trajectory is clearly recognizable: in the opening section, John is an unemployed intellectual who admits to still being 'a child' (14), a son living at home with his father. A few chapters later, it is the end of John's 'prolonged childhood' that marks the ending of the book. Nostalgia permeates its closing section as his father becomes older and needier. The two men's mundane and uneventful routine is interrupted by a sudden cancer diagnosis. In the aftermath of a larynx surgery and amidst cancer treatment, John's father is left unable to talk and take care of himself, and John is faced with a choice: he can either abandon his own literary ambitions and become a full-time caregiver or 'alternatively, if he will not be a nurse, he must announce to his father: I cannot face the prospect of ministering to you day and night. I am going to abandon you. Goodbye. One or the other: there is no third way' (266). This is the closing sentence of the book. Of course, John's feeling that he needs to make a drastic choice to either abandon his father tout court or devote his entire life to him sounds more like a symbolic crossroads than a realistic necessity. Nevertheless, his dilemma is posited as an either/or situation, and since *Summertime* depicts the Coetzee character as a world-famous, successful author, readers are led to assume that John's choice was to forgo filial responsibility in order to focus on his writerly ambitions instead.

When Coetzee-the-character stops figuring as a filial figure, he becomes an author – the dead author whose life Mr Vincent purposes to reconstruct, and therefore a spectral presence in the conversations of those who remember him, much like Derrida's Freud. At the same time, the posthumous situation implies the loss of authorial authority and mirrors Roland Barthes's famous argument in 'The Death of the Author' that 'where interpretation of a literary text is concerned the author is not a supervisory limit to it but an absence and a silence, always already dead insofar as it is the reader who inherits the text to settle its meaning'.[20]

The Childhood of Jesus is also haunted by a kind of absence that has to do with both authorship and paternity. We know that Simón is not David's father, and that his responsibility towards the boy does not seem to imply any sort of authority over him. Moreover, while all the main characters can be loosely traced back to evangelical *personae*, no God-like figure is ever detected. God the Father holds no authoritative place in Coetzee's allegorical Gospel, and there is no authorial voice to guide Simón's rambling quest. Paternal authority is irredeemably lost, as is David's missing letter: the word of law, presumably written in a forgotten mother tongue, is the only archival document from a world that is now lost to memory.

In his discussion of death in Coetzee's fiction, Chris Danta states that the prospect of death – the short time and limited space that characters often perceive before them – defines Coetzee's fiction (2018: 3). In fact, Danta argues that 'Coetzee as a storyteller ... borrows his authority from the prospect of death' (2018: 2). However, *Summertime* and *The Childhood of Jesus* are different kinds of narratives: death has already occurred off-stage before they begin, and authority has already been lost. Once again, the post-mortem situation is aptly described by an analogy between Coetzee's work and Roland Barthes's:

> to write is in a sense to become 'still as death,' to become someone to whom the last word is denied; to write is to offer others, from the start, that last word. For the meaning of a work (or of a text) cannot be created by the work alone; the author never produces anything but presumptions of meaning, forms, and it is the world which fills them.[21]

The Derridean depiction of archival memory in Coetzee's work indeed functions as Barthes describes: it never ceases to generate new commentary, which it then goes on to incorporate, thereby changing its internal structure again and again. As a result, it undermines its own authority from within; it does not present readers with ultimate and authoritative accounts of facts, but rather offers them the last, interpretative word.

Notes

1 In an interview with Elleke Boehmer, David Attwell remarks upon the general unanimity in the community of Coetzee scholars on some key stances, including this one. See Boehmer (2010: 60).
2 See Lodge (2003: 6) or Herford (2003: 6).
3 See Lynn (2005: 130) or (Attwell 2008: 229).
4 See Shillingsburg (2006: 13) and Northover (2012).
5 See Boehmer (2010: 60) as well as López (2011: xviii).
6 'Allusions to other writers ... are brought in only once the work has found its own legs. ... Typically, the novels begin personally and circumstantially, before being worked into fiction. ... Coetzee's writing is a huge existential enterprise, grounded in fictionalized autobiography' (Attwell 2015: 20, 25–6).
7 Arguably, Coetzee's most famous work dealing with father–son relationships is *The Master of Petersburg* (1994), in which a fictionalized Dostoevsky mourns his stepson's death

in 1860s Saint Petersburg. The novel, published five years after the death of Coetzee's son Nicolas, obviously bears biographical and documentary significance. In David Attwell's words, 'certain passages … are written straight out of a father's grief' (2015: 196). Differently from *Summertime* and *The Childhood of Jesus*, however, *The Master of Petersburg* depicts a father losing a son, not a son managing the lack or loss of a father figure and the symbolical connections to authority and personal origins that entails.

8   Archival evidence proves that Coetzee's first wife did appear in the first drafts of *Summertime*; however, she disappeared from the narrative once Coetzee decided to change the time frame (see Attwell 2005: 181). Biographical gaps in the published work may not have been gaps in the earlier version.

9   Coetzee (2013: 1). Simón uses similar words to describe David on other occasions as well: see, e.g., pages 28, 33, 53 and 207.

10 See pages 27, 63, 87, 91, 157, 161, 165, 171, 175, 237 and 238.

11 See pages 20–1, 60, 133, 156 and 208.

12 This feeling of *after-ness* can be seen as an ironic counterpart to what Jan Wilm describes as Coetzee's *Vorlass* (2017: 217). While *The Childhood of Jesus* presents us with an afterworld that has lost any connections to its origins, *Summertime* (much like the actual Texas archive) evokes a literary afterlife that begins before the author's actual death. Boundaries between fictional and autobiographical work are thus blurred, reinforcing Coetzee's famous statement in *Doubling the Point* that 'writing writes us' (1992: 18).

13 See Kannemeyer (2012: 423) and 425 for some examples.

14 Derek Attridge (2004: 138–41) comments on Coetzee's highly recognizable, and yet idiosyncratic, rendering of the confessional mode by comparing *Boyhood* and *Youth* to Augustine's and Rosseau's *Confessions*, Proust's *Recherche*, and 'two obvious precursors that narrate the childhood of a writer with exceptional gifts' (141): *The Education of Henry Adams* and Joyce's *A Portrait of the Artist as a Young Man*. Some of those works are mixtures of facts and fictions and others use the third person, but none is written in the present tense. According to Attridge, it is precisely the simultaneous employment of the third person and of the present tense that marks Coetzee's singularity.

15 *Boyhood* and *Youth* have variously been described as both fiction and non-fiction – more specifically, as *memoirs*, fictionalized *memoirs*, autobiography, fictionalized autobiography, *autre*biography and possibly other labels.

16 See Crewe (2013: 11–13).

17 See Clarkson (2014: 264) ('the question of the self in writing is addressed with such critical and creative acuity throughout Coetzee's oeuvre that the work of any other biographer would in some sense seem to be pre-empted') and Dooley (2013: 19).

18 The dialogical, mutually reshaping nature of Coetzee's unfinished archive and equally unfinished fictional oeuvre is discussed by Jan Wilm in his essay 'The J.M. Coetzee Archive and the Archive in J.M. Coetzee' (2017: 222).

19 Danta also comments on more ambiguous 'death-in-life' situations, when characters become ghostly figures after a symbolic death happens inconspicuously, like 'a mere hiccup in time after which life goes on as before' (2009: 4). Alice Brittan makes entirely similar remarks on David Lurie's existential condition in *Disgrace*: according to her, Lurie is 'posthumous from the novel's opening pages' (2010: 484), and after being attacked he becomes 'as evanescent as the dead', with 'no self to speak of' (483).

20 See Powers (2016: 324).

21 Barthes (1972: xi). The analogy with Coetzee's work was posited by Donald Powers (2016: 324).

References

Attridge, D. (2004), *J.M. Coetzee and the Ethics of Reading: Literature in the Event*. Chicago: University of Chicago Press.
Attridge, D. (2010), *Reading and Responsibility: Deconstruction's Traces*. Edinburgh: Edinburgh University Press.
Attwell, D. (2008), 'Coetzee's Estrangements', *Novel*, 41 (2/3): 229–44.
Attwell, D. (2015), *J.M. Coetzee and the Life of Writing: Face to Face with Time*. Oxford: Oxford University Press.
Barthes, R. (1972), *Critical Essays*. Evanston, IL: Northwestern University Press.
Barthes, R. (1977), 'The Death of the Author'. In: S. Heath, ed., *Image, Music, Text*. London: Fontana Press, 142–8.
Bellin, R. (2013), 'A Strange Allegory: J.M. Coetzee's *The Childhood of Jesus*', *Los Angeles Review of Books*, 6 November 2013. Available online: lareviewofbooks.org/article/magical-child-troubled-child-on-jm-coetzees-the-childhood-of-jesus/#! (accessed 7 November 2018).
Boehmer, E. (2010), 'Doubling the Writer: David Attwell on His Textual Dialogue with J.M. Coetzee', *Wasafiri*, 25 (3): 57–61.
Brittan, A. (2010), 'Death and J.M. Coetzee's *Disgrace*', *Contemporary Literature*, 51 (3): 477–502.
Chapman, M. (2010), 'The Case of Coetzee: South African Literary Criticism, 1990 to Today', *Journal of Literary Studies*, 26 (2): 103–17.
Clarkson, C. (2014), 'J.M. Coetzee: 'n Geskryfde Lewe. / J.M. Coetzee: A Life in Writing', *Life Writing*, 11 (2): 263–70.
Coetzee, J. M. (1974), *Dusklands*. London: Vintage Books.
Coetzee, J. M. (1992), *Doubling the Point: Essays and Interviews*, ed. David Attwell. Cambridge, MA: Harvard University Press.
Coetzee, J. M. (2009), *Summertime: Scenes from Provincial Life*. London: Harvill Secker.
Coetzee, J. M. (2013), *The Childhood of Jesus*. London: Harvill Secker.
Crewe, J. (2013), 'Arrival: J.M. Coetzee in Cape Town', *English in Africa*, 40 (1): 11–35.
Danta, C. (2009), 'Coetzee's Animal Afterlives', *Southerly*, 69 (1): 1–8.
Danta, C. (2018), 'Eurydice's Curse: J.M. Coetzee and the Prospect of Death', *Australian Literary Studies*, 33 (1): 1–17.
Derrida, J. (1995), 'Archive Fever: A Freudian Impression', *Diacritics*, 25 (2): 9–63.
Dooley, G. (2013), 'An Arched Bow: Review of *J.M. Coetzee: A Life in Writing* by J.C. Kannemeyer', *Australian Book Review*, February: 19–20.
Farago, J. (2013), 'J.M. Coetzee's Stunning New Novel Shows What Happens When a Nobel Winner Gets Really Weird: Review of *The Childhood of Jesus* by J.M. Coetzee', *New Republic*, 14 September. Available online: newrepublic.com/article/114658/jm-coetzees-childhood-jesus-reviewed-jason-farago (accessed 7 November 2018).
Herford, O. (2003), 'Tears for Dead Fish: Review of *Elizabeth Costello: Eight Lessons* by J.M. Coetzee', *Times Literary Supplement*, 5 September. Available online: www.the-tls.co.uk/articles/private/tears-for-dead-fish/ (accessed 7 November 2018).

Kannemeyer, J. C. (2012), *J.M. Coetzee: A Life in Writing*, trans. Michiel Heyns. London: Scribe.

Kepnes, S. (1996), 'Review of *Freud's Moses: Judaism Terminable and Interminable* by Yosef H. Yerushalmi', *Journal of the History of the Behavioral Sciences*, 32 (April): 193–6.

Lawlor, L. (1998), 'Memory Becomes Electra: Review of "Archive Fever: A Freudian Impression" by Jacques Derrida', *Review of Politics*, 60 (4): 796–8.

Lodge, D. (2003), 'Disturbing the Peace: Review of *Elizabeth Costello: Eight Lessons* by J.M. Coetzee', *New York Review of Books*, 50 (18): 6–11.

López, M. J. (2011), *Acts of Visitation: The Narrative of J.M. Coetzee*. Amsterdam: Rodopi.

Lynn, D. H. (2005), 'Love and Death, and Animals too', *Kenyon Review*, 27 (1): 124–33.

Northover, R. A. (2012), 'Elizabeth Costello as a Socratic Figure', *English Studies in Africa*, 39 (1): 37–55.

Oates, J. C. (2013), 'Saving Grace: Review of *The Childhood of Jesus* by J.M. Coetzee', *New York Times*, 29 August. Available online: www.nytimes.com/2013/09/01/books/review/j-m-coetzees-childhood-of-jesus.html (accessed 7 November 2018).

Powers, D. (2016), 'Beyond the Death of the Author: Summertime and J.M. Coetzee's Afterlives', *Life Writing*, 13 (3): 323–34.

Shillingsburg, P. (2006), 'Textual Criticism, the Humanities and J.M. Coetzee', *English Studies in Africa*, 49 (2): 13–27.

Wilm, J. (2016), *The Slow Philosophy of J.M. Coetzee*. London: Bloomsbury Academic.

Wilm, J. (2017), 'The J.M. Coetzee Archive and the Archive in J.M. Coetzee'. In: Patrick Hayes and Jan Wilm, eds, *Beyond the Ancient Quarrel: Literature, Philosophy, and J.M. Coetzee*. Oxford: Oxford University Press, 215–31.

Yerushalmi, Y. H. (1991), *Freud's Moses: Judaism Terminable and Interminable*. New Haven, CT: Yale University Press.

Part Two

History, politics and the archive

# 4

Writing, politics, position: Coetzee and Gordimer in the archive

Andrew van der Vlies

An attentive reader of J. M. Coetzee's sixth published fiction, *Age of Iron* (1990), who is also au fait with the oeuvre of Nadine Gordimer, could be forgiven for pausing over what might appear to be allusions to the work of Coetzee's countrywoman – nearly two decades older and at this point still more internationally renowned (she would be awarded the Nobel Prize for Literature the following year).[1] Might the moment in which Coetzee's protagonist Mrs Curren thinks of her unkempt house as 'a late bourgeois tomb' (1990: 137) be an intentional echo of the title of Gordimer's 1966 novel, *The Late Bourgeois World*, in which another female narrator (first name Liz[2]) begins to understand the nature of her complicity with injustice? When Mrs Curren compares the body of a teenager shot by the police to 'pig iron' (114), or feels as though she is 'walking upon black faces' (115), might our reader recall these images from Gordimer's *The Conservationist* (1974) (though Mrs Curren would perhaps strike this reader as more knowing than Mehring, Gordimer's protagonist in that novel)? Mrs Curren certainly demonstrates an awareness of what Stephen Clingman, in his seminal 1986 study of Gordimer's fiction as 'history from the inside', characterizes as the 'destabilization of a whole framework of reality and its eventual displacement' (1993: 155). While legible in *The Conservationist*, indeed in any Gordimer novel, this awareness is not always evident with such clarity to Gordimer's characters, those like Bam and Maureen Smales in *July's People* (1981), whose obsessive shortwave-radio listening might come to our reader's mind, too, when reading of Mrs Curren doing the same in *Age of Iron*.

It is not new to suggest that Coetzee and Gordimer were engaged with or even influenced by each other's work. Several scholars have made comparisons between *July's People* and Coetzee's novels of the early 1980s, though without suggesting direct allusion one way or the other.[3] Lars Engle (2010) makes a case for Gordimer's *None to Accompany Me* (1994) being a subtext for *Disgrace* (1999), while being careful not to suggest deliberate intertextuality; Coetzee is responsive to the *kind* of political directness associated with Gordimer's work, Engle instead argues.[4] David Attwell has suggested that, alongside Coetzee's own mother, Gordimer may have been a key influence on several of his 'female fictional authors', especially Elizabeth Costello

(2015: 115). Attwell cites a research visit Coetzee made to the Gordimer papers in the Lilly Library in Bloomington, Indiana, while preparing to write *The Lives of Animals* (1999).[5] Engagements with Gordimer – in drafts of the fiction and in other archival writing – predate this trip, however.

In what follows, I describe some of these traces in support of a contention that the allusions noted by the hypothetical reader above are entirely well founded. I wish, however, to add some caveats to a description of the archive's confirmation of the importance of Gordimer's work for Coetzee's own: such trails might also blind us to other links and connections and, insofar as fiction does something *different* (from letters, essays, or talks, for example), we ought to guard against relying too heavily on archival material for interpretations of the published works of fiction themselves. How might these examples instead offer both a necessary expansion of our understanding of literary networks in a particular time and place, and suggest that caution is required in this season of archival turns – and returns – in what can by now be called 'Coetzee Studies'?

* * *

As I have noted elsewhere, the trajectory of characters in Gordimer's novels from the 1960s through the early 1990s is almost always from a position of discomfited liberal humanism to profound disillusionment, a dysphoria that prompts a realization of the inevitability of the end of white rule (Van der Vlies 2014: 102–3). Coetzee's *Age of Iron* enacts through its very form, a letter to an émigré daughter, a thoroughgoing critique not only of the stability of any position from which a writer like Coetzee – and crucially also like Gordimer – might represent this realization about (or similar analysis of) white complicity, but indeed also of the efficacy or ideological incorruptibility of political praxis tout court. Coetzee's novel takes the position of the liberal white person of conscience, so often the focus of Gordimer's fiction, too, to what might be described as its logical end point – a deathbed. It is as if the trope of the moribund body politic beset by an array of morbid symptoms, borrowed from Antonio Gramsci's analysis of late capitalism (Gordimer would popularize Gramsci's use of the term 'interregnum' as description for late-apartheid South Africa), is in fact embodied in Mrs Curren's cancer-ridden frame.[6]

As Carrol Clarkson notes, that this destabilization extends to all narrative positions is likely at the heart of Gordimer's unease with what she understood to be the eponymous protagonist's disavowal of revolutionary agency in Coetzee's 1983 novel, *Life & Times of Michael K*. Gordimer's review of the novel, in the *New York Review of Books* in 1984, while voicing appreciation for the book, also expressed unease at Coetzee's portrayal of his protagonist as a victim. Michael K is a mixed-race, cleft-lipped gardener caring more for pumpkin seeds than revolutionary struggle; he wishes to be left alone to answer only to the seasons, free from the designs either of the white-ruled state disintegrating around him (in Coetzee's dystopian depiction of a near future) or of the black liberation-movement fighters struggling for a new dispensation. This representation, Gordimer wrote, was 'a challengingly questionable position for a writer to take up in South Africa' in that moment (1984: 4). Given that Gordimer's 'literary touchstone' was 'the realist novel', Clarkson suggests, 'the absence of a realist representation of the daily lives and ideological commitments of political activists in South Africa', and in particular a representation of black subjects with agency, would likely have struck her as 'a breach in the responsibility of the South African writer' (2017: 203).[7]

By the middle of the 1980s, the decade of the death-throes of the apartheid state, marked by states of emergency, township violence and proxy Cold War border conflicts, Gordimer and Coetzee, widely recognized as South Africa's two pre-eminent white Anglophone novelists, were often taken to occupy divergent positions on the question of the writer's responsibility to society. Indeed scholars frequently take Gordimer's review of *Life & Times of Michael K* as a starting point in drawing the comparison.[8] But if Coetzee scholars felt the need to nuance and defend what was too often and too easily cast as the author's (or sometimes, defensively, *their* author's) reluctance to enter the political fray, so too did proponents of Gordimer's work feel compelled, as the hoped-for final days of apartheid arrived, to reassess their critiques of Coetzee. Stephen Clingman, for instance, in a 1992 Prologue to the second edition of his study of Gordimer's fiction, despite still arguing that her oeuvre had 'always been tied much more urgently than Coetzee's to the idea of political obligation and responsibility' (1993: xii), is at pains to suggest that the two authors' writing was becoming increasing more alike. While *Age of Iron*, then 'Coetzee's most recent novel,' came 'closer than ever to the urgencies of political consciousness even as he doubts its priorities', Clingman wrote, Gordimer was herself beginning 'to raise her own questions more insistently'; they 'begin to meet at the same place from their different directions, and there are "double-graphs" across and within both their fictions' (xxxiii). What Clingman notices is not – or is not *only* – a growing similarity between these writers' senses of the kind of work demanded by a turn in the country's politics, even a turn that, while long desired, would inevitably take an unpredictable course. Instead it is the visibility of an engagement by Coetzee with Gordimer's example, one that had been ongoing for two decades, which has come more clearly into focus. While we know that Coetzee had been following Gordimer's work and its reception during this decade (he published a review of Michael Wade's study of Gordimer's fiction in 1980), the archive reminds us of more frequent and sometimes difficult engagements between the writers.

As Attwell (2015) has demonstrated, Coetzee's novels grew differently each time, with allusions and references often inserted after a novel had found its near-final shape. In the case of *Age of Iron*, however, manuscript drafts in the Harry Ransom Center in Austin, Texas, show that, from the earliest stages, Gordimer and her work were significant foils. At one point in May 1987, Coetzee thinks of the novel-in-progress as 'in a sense an anti-*July's People*' (HRC, CP, 33.7: 08-05-1987). Later, in a notebook kept during the final stages of composition, he expresses doubts that its many classical allusions are working, and wonders about his protagonist whether it might work better to

> Make her a writer. Base her on Gordimer? She writes novels, has cancer, faces the failure of her career.
>
> (HRC, CP, 17.2: 20-11-1989)

As early as the second draft, in a section dated 23 September 1987 (the manuscript was begun in May), the protagonist – at this point a man – tells his domestic worker that he and she are not unlike characters in Gordimer's fiction:

'Florence,' I said, 'there is a writer who lives in Johannesburg, called Nadine Gordimer, who writes about people like us. She writes about people who talk like us. It is a very humiliating experience to read about oneself in her books. We must try not to be like people in the books Mrs Gordimer writes.'

Florence looked at me with real interest. 'She writes about you and me, this Mrs Gordimer.'

'She writes about us, all the time. She gives us different names, but she writes about us. She writes about us because there are so many of us, all over this country, talking together like we do. Florence, it's no good. We must try to talk a different way. We must put this Mrs Gordimer behind us. Florence, you mustn't pretend that you don't know what I'm talking about. You know very well what I'm talking about.'

(HRC, CP, 14.1: 23-09-1987)

None of these direct allusions survives in the final text. Those that remain are considerably more wry: Gordimer, for example, was a cat owner, and Mrs Curren's invocation of a late bourgeois tomb (quoted earlier) is prompted by the 'smell of cat urine' (1990: 150). We might note, too, the dilemma that Coetzee is exploring at this point in the composition process, dramatizing entrapment in precisely that master–servant dialectic that animates *July's People*, or that Gordimer explores in any number of short stories (and which Coetzee staged very differently in *In the Heart of the Country*).

Why might Coetzee have been contemplating such writing back, if that is what this is? Gordimer's narrating voices, often cast in conspicuously difficult, late-modernist, free-indirect discourse, are not those of writers per se. Mrs Curren *is* a writer, however, most obviously of letters to an absent daughter. She is also a self-conscious worrier about the efficacy of language, drawing frequent attention to the limits of representation and implicitly of realism itself: recall how she questions the status of her imagining of an encounter between Florence and Florence's husband, William (43–4), or dwells on the difficulty of communication, resorting to making 'sprawling, sliding characters, meaningless' on the wall (182).[9] Writing itself, then, its costs and commitments, are here at stake, as is Coetzee's concern – in view from the very first fictions, but evident in newly compelling ways in *Life & Times of Michael K*, *Foe* and *Age of Iron*, the novels written during the 1980s – with the strangeness of the literary, with literary writing's insistence on its own rules and procedures, on what Coetzee would characterize in his November 1987 *Weekly Mail* Book Fair address, 'The Novel Today' (delivered some months into the writing of the early manuscript drafts of *Age of Iron*), as its refusal to be subsumed 'under history', of being made to stand in a position of 'supplementarity' to historical discourse (1988: 2). The novel, he insisted, operated according to rules different from those governing public speech. In short, Coetzee was becoming increasingly convinced during this period that there was no way to speak directly in his own voice without such speech being always already undermined or co-opted to unsustainable positions; there was no public language uncontaminated by politics in which to speak. Concomitantly, literature that sought to address public-political issues directly would run into the same problems. As Coetzee would say nearly two decades later, in a terse response to a question about the difficulty or otherwise of taking up public-intellectual positions in writing, 'it is hard for fiction to be good fiction while it is in the service of something else' (2006: 21).[10]

The archive gives us a glimpse of two particular moments during this period in which we see Coetzee attempting to navigate the demands made on him to speak publicly in this way. In each, it is Gordimer to whose example he turns in order to think his way towards a tenable position. In the first instance, the writers are brought together in public and cast inadvertently on opposite sides of a controversy whose fallout they subsequently attempt to address in private correspondence – a privacy, it should be noted, in effect refused by the accessibility of the archive. In the second instance, Coetzee attempts to engage not with Gordimer herself, but with the example of her work, and in a way that casts light rather more usefully on the reason for what I have suggested are occluded engagements with her in the published text of *Age of Iron*. Fiction, it will emerge, is where Coetzee finds that he might stage positions taken without being forced into himself taking positions.

* * *

The first moment is that of the public disagreement that occurred between Coetzee and Gordimer in late October 1988 over the withdrawal of an invitation to Salman Rushdie to speak at the *Weekly Mail* Book Fair in Cape Town that year. Rushdie's new novel, *The Satanic Verses*, then eliciting condemnation from some Muslim communities, had just been published. When the scale of the objections to Rushdie's attendance raised by representatives of some South African Muslim communities became clear, the Congress of South African Writers (COSAW) tried to broker an agreement that would recognize a right to protest *and* allow the appearance to take place. When it became clear that neither Rushdie's nor audience members' safety could be guaranteed, COSAW reluctantly concluded that the invitation should be withdrawn.

Coetzee had been scheduled to be in conversation with Rushdie at the University of Cape Town's Baxter Theatre. On hearing of the withdrawn invitation, he threatened to pull out of the event himself, but agreed, after seeing the *Weekly Mail*'s statement, to appear in order that he might make clear his own position on the matter. When he took to the stage, it was to deliver a scathing critique of the organizers' decision, one that warned against 'alliances' with fundamentalists: 'Fundamentalism means nothing more or less than going back to an origin and staying there', he suggested; 'it stands for one founding Book and after that no more books' (qtd in Kannemeyer 2012: 410).[11] Gordimer, a leading COSAW member who had worked behind the scenes to attempt to rescue the event in some form, had travelled to Cape Town to make the union's case clear and was wounded by the sharpness of Coetzee's riposte. The archive includes an exchange of letters in the weeks following in which Coetzee attempts to clarify his position.

On 5 November 1988, Coetzee wrote to Gordimer to emphasize that he had assumed that she was aware of his opposition to the cancellation of Rushdie's invitation. He apologizes for what she took as 'the unexpectedness' of what he is careful to call his 'attack on the COSAW decision'. 'As for the substance of the attack,' he continued, 'I remain unrepentant' (HRC, CP, 73.5: 05-11-1988).[12] Gordimer responded three weeks later: 'It was the Muslim community who prevented Salman Rushdie from coming to South Africa, not COSAW and the Weekly Mail'

(Gordimer in Coetzee, HRC, CP, 73.5: 29-11-1988).[13] She is eager to acknowledge the spirit in which Coetzee had written, and notes that she 'resented very much' how the press had cast their comments. The *Tribune* had reported them as being 'in a "bitter" exchange', but, she continues,

> It wasn't so. But what can one do with journalists when they want to invent a good story? Let it go to line the drawers or light the fire. They're not going to make enemies out of us, believe me.
>
> (ibid.)

The letter is signed 'Affectionately'. Coetzee responds equally warmly, in mid-December, closing with these lines:

> Allow me to say (since there are not many openings for saying this kind of thing) that if on occasion it may seem to you that you have lost touch with whites, even 'good' whites, it is because you have travelled so much farther down a road which they too, in the end, will have to cover, that you are, at times, no longer in sight. (I say this as someone who is himself lagging behind, but trying to keep you and your example in view.) With warmest affection.
>
> (HRC, CP, 73.5: 14-12-1988)

Gordimer responded in a handwritten postcard three days later, thanking Coetzee for '[a] remarkable letter, which I'll not forget; and support for which I'm grateful' (Gordimer in Coetzee, HRC, CP, 73.5: 17-12-1988).

But ten days before Gordimer's first response, on 19 November 1988, Coetzee had written the following in one of the notebooks he kept during the composition of *Age of Iron*:

> Have been reading interview with Joseph Brodsky. I certainly won't make anything of the current book unless I have the courage to write for that kind of reader. The pressure for so-called relevance in SA too much for me. That is to say, I am capitulating before it.
>
> (HRC, CP, 33.6: 19-11-1988)

We might speculate about whether this is a comment about the progress of the manuscript, or indeed at least in part a reflection on his having been drawn into a public argument, into speaking in the kind of public forum *as author* rather than letting *writing* speak for itself. The notebook continues:

> The book will only work if I work on things like *angelhood*. And perhaps not even then.
>
> The cancer as an *index*. A heightened feeling of the death in her. Logic: we all have cancer. In all of us the body is consuming itself. Therefore: when she is herself – i.e. when she is *writing* – she is there, she is strong.
>
> (ibid.)

The act of writing, a commitment to it in the face of the undoubted urgency of other claims, claims for other kinds of action, is clearly at issue for Coetzee here.

The final text of *Age of Iron* bears a trace of Coetzee's sense of the 'pressure for so-called relevance' in Mrs Curren's own wrestling with what she calls 'urgency':

> 'I am sorry if I am not making sense,' I said. 'I am trying my best not to lose direction. I am trying to keep up a sense of urgency. A sense of urgency is what keeps deserting me. Sitting here among all this beauty, or even sitting at home among my own things, it seems hardly possible to believe there is a zone of killing and degradation all around me. It seems like a bad dream. ... With relief I give myself back to the ordinary. I wallow in it. I lose my sense of shame, become shameless as a child. The shamefulness of that shamelessness: that is what I cannot forget, that is what I cannot bear afterwards.'
>
> (1990: 109)

It is when she is writing that Mrs Curren is herself, Coetzee realises (HRC, CP, 33.6). When she speaks, as we see her representing herself (*writing* herself) doing, she finds speech inadequate, or rather finds that 'a sense of urgency is what keeps deserting me'. Not to speak in this way, but rather to write (and the conceit is that what we read is to be imagined as her writing), is 'shameful' insofar as it requires shamelessness to think one *can* write in the midst of injustice and death. Mrs Curren cannot speak in good faith and in a language unmediated by the competing discourses of the regime and the liberation movement about what she has witnessed on the Cape Flats; she can only focus on her own struggle, look into her own heart, and express this dilemma through writing. Writing itself is thus an instantiation of shame, as Tim Bewes posits it (2007: 153).[14]

While the archive shows that Coetzee attempted to re-establish a relationship of cordiality with Gordimer after the *Weekly Mail* Book Week fallout, it also confirms that his displeasure at having been drawn into a public disagreement – acceding to the demands of urgency and relevance – lingered. In *Diary of a Bad Year*, in the strong opinion 'On Harold Pinter', J. C. reflects that 'when one speaks in one's own person ... using the rhetoric of the agora, one embarks on a contest which one is likely to lose because it takes place on ground where one's opponent is far more practised and adept' (2007: 127). In the draft diary entry in which this reflection first took form, dated 9–10 December 2005, soon after Pinter's Nobel Lecture, Coetzee himself reflects on how he had chosen not to speak in the way that Pinter did when he had given his own Nobel Lecture two years previously. And it concludes with a reflection, which does not make it into *Diary of a Bad Year* (as distance grew between Coetzee and his fictional character), that it was in fact in what he calls 'confrontations with Nadine Gordimer' in the 1980s that this lesson was learned (HRC, CP, 42.3: 9/10-12-2005).[15] 'Behind the lingering resentment', David Attwell suggests in commenting on this draft material, 'is a sense that when Gordimer adopted the role of prophet, she went off key' (2015: 42–3). It was this that Coetzee resolved to avoid.

* * *

The second moment I refer to above came some four months later, in early 1989. Coetzee was in the United States as a visiting professor at Johns Hopkins University in Baltimore and, on 12 April, delivered a talk about five South African writers, using each as proponent of a position in 'the field of literature and politics in South Africa'. He would 'not', Coetzee announced, 'be talking about myself or my own work' (HRC, CP, 65.2: 12-04-1989), and yet, in speaking of the field in such Bourdieu-like terms, he sketches precisely the possibilities for position-taking that structure his own sense of the dangers of being drawn into ascribable polemic.

Three of the writers about whom he speaks – Hein Willemse, André Brink, and Breyten Breytenbach (all writers in Afrikaans) – need not detain us further, nor need we consider in detail his comments about Mothobi Mutloatse, who serves as key example of Black Consciousness writing. Rather, it is what Coetzee has to say about Nadine Gordimer – and specifically her *response* to Black Consciousness – that is worth considering. Coetzee sketches the development of Gordimer's position on the responsibilities of the writer through four key essays, from the mid-1970s to the mid-1980s. He had in fact published a warm review of the recent – 1988 – collection, *The Essential Gesture*, in which these had reappeared,[16] but in this talk characterizes Gordimer's shift from the earlier to the later essays as a mark of impasse. In 'A Writer's Freedom' (1975), for example (Coetzee writes), we see Gordimer resisting 'pressure from the political Left that she writes books in a more popular or even populist mode' (HRC, CP, 65.2: 12-04-1989). Later – 'Living in the Interregnum' (1982) is the key example – Gordimer seems caught between 'a disappointed realization' about the divergent paths white and black writers would likely have to tread, black writers insisting on communal identification while white writers hold fast to the dilemmas of the individual conscience.[17] Coetzee notes a divided sense about Gordimer's own 'agony' over whether it was possible to be committed to the ideal of black liberation *and* 'to an art which is essentially, or at any rate is branded by black writers as being, Western and bourgeois in its inspiration' (HRC, CP, 65.2: 12-04-1989). The watershed, he notes correctly, is the 1976 Soweto student rising, after which Gordimer finds it impossible to continue to advocate that writers – white *and* black – answer only to their own freedom to write as they like.[18]

One reason for the double-bind into which insistence on a double fidelity leads Gordimer, Coetzee would note in a 1997 essay on Gordimer's relationship to Turgenev, is that she was always speaking to a divided 'imaginary audience': 'inside South Africa, to a radical intelligentsia, mainly black; outside South Africa, to a liberal intelligentsia, mainly white; each (as she was acutely aware) listening with one ear to what she was saying to them, with the other ear to what she was saying to the other half' (2001: 272).[19] What comes to interest Coetzee later, when he publishes his essay on Gordimer and Turgenev (in effect, as far as I can tell, repurposing the Gordimer sections of his 1989 Hopkins talk in the process), is how she positions herself in relation to the Russian author's negotiation of the demands of radical politics and an insistence on individual expression.[20] In 'A Writer's Freedom', Gordimer had pointed to Turgenev's 1862 novel *Fathers and Sons* as the epitome of the kind of balance she valued: Turgenev had made his sympathy with revolutionary causes clear, and yet presented his revolutionary hero as flawed. '[A] writer has to reserve the right to tell the truth as he sees it, in his own words, without being accused of letting the side down', she had written (1989: 107).[21] 'After 1976,' Coetzee notes (in 1997), the ground shifted. In the new, charged atmosphere, Turgenev was set aside (too politically cautious? Too comfortable in his exile?). The question of whether European models were still viable in Africa was subsumed under a more complex, more personal, more urgent question: how to continue to manage a double discourse in which she could claim for the artist the role of both lone Shelleyan visionary and voice of the people, without being driven to accept a hierarchy of high art and popular art, one standard for herself and like-minded Eurocentric writers, another for black African writers.

(2001: 283)

The key thing for Gordimer, Coetzee observes, was this tortuous balancing act in which she claims a double fidelity, 'to a transcendental vocation' *and* 'to the people and to history' (2001: 282), a balancing act that no doubt arose from Gordimer's commitment to continue to speak out, and also her experience of Black Consciousness as a complicating factor in any act of representation, understood in all its complexity.[22]

Coetzee himself felt drawn reluctantly into public statements of the kind Gordimer made more willingly in her essays. I have already discussed the contretemps with Gordimer over Rushdie in 1988 and mentioned his 'The Novel Today' address from the year before that. But Coetzee would later regret these interventions, seeking to refuse definite positions, even while recognizing any claim to a non-position as itself a position. He would go on to develop this notion more explicitly in the years following, drawing on Desiderius Erasmus as example in an essay published in January 1992 and later included in the 1996 collection *Giving Offense*.[23] The complexities of positionality are clearly being worked out, however, in relation to Gordimer: the archive reveals this clearly in relation to the Hopkins event(s), though they will be dramatized most effectively in his fiction.[24] Two days before the 1989 Hopkins talk Coetzee had in fact given a reading in lieu of the named – Hinkley – lecture required by his visiting position.

The reading was from work then in progress, which would be published the following year: a draft of *Age of Iron*. First, Coetzee noted, he needed to 'set out a context that may be unfamiliar' to the audience, that of 'the debate (if that is the word) within which writing is carried on in South Africa today' (ibid.). He juxtaposed black-liberation aesthetics with Gordimer, who, 'through her fiction, her criticism and her public statements', had 'done more than anyone to explore the workings of the political conscience in South Africa' (ibid.). Yet, he added, Gordimer's 'political ideals' were 'not significantly to be distinguished from Motloatse's', the representative Black Consciousness writer Coetzee would discuss in his talk, which is to say that Gordimer had found herself backed into a corner, had come to a 'brink or impasse of some kind, from which [her] thinking baulks and retreats' (HRC, CP, 65.2: 10-04-1989). Here we might perhaps think of the many thresholds and crossings, structured by Classical allusions, in *Age of Iron*. Mrs Curren refuses precisely the same crude 'either/or' opposition between a commitment to oppose apartheid and the kind of 'fusion of and tension between inward and outward, private and public' (HRC, CP, 65.2: 10-04-1989) that defines her commitment to liberal arts, Classics and interiority, just as it defines Gordimer's work in Coetzee's formulation of the dilemma.

> Commitment to the fight against racism – Gordimer's first absolute – requires, as she says clearly, here and elsewhere, a commitment to a black-led future. But must that commitment, she goes on to ask herself, include commitment to a revolutionary aesthetic which seems to demand that she either deny that fusion of and tension between inward and outward, private and public, that defines her art, or be rejected as just another saleswoman for an alien colonizing culture?
>
> (HRC, CP, 65.2: 10-04-1989)

Gordimer's claim that '"In South Africa there is no longer any room for private life. Everything is political now"' (Coetzee quotes from memory) has, he says, come back to haunt her – 'the chickens come home to roost':

> As she is in the process of recognizing here, in a liberated South Africa there may be no room for the kind of books she writes; or rather, in a liberated South Africa, even in a South Africa on its way to liberation, the kind of book she writes may no longer be accorded the power to define its own room, but will be born into a pre-existing room, perhaps even the room set aside for literature of the late bourgeois world.
>
> (HRC, CP, 65.2: 10-04-1989)

But why, he asks, is he talking about Gordimer? What does it have to do with the text from which he is about to read (*Age of Iron*)? 'I will answer simply', Coetzee continues: 'In South Africa to write about the lives of white people, of old people, perhaps even of women, is a political position taken' (HRC, CP, 65.2: 10-04-1989). Many other things are similarly 'political position[s] taken', he observes, including 'to write a cadenced prose', or 'to travel to the United States and address an audience there and report that in South Africa to write about the soul or the music of Bach is a political position taken' (this too 'is a political position taken'). Taking political positions is not the problem: it is rather that 'the positions are always already-taken by the time' the writer is able to 'get there' (ibid.). This is an extraordinary statement of Coetzee's understanding of what it means to take a position:

> To want to take your own position is a position already taken. To enter upon discourse on the already-taken is a position already taken.
>   There is no discourse one can enter or enter upon to enable one to transcend this overmastering and – I use the word deliberately – colonizing critique which pre-scribes every position.
>
> (HRC, CP, 65.2: 10-04-1989)

Referring, when he gave the talk (two days later), to the reading from *Age of Iron* that he had introduced with these words, Coetzee would characterize his work-in-progress as one '[in] which I address' 'the question of the position of the writer in the political context of South Africa' 'in the medium I know best': 'fiction – ... the medium, furthermore, which I regard as the right one for the novelist to use' (HRC, CP, 65.2: 12-04-1989).

* * *

Coetzee's relationship with Gordimer is, I argue, significant in ways that scholars have not adequately considered, or at least not in the kind of detail that access to the archive now allows. Certainly, much of what is discussed above was available to Kannemeyer, whose index entries to Gordimer are not tremendously illuminating, and to Attwell, who had not the space to follow every lead and has tended in discussing Coetzee's relationship to Gordimer either to focus exclusively on published essays (2018), or to make only tangential references as they pertain to his focus on the compositional processes (2015). These very different treatments of the archive, in service of something like a standard author's biography and of a critical biographical treatment of the writing, pose a crucial question about scholarly use of the great plenitude of material available to anyone with the means to travel to Austin, Texas, to consult the Coetzee papers at the Harry Ransom Center. What do we *do* with what is in the archive, how do we use it, for what kinds of interpretative processes should we rely on it?

Considering some of these questions, Jan Wilm asks what the dual 'epistemic and hermeneutic promise' might be of the 'candid nature of an archive of an author whose public persona as well as his fictions are marked (and perhaps shaped) by elusiveness, vagueness, and even aloofness?' (2017: 218). Wilm offers some answers, generally issuing a healthy caution about the uses to which we put what the archive appears to reveal and observing that it is the fiction that must, ultimately, have final authority.[25] Yet he casts the question in such a way as to recapitulate as wilful obfuscation what I think the archive *does* confirm – but more importantly what the representation of the dilemmas of characters in the fiction presents, indeed what the careful undermining of narrative certainty that is so often at the heart of the *form* of a Coetzee fiction insists upon: a principled recognition of the impossibility of maintaining ownership (epistemic authority, hermeneutic fixedness) over any 'position'. That 'the positions are always already-taken by the time I get there' (HRC, CP, 65.2: 10-04-1989) is a lesson Coetzee learned, I contend, in large measure from his observation of and engagement with the example of Nadine Gordimer.

It is perhaps worth noting in conclusion that these two giants of South African letters continued a warm correspondence well beyond the difficult political period discussed above. In November 1999, for example, Gordimer writes to express her admiration for *Disgrace*, published a few months previously. It is telling perhaps that even while addressing this most recent fiction, which she calls 'wonderfully disturbing' (adding 'which I believe fiction should be, and only the very best is'), Gordimer also feels the need to return to *Life & Times of Michael K*, to which she had had such a troubled response a decade and a half before.

> Years ago, when you wrote *The Life & Times of Michael K.*, your man and his mother in the wheelbarrow were nobodies in particular, but their story was the overarching happening of the time, the removals, displacement, dismemberment of a country's people. The rape of your professor's daughter: it's the surfacing, within the consciousness of two individuals, daughter and father, out of the strange miasma of inexplicable sexual crimes in which we are floundering. Inexplicable? Yes. They can't be completely explained, as I often do, and your book implies, by the return of the repressed: in more down-to-earth terms, the revenge of the past.
>
> (Gordimer in Coetzee, HRC, CP, 75.4: 22-11-1999)

Gordimer is drawn to insist on the author's direct engagement with society and politics in these novels even if such concerns seem occluded in the text, perhaps even a characteristic of its unconscious, and only barely understood – if at all – by its characters. This is not to say that she is making an argument about intention; indeed, she offers a fascinating account of the writer as what she calls 'a medium in response to the table-tapping of our contemporary society' (ibid.), the writer as seer or prophet, which Elizabeth Costello rehearses (with a similar self-defensiveness) in Coetzee's eponymous 2003 novel.

> You and I, for example, are writing each in our own solitude 'within' the same time and place, but we seldom meet and we therefore don't exchange spontaneous responses to what is happening around us and the shifts of perception occurring in consequence, in ourselves. But we receive, perceive, these happenings that create certain re[s]ponses in the society, the country we share; they take form through the imaginary people we create, feel towards the kind of solutions to the present people seek, maybe hope for, maybe count on.
> (Gordimer in Coetzee, HRC, CP, 75.4: 22-11-1999)[26]

Coetzee's response is warm and revealing, confirming his sense that to write is to refuse the logic of position taking:

> I couldn't agree with you more about not being in control – ultimately in control – of one's fictional world. I find it astonishing that critics and interviewers cannot or will not accept this. One of the reasons why I dodge interviews is that I find myself continually pushed or dragged into what feel like betrayals of the people I have created – into giving interpretations of them when their motives are as mysterious to me as the motives of 'real' people around me.
> (HRC, CP, 85.5: 9-12-1999)

Characteristically, despite this apparent agreement with Gordimer, evidencing complete consistency with his position in respect of the non-position, Coetzee refuses the interpretation Gordimer wants – perhaps born of a desire to revise her earlier reading of *Life & Times of Michael K* – to put on *Disgrace*:

> One writes, most of the time, in order to move beyond whatever it is that grips one's imagination, to purge oneself of that particular set of obsessions. Which is preliminary to saying that it's hard for me to know whether what people say about 'Disgrace' is right or not. I can't think my way back into it, and don't want to.
> (HRC, CP, 85.5: 9-12-1999)

Notes

1 Research for this article was supported by a Harry Ransom Center Research Fellowship in the Humanities, supported by the Andrew W. Mellon Foundation Research Fellowship Endowment, in July 2015. The author thanks John Coetzee for permission to quote from

unpublished material, and Stephen Clingman, Lucy Graham, Patrick Flanery, and the editors and readers, for feedback. The essay is for Malvern van Wyk Smith.
2 Coetzee refers to Mrs Curren in an interview in *Doubling the Point* as Elizabeth (1992: 340), though the name appears nowhere in *Age of Iron*, where we have only her initials, EC (1990: 38). In draft 5, she is *Evelyn* ('Her name is evidently *Evelyn Curren*') (HRC, CP, 14.2: 24-12-1987).
3 See Rich (1984) and Zimbler (2014: 135–41) for just two, thirty years apart.
4 Specifically, Engle suggests that *Disgrace* 'rewrites' Gordimer's 'hopeful emotional register' (2010: 110), responding instead with a 'guarded pessimism' (118). He sees parallels in the authors' treatment of white lesbians raising a black or mixed-race child (117), and suggests that 'it is very tempting to approach some of the plot elements in *Disgrace* that lend themselves to political allegorization as revisionary allusions to allegorical treatments of *None to Accompany Me*, a book that embraces its own political message-bearing' (124). See also Engle's comparison of engagements with the canon in *Age of Iron* and Gordimer's *My Son's Story* (2002).
5 Gordimer's notebooks, Attwell observes, 'record her reflections on reading Sartre, Camus, Merleau-Ponty and others on violence, on "ends and means"; Coetzee would' apply this position to animals and have Costello take it up on the platform' (2015: 217–18). Attwell qualifies his suggestion of influence by noting that 'without having to refer to either Vera or Gordimer, there is Coetzee's own shrewd sense that the female narrator is a strategic way of positioning oneself on the margins of authoritative traditions' (2015: 166). Attwell has recently given an account of Coetzee's engagement with Gordimer, including his critique of her reading of Turgenev (Coetzee 2001: 268–83). See Attwell (2018: 285–9).
6 Gramsci's diagnosis – 'The old is dying and the new cannot be born; in this interregnum there arises a great diversity of morbid symptoms' – gave its title to Gordimer's 1982 speech, later an essay, about the costs of living in South Africa as a person of conscience (1989: 262–3), and provided the epigraph for her novel *July's People* (1982: iii). On Mrs Curren's cancer, see Van der Vlies (2017: 45, 52), Probyn (1996) and Neill (2016: 98).
7 As Clarkson notes, 'Gordimer's criticism follows on from a tacit assumption that politically engaged writing must play out at the level of political *themes* and that the characters should hold explicit political views' (2017: 203). For Gordimer, 'the explicit political themes of the story and whatever solutions they offer take precedence', Clarkson observes, whereas, by contrast, Coetzee's work is characterized by its 'relentless enquiry into … the modes of telling that both enable and constrain the writer or the artist within a particular socio-historical context' (205).
8 See, e.g., Hewson (1988).
9 See Van der Vlies (2014) further.
10 Gordimer, of course, had said something very similar in her Nobel lecture in 1991, citing Gabriel García Márquez's dictum that 'the best way a writer can serve a revolution is to write as well as he can'. See Gordimer (2010: 493).
11 For a full text of Coetzee's remarks, see Kannemeyer (2012: 658–61, n91).
12 Coetzee explains that he had been told early on Wednesday, 2 November, that the invitation to Rushdie had been withdrawn, that he had threatened to pull out of the festival but had been asked to wait until the newspaper had released a statement. This he had seen that evening, and while feeling it might have been clearer about its opposition to the withdrawal, because the statement made clear that the paper was against it, he decided he would go ahead with his appearance. He assumed that

everyone – including Gordimer – had understood these circumstances (HRC, CP, 73.5: 5-11-1988).

13 'I came in all innocence and ignorance to the scaffold, believing that we were going to discuss the deplorable actions of the religious extremists and their city father supporters' (Gordimer in Coetzee, HRC, CP, 73.5: 29-11-1988). Gordimer goes on to say that she thinks the *Mail* statement disingenuous, though she will not say so publicly as they are 'too hard-pressed by too many enemies for any of us to join in the destruction' (ibid.).

14 I have discussed Bewes's engagement with Coetzee and shame elsewhere (Van der Vlies 2017: 52).

15 Coetzee describes these as 'the controversy over the invitation to Salman Rushdie to visit South Africa' and her review of *Life & Times of Michael K* (HRC, CP, 42.3: 9/10-12-2005).

16 See Coetzee (1992b: 387–8).

17 The other essays discussed are 'Relevance and Commitment' (1979), and 'The Essential Gesture' (1984). All are collected in Gordimer (1989).

18 Gordimer put it thus in 'The Essential Gesture': 'The writer is eternally in search of entelechy in his relation to his society. Everywhere in the world, he needs to be left alone and at the same time to have a vital connection with others; needs artistic freedom and knows it cannot exist without its wider context; feels the two presences within – creative self-absorption and conscionable awareness – and must resolve whether these are locked in death-struggle, or are really fetuses in a twinship of fecundity. Will the world let him, and will he know how to be the ideal of the writer as a social being?' (1989: 299–300).

19 This is true, though it is telling that Coetzee does not pay much attention to the specific audiences to whom Gordimer addresses each of the four essays he cites: 'A Writer's Freedom' (1975) was an address at the Durban Indian Teachers' Conference in December 1975 (and first published in *New Classic* 2 in 1975); 'Relevance and Commitment' was an address at a conference on the 'State of the Art in South Africa', given at the University of Cape Town in July 1979, thereafter at the Radcliffe Forum at Harvard (that October) and as the Neil Gunn Fellowship Address at the University of Edinburgh (in 1981) (published in slightly different form as 'Apprentices of Freedom' in *New Society* 24–31 December 1981); 'Living in the Interregnum' was the William James Lecture at NYU's Institute of the Humanities (14 October 1982) (published in the *New York Review of Books* 20 January 1983); 'The Essential Gesture' was a Tanner Lecture on Human Values delivered at the University of Michigan on 12 October 1984 and included in a volume of those lectures published inter alia by Cambridge University Press in 1985, as well as being published in different form in *Granta* magazine in Spring 1985. See Gordimer (1989: 323, 326, 337, 339).

20 The essay, 'Gordimer and Turgenev', is included in Coetzee (2001), but was first published in Reckwitz, Reitner and Vennarini (1997). Coetzee's reading notes preserved in the Ransom Center include several folders (box 68.1, 68.2) of photocopied pages from works on Turgenev; some of these include photocopies of work on Gordimer.

21 Although, as Coetzee will point out, citing not *Fathers and Sons* itself, but later paratexts in which Turgenev had defended himself against attacks from the left (Coetzee 2001: 272, 280–1). Indeed, Gordimer ends the 1975 essay with a quotation from Turgenev's 'Apropos of Fathers and Sons' (Gordimer 1989: 110).

22 Both as *vertreten* and *Darstellung*, to reference Spivak's unpacking of the problematics of speaking for others at around the same time. See Spivak (1988: 275).
23 See Coetzee (1996). I discuss Coetzee's negotiation of the problematics of the position and the *non*-position alike further in Van der Vlies (2017: 66–7), and discuss this in relation to his use of various speaking personae (as well as writer-surrogate characters) in Van der Vlies (2020).
24 Attwell observes that 'like his fictional Dostoevsky' in *The Master of Petersburg* (1994), Coetzee 'found a way "to live through the madness of our times … to wrestle with the whispering darkness, to absorb it, to make it his medium"' (2018: 289; quoting from Coetzee 1994: 235).
25 In other words, we should use the archive 'not to move away from the literary work but rather towards it' (2017: 224). This is an eminently sensible position, though I take issue with Wilm's characterization of it as an endorsement of 'surface reading'.
26 Gordimer writes earlier in the letter:

> People may argue about your 'intention', what your novel is 'about'; it will never be understood that we writers – a writer is the medium, in the sense of possessed (without the mystification implied) of what is happening in our society, transformed by the imagination from the general to the particular: the people we invent. (Gordimer in Coetzee, HRC, CP, 75.4: 22-11-1999)

References

Attwell, David (2015), *J. M. Coetzee and the Life of Writing: Face to Face with Time*. Oxford: Oxford University Press.
Attwell, David (2018), 'J. M. Coetzee's South African Intellectual Landscapes'. In: Tim Mehigan and Christian Moser, eds, *The Intellectual Landscape in the Works of J. M. Coetzee*. Rochester: Camden House, 274–93.
Bewes, Timothy (2007), *The Event of Postcolonial Shame*. Princeton: Princeton University Press.
Clarkson, Carrol (2017), '"Wisselbare Woorde": J. M. Coetzee and Postcolonial Philosophy'. In: Patrick Hayes and Jan Wilm, eds, *Beyond the Ancient Quarrel: Literature, Philosophy, and J. M. Coetzee*. Oxford: Oxford University Press, 199–214.
Clingman, Stephen (1993), *The Novels of Nadine Gordimer: History from the Inside*, 2nd edn. London: Bloomsbury.
Coetzee, J. M. 'J.M. Coetzee Papers'. Austin, TX: Harry Ransom Center.
Coetzee, J. M. (1980), 'Michael Wade: *Nadine Gordimer*', *Research in African Literatures*, 11(2): 253–6.
Coetzee, J. M. (1983), *Life & Times of Michael K*. London: Secker & Warburg.
Coetzee, J. M. (1988), 'The Novel Today', *Upstream*, 6(1): 2–5.
Coetzee, J. M. (1990), *Age of Iron*. London: Secker & Warburg.
Coetzee, J. M. (1992a), 'Erasmus: Madness and Rivalry', *Neophilologus*, 76(1): 1–18.
Coetzee, J. M. (1992b), *Doubling the Point: Essays and Interviews*, ed. David Attwell. Cambridge, MA: Harvard University Press.
Coetzee, J. M. (1994), *The Master of Petersburg*. London: Secker & Warburg.
Coetzee, J. M. (1996), *Giving Offense: Essays on Censorship*. Chicago: University of Chicago Press.

Coetzee, J. M. (1999), *Disgrace*. London: Secker & Warburg.
Coetzee, J. M. (2001), *Stranger Shores: Essays 1986–1999*. London: Secker & Warburg.
Coetzee, J. M. (2003), *Elizabeth Costello*. London: Secker & Warburg.
Coetzee, J. M. (2006), 'J. M. Coetzee in Conversation with Jane Poyner'. In: Jane Poyner, ed., *J. M. Coetzee and the Idea of the Public Intellectual*. Athens: Ohio University Press, 21–4.
Coetzee, J. M. (2007), *Diary of a Bad Year*. London: Harvill Secker.
Engle, Lars (2002), 'Western Classics in the South African State of Emergency: Gordimer's *My Son's Story* and Coetzee's *Age of Iron*'. In: John Burt Foster Jr and Wayne J. Froman, eds, *Thresholds of Western Culture: Identity, Postcoloniality, Transnationalism*. London: Continuum, 114–30.
Engle, Lars (2010), '*Disgrace* as an Uncanny Revision of Gordimer's *None to Accompany Me*'. In: Graham Bradshaw and Michael Neill, eds, *J. M. Coetzee's Austerities*. Farnham: Ashgate, 107–25.
Gordimer, Nadine (1966), *The Late Bourgeois World*. London: Victor Gollancz.
Gordimer, Nadine (1974), *The Conservationist*. London: Jonathan Cape.
Gordimer, Nadine ([1981] 1982), *July's People*. London: Penguin.
Gordimer, Nadine (1984), 'The Idea of Gardening: *Life and Times of Michael K* by J. M. Coetzee', *New York Review of Books*, 2 February: 3–6.
Gordimer, Nadine ([1988] 1989), *The Essential Gesture: Writing, Politics and Places*, ed. Stephen Clingman. London: Penguin.
Gordimer, Nadine ([1992] 2010), 'Turning the Page: African Writers on the Threshold of the Twenty-First Century', *Telling Times: Writing and Living, 1950–2008*. London: Bloomsbury, 485–93.
Hewson, Kelly (1988), 'Making the "Revolutionary Gesture": Nadine Gordimer, J. M. Coetzee and Some Variations on the Writer's Responsibility', *ARIEL: A Review of International English Literature*, 19: 55–72.
Kannemeyer, J. C. (2012), *J. M. Coetzee: A Life in Writing*, trans. Michiel Heyns. Jeppestown: Jonathan Ball.
Neill, Michael ([2010] 2016), '"The Language of the Heart": Confession, Metaphor and Grace in J. M. Coetzee's *Age of Iron*'. In: Graham Bradshaw and Michael Neill, eds, *Coetzee's Austerities*. Abingdon: Routledge, 79–106.
Probyn, Fiona (1996), 'Cancerous Bodies and Apartheid in Coetzee's *Age of Iron*', *Antithesis*, 18(1): 105–20.
Reckwitz, Erhard, Karin Reitner and Lucia Vennarini (eds) (1997), *South African Literary History: Totality and/or Fragment*. Essen: Die Blaue Eule.
Rich, Paul (1984), 'Apartheid and the Decline of Civilization Idea: An Essay on Nadine Gordimer's *July's People* and J. M. Coetzee's *Waiting for the Barbarians*', *Research in African Literatures*, 15: 365–93.
Spivak, Gayatri Chakravorty (1988), 'Can the Subaltern Speak?' In: Gary Nelson and Lawrence Grossberg, eds, *Marxism and the Interpretation of Culture*. London: Macmillan, 271–313.
Van der Vlies, Andrew (2014), '"[From] Whom This Writing Then?": Politics, Aesthetics and the Personal in Coetzee's *Age of Iron*'. In: Laura Wright, Elleke Boehmer and Jane Poyner, eds, *Approaches to Teaching Coetzee's* Disgrace *and Other Works*. New York: MLA, 96–104.
Van der Vlies, Andrew (2017), *Present Imperfect: Contemporary South African Writing*. Oxford: Oxford University Press.

Van der Vlies, Andrew (2020), 'Publics and Personas'. In: Jarad Zimbler, ed., *The Cambridge Companion to J. M. Coetzee*. Cambridge: Cambridge University Press, 234–48.

Wilm, Jan (2017), 'The J. M. Coetzee Archive and the Archive in J. M. Coetzee'. In Patrick Hayes and Jan Wilm, eds, *Beyond the Ancient Quarrel: Literature, Philosophy, and J. M. Coetzee*. Oxford: Oxford University Press, 215–31.

Zimbler, Jarad (2014), *J. M. Coetzee and the Politics of Style*. Cambridge: Cambridge University Press.

5

Out of the dark chamber: Violence and desire in the textual history of *Waiting for the Barbarians*

Hermann Wittenberg

1. Introduction

In his assessment of J. M. Coetzee's third book, *Waiting for the Barbarians* (1980), Derek Attridge offers an important corrective to overly narrow interpretations that read the novel as a thinly disguised allegory of the political situation in South Africa. 'The urge to allegorise Coetzee', argues Attridge, is 'rooted in the formidable power of this traditional trope to make sense of texts that, for one reason or another, are puzzling when taken at face value' (2004: 39). In his detailed reading of the vexing episode in which the Magistrate encounters the barbarian girl for the first time in his quarters, Attridge argues that 'the experience of such passages complicates any process of allegorical transfer' (2004: 45). The scene, which does not follow the conventional script of exploitative sexual conquest of a young native woman by an older, powerful man, does not neatly fit into political schemes of reading that many critics have advanced about the novel's critique of imperialism or of the repressive politics of the apartheid state. Nevertheless, Attridge calls this scene, charged as it is with suppressed eroticism and self-conscious guilt, an example of 'an ethically charged event' (2004: xii) that discloses vital insights into the relationship between self and other. Indeed, the Magistrate's responses towards both state violence *and* the private world of desire are key to an understanding of the ethical structure of the novel as a whole. This is not to suggest that politically charged interpretations of the novel have a lesser validity than approaches that emphasize individual ethical responsiveness, but that both are interlinked, and that the archival history of the book shows that these two concerns are inseparable. This chapter will therefore look more carefully at the complex compositional history of *Waiting for the Barbarians* in the archive in order to show how Coetzee's critical engagement with coercive South African politics and the deeply personal world of human desire work together in giving the story its distinctive shape and focus. As the chapter will show, the public domains of politics and the private worlds of erotic desire became problematically entwined in the writing of the novel, and the displacement of the story to a far-off setting, to a geographically and temporal distant location, was one of the solutions through which the nexus of politics and desire could be untangled. Ultimately, Coetzee could not write a story in which both Eros and violence could inhabit the same space, and an exogenous setting offered a route out of this contradiction.

I have written elsewhere how and where Coetzee found the novel's distinctive locale, and the complex ways in which the specificity of an actual geographic location in China's Taklamakan desert became both appropriated and disguised (Wittenberg and Highman 2015). Coetzee wanted to write about South Africa, and was indeed compelled to do so by the urgency of the historical moment, but he ultimately found it impossible to write a book that was a story of love and desire at the same time as a story of violent revolution. In this chapter, the focus will though be on the way the novel's content and form arose out of a complex process in which autobiography, politics and aesthetic choices became entangled, giving rise to a story that registered the violence of late apartheid, but also delinked itself from its corrosive influence. The archival story of *Waiting for the Barbarians* has been comprehensively told in David Attwell's authoritative and wide-ranging *J.M. Coetzee and the Life of Writing* (2015), detailing how 'the novel's emergence took the form of a simultaneous, seemingly contradictory, two-way process: both a distancing – into an unspecified empire at an unspecified moment in history – and a homecoming into the violence of apartheid in the period of its climactic self-destruction' (113–14). The account in this chapter follows similar paths of reading but also seeks to develop a more complex and detailed analysis of the novel's genesis in a simultaneous engagement and disavowal of violence, taking into account material in the manuscripts and notebooks that have not yet been subjected to careful scrutiny.

2. Writing the revolution

With the previous two books, *Dusklands* (1974) and *In the Heart of the Country* (1977), Coetzee had either written fictions that were firmly situated in a historical South African past, or set in another geopolitical context altogether. Perhaps with the exception of the abandoned 'Burning of the Books' project, Coetzee had avoided tackling the present history of his country directly. Reflecting critically on this state of affairs, Coetzee summed up his attitude as follows: 'What has happened between *Dusklands* and now is that I have become unpolitical. The revolutionary setup behind BoB ['Burning of the Books'] doesn't fire me. I can now see that D [*Dusklands*] was a product of the passionate politics of 1965–71, USA' (HRC, CP, 33.3: 28-6-1974).

As recounted in the autobiographical memoir, *Youth*, the young Coetzee had earlier encountered a threatening revolution in South Africa in 1960, witnessing a mass march of about thirty thousand people from Langa which was winding its way past the university to the city centre:

> *Africa for Africans!* says the PAC. *Drive the whites into the sea!* Thousands upon thousands, the column of men winds its way up the hill. It does not look like an army, but that is what it is, an army called into being of a sudden out of the wastelands of the Cape Flats. Once they reach the city, what will they do? Whatever

it is, there are not enough policemen in the land to stop them, not enough bullets to kill them.

(2002: 38)

Coetzee's autobiographical protagonist could not then conceive of 'standing against them when you do not believe in what you are standing for' (39). In the revolutionary climate in the wake of the Sharpeville massacre, the only option, apart from being conscripted into the apartheid army, was an escape to London. Not able to imagine himself fighting *against* the revolution to defend the status quo of white privilege, he would now, on his return to the country a decade later, also not find it easy to stand *with* the revolution and become enlisted in the battle to liberate the country. Despite an involvement in leftist anti-Vietnam campus activism, Coetzee found it difficult, on his return early in 1971, to transfer this progressive, activist stance to the South African situation. As he noted privately: 'Ever since I moved back to SA my attitude towards the revolution has become more ambivalent. And in parallel with this movement, my fervour as a writer has waned' (HRC, CP, 33.3: 4-11-1974).

Two very different sets of events were to force a change in Coetzee's position in this regard, enabling him to recover his 'fervour as a writer' and make the politics of South Africa, and indeed the revolution, a central idea in his fictions. The first set of events was his embroilment with the censorship authorities. While he told David Attwell that 'at a practical level I hardly suffered at all' (1992: 298), it is clear that for Coetzee censorship was a deeply personal matter that violated his privacy intimately: 'Being subjected to the gaze of the censor is a humiliating and perhaps enraging experience. It is not unlike being stripped and searched' (299). Reflecting on the effect of censorship, Coetzee recognized that 'writing under threat also has uglier, deforming side effects that it is hard to escape' (300). The 'side effects' Coetzee was referring to concerned a perverse incitement to write about the very topics that were officially banned. Thinking back on the conditions under which he was writing his third and fourth novels, Coetzee acknowledged that 'the concentration on imprisonment, on regimentation, on torture in books of my own like *Waiting for the Barbarians* and *Michael K* was a response – I emphasize, a *pathological* response – to the ban on representing what went on in police cells in this country' (300). As we will see, Coetzee own recognition of a '*pathological* response' to the turbulent and violent times he was writing in manifested itself in the form of 'uglier, deforming side effects' whose traces are visible in the manuscript versions.

The second, far more momentous set of events that propelled Coetzee towards a direct engagement with South African contemporaneity was a marked shift in the political climate of the country. When Coetzee returned to South Africa early in 1971, Nationalist white rule was firmly entrenched, and most of the black political leadership was either in jail or in exile, including Philip Kgosana, the leader of the great mass march that the young Coetzee had witnessed eleven years earlier. The government was confidently implementing the grand apartheid vision, and isolated forms of activism were ruthlessly nipped in the bud by the security forces. But after the decade-long repressive inertia which followed the post-Sharpeville clampdown and the imprisonment of black leadership, the country dramatically erupted into politics again. In June 1976, thousands of Soweto students took to the streets to protest against compulsory tuition in the medium of Afrikaans. Catalysed by the student revolt, there was soon a country-wide resurgence of mass marches, demonstrations and political activism. Hundreds of protesters lost their lives, mostly at the hands of the police, and various repressive measures were enforced such as bannings, newspaper closures, and mass arrests of labour, student and church leaders. In the aftermath of the Soweto rebellion, and in the context of the collapse of the Portuguese colonial empire in the adjacent territories of Mozambique and Angola, the prospects of revolutionary change in South Africa had increased markedly, developments which the state responded to with more repressive legislation, additional police powers, extrajudicial killings of activists, extended conscription and increased military spending. It was also in this period that the Bureau of State Security (BOSS) was established, whose influence and powers soon pervaded all areas of government. BOSS can be seen to be one of the models for the sinister Third Bureau in *Waiting for the Barbarians*.

By the time *In the Heart of the Country* was published in 1977 and Coetzee was attempting to write his third novel, the political scenario in the country had thus shifted decisively, with government in the hands of hawkish securocrats, and activism in the townships strongly inflected by Black Consciousness ideology. One of the key figures in this regard was Stephen Biko who championed the newly awaked struggle for freedom. As we shall see, it was Biko's arrest and subsequent death in detention on 12 September 1977 that was the seminal event that gave shape to *Waiting for the Barbarians*. With Biko's death, a tipping point had been reached that not only shifted the politics of South Africa decisively towards an escalation of popular resistance (and concomitant state repression), but also precipitated a catalytic shift in Coetzee's creative practice.

3. Last days and epochal endings

Coetzee had begun thinking about a novel a few months earlier already, well before Biko's death. On 11 July 1977, he sketched out the outline in his notebook:

> The time: the middle of a revolutionary war in S. Africa (the war remains throughout in the background). The place: an island transit camp for aliens waiting for transport out of the country – Robben Island, the prison now a tired hotel, with a launch bringing out supplies daily. Planes are not flying (no refuelling facilities, the north too dangerous). The man and the woman meet. Both hold British passports and are returning to Britain (where they have no roots). The man is 50, an academic working on a translation and edition of a narrative of the fall of Constantinople. The woman is 21/22, she has left her husband (or he is dead).
> (HRC, CP, 33.3: 11-6-1977)

In the notebook entries in the weeks to come, the story began to evolve, but when Coetzee eventually began drafting the beginnings of the novel in September of that year, the core narrative set in revolutionary times remained intact. As can be seen in the first pages of the manuscript, South Africa is in the midst of a civil war, with floods of white refugees having fled the country. The authorities have designated Robben Island as an embarkation point for the last stragglers awaiting rescue by UN chartered ships. The novel's protagonist is Manos Milis, a middle-aged university professor of Greek descent, one of the refugees waiting interminably for the boat. In a politically charged act of envisaging, Coetzee's narrative transformed the notorious apartheid prison island into a bleak camp for white refugees who no longer have a home in Africa, but cling tenuously to its shores in the vain hope for repatriation. The scenario effects a neat reversal of South Africa's colonial history: the European settlers who had arrived some 350 years earlier on the Cape shore, now find themselves driven back to the coast awaiting an uncertain future beyond the sea. We need to remember that at the time Coetzee was writing, Robben Island still housed scores of South Africa's most prominent black political prisoners, among them Nelson Mandela and several other leading activists. Like no other place in apartheid South Africa, the highly symbolic carceral site of Robben Island encapsulated the denial of freedom, and Coetzee's narrative of its radical transformation was an audacious act of reimagination with political significance.

But the stasis of the Robben Island camp situation made it difficult to develop a storyline that would transcend the deadlocked settler–native dialectic, and Coetzee soon abandoned this version. An earlier notebook entry already anticipated the impossibility of a narrative resolution outside of South Africa. 'Drop the London angle entirely,' he wrote (HRC, CP, 33.3: 5-8-1977). The book clearly had to remain anchored in Coetzee's own troubled land: instead of evading the trauma of South Africa, a narrative had to be found that could work through the political and personal questions that were beginning to pose themselves with urgency. Unlike an earlier escape from a South African revolution in 1961, in this fictional scenario Coetzee remained committed to an engagement with his country.

In his next version, Coetzee placed Milis and his fellow refugees in a quarantined zone in Cape Town harbour, living in the bowels of an ominously named ship:

> The ship that was due to take them to safety away from civil war in South Africa was the ANACONDA, registered in Panama, chartered by UNRRA. In the first year of the emergency, when South African air space had been closed, a quarter of a million holders of foreign passports, primarily Europeans, had been evacuated out of South African ports. Now, in the second year, only the old, the complacent, the eternally hopeful, the greedy remained. In the six weeks that the ANACONDA had stood in Cape Town harbour, not more than three hundred passengers had boarded.
>
> The ANACONDA was likely to stand in the harbour indefinitely. The ship was hostage in a dispute about refuelling which neither side felt any pressure to resolve.
> (HRC, CP, 5.1: 7-9-1977)

Stuck in this bureaucratic limbo, Milis quite happily follows his scholarly inclinations by translating Kristoboulos's history of the fall of Constantinople. The choice of text is not accidental: the fall of the moribund Byzantine empire and the violent transition to a new political order had resonance for the imagined fall of the white republic.

Michael Kristoboulos was, moreover, a curiously hybrid historical figure. He was an eyewitness to the conquest of the city by the Ottomans in 1453, but his vivid account of the dramatic battle followed the action from the point of view of the invader. Although he was a Greek, and would perhaps more naturally have been expected to side with Christian Byzantium, Kristoboulos had chosen the employ of Mehmet II.

How the Kristoboulos chronicles would function in the envisaged novel was however not quite settled for Coetzee: 'Precisely what role Kristoboulos will play is not yet clear. The text is the only thing the man is allowed to take with him to the camp' (HRC, CP, 33.3: 30-9-1977). As the story evolved, Manos Milis's night-time translation work on Kristoboulos may have stood for civilized values which *contrasted* with the ugly daytime encounter with violence and death. By this time, the narrative is set in a camp, reminiscent of the concentration camps in Nazi Germany:

> He is sentenced for looting, having no paper, breaking the curfew, etc. He is sent off to a miscellaneous camp/prison. He volunteers for toilet duties, eventually for disposal of the dead. This brings down on him the execration of his fellow-prisoners. However, his mind is not changed: what he needs is to do what no one else will do – perform the rites for the corpse.
>
> (HRC, CP, 33.3: 28-8-1977)

As reflected in the manuscript's early title, 'Disposal of the Dead', Milis is increasingly obsessed with corpses and the matter of their proper burial. His need to 'perform the rites for the corpse' echoes not only Antigone's plight in Sophocles's drama, but is also a politically charged concern in a country which had seen thousands of police casualties in the aftermath of the Soweto uprising, and ongoing deaths in detention, unexplained disappearances, and targeted political assassinations. The scholarly routines of reading and translating Kristoboulos in the evenings, juxtaposed with the daily chores of tending to violated corpses, produce a form of inner liberation for Milis: 'Out of this kind of regimen varied in the evenings of translation *without a dictionary* (plus usual problems of no paper, etc.) comes a shift in his spiritual state' (HRC, CP, 33.3: 10-8-1977). In Milis's devotion to the practice of translation in the midst of war, Coetzee may also have played with the doubled etymological roots of the word. The word 'translation' does not only refer to the practice of turning one language to another but also means 'to bear, to convey, or remove from one person, place or condition to another'. The parallels between textual translation and the practice of conveying bodies are furthermore amplified by an archaic set of meanings that develop a particular resonance in the context of Biko's martyrdom: translation also means 'to remove the body or relics of a saint (or hero) from one place of internment or repose to another' (*Oxford English Dictionary*). In seeking a proper resting place for the maimed bodies, Milis is thus in this doubled sense a translator.

As Coetzee noted of his protagonist, 'The one role he can see for himself in a war-struck country is that of burier of the dead' (HRC, CP, 33.3: 10-8-1977). Not being able to fight either for or against the revolution, Milis compensates by tending to the mutilated bodies, paying them their last respects. In another version, Milis memorizes a mental map of the locations of buried bodies:

What he commits to memory is, in effect, a detailed plan of all the graves of prisoners done away with. One day, under some kind of provocation, (what?), he reels the entire plan out on paper. It is this which is discovered and reveals him to be dangerous. He is rushed through a trial and condemned. Perhaps in the very instant between the raising of the guns and his death, the whole opening of the novel is rewritten.

(HRC, CP, 33.3: 3-9-1977)

In Coetzee's morbid imagination, the country has been transformed into nightmarish land of camps, barbed wire and makeshift grave yards in which the victims of brutality are secreted away. But Coetzee was not only writing about death, he was also writing himself into a dead end. The novel was not proceeding well, impossibly reduced to the singular moment between 'the raising of the guns and his death'. Coetzee may have been thinking here of Borges's short story 'The Secret Miracle' in which the writer Jaromir Hladik is facing the Nazi executioners (Borges 2000). He miraculously experiences the seconds before his death as an entire year – enough time to complete the unfinished play. Just like the fictional Czech playwright in Borges's story who struggled to complete the third act until he faced death, Coetzee was trying to conceptualize his novel in the face of violent times. Trapped in inward-looking, hyper self-conscious language, Coetzee was evidently not finding a mode of storytelling that could move his narrative forward. Moreover, he was slipping back into a mode reminiscent of the previous novel. Writing about this impasse in his notebook, Coetzee expressed his distress:

> After 22 pages, no lift-off yet. It would seem that I can get nowhere unless the whole thing turns into a drama of consciousness a la *In the Heart*. But I cannot face the project of writing at that hysterical intensity again. Once is enough.
>
> (HRC, CP, 33.3: 10-10-1977)

Coetzee clearly had no desire to write another novel primarily located in the consciousness of his protagonist, impossibly playing itself out in the mind of a man during the last few seconds of his life as he is facing death. The project was in danger of petering out. A week later he wrote in despair, 'Throw the whole thing up' (HRC, CP, 33.3: 19-10-1977), and attempted to write the novel as a montage of stories told by women narrators. One of these narratives is a nightmarish fragment where two women encounter a wounded man running away from the police, the sore on his back covered by flies:

> Then you noticed that the flies were not only following him, they were clustering on his back. When you slowed down enough, you could see a sticky redness beneath them. You thought to yourself, 'He is carrying a slab of meat on his back!' That is what you said: 'Look – it is meat they are after!' Then you realised that the meat was part of him.
>
> (HRC, CP, 5.1: 23-10-1977)

The vividness of Coetzee's imagination is suggestive of a dream, and the narrator has visions of being smothered:

You even dreamed about him, and about the flies. But in your dreams the flies become bees. The bees settled all over you, on your face, on your eyelid, until there was no light. You felt the soft, palpitating humming weight upon you. When you opened your mouth to scream, the bees filled it at once.

(HRC, CP, 5.1: 25-10-1977)

Coetzee's story is rich in substitutive figurative transformations, producing a disturbing identification between the man trailed by flies and the woman suffocated by bees, filling her mouth and silencing her voice. The phantasmagorical story must also be read against an event which was to have a direct impact on the emerging novel. Written a few weeks after Biko's death – he was the fortieth person to die in police custody that year – these scenes clearly articulate Coetzee's sense of dead ends.

4. Dead ends of desire

It is at this point that Coetzee abandoned this version of the novel, despite having created the beginnings of a potentially compelling work of fiction. Moreover, in writing prose with strong surreal features, Coetzee had achieved a remarkably unambiguous engagement with the events unfolding in his country, without lapsing into predictable politically correct realism. But writing in his notebook at this time, Coetzee recorded his sense of a dead end: 'Abandon everything I have done thus far. There is no interest in the story' (HRC, CP, 33.3: 6-11-1977). The reasons for this standstill are complex and difficult to discern, but may have to do with a tension between outer and inner pressures impinging on the creative process. On the one side, the dismal political scenario of torture, death and repression pressed itself in on the writing, creating morbid, deforming effects. On the other hand, impermissible erotic desire welled up in the story from within, threatening to propel the narrative towards violent ends that could not easily be contained. Ultimately, such a containment was achieved by transforming the dangerous nexus of violent desire and impotent political guilt into a fictional world that needed to be necessarily displaced, and was therefore located in a remote, geographically indistinct setting. The event that catalysed this decisive shift from home to an elsewhere was, paradoxically, the effect of Biko's murder. Biko's impact on the novel was less his death in detention on 12 September 1977, but more a subsequent high-profile official inquest hearing that was held in the last two weeks in November. It was the public unmasking of Biko's police torturers and an unveiling of the state machinery that killed people behind closed doors, which gave the embryonic novel an object on to which it could transfer its aggressive energies, allowing Coetzee to disentangle the problematic nexus of violence and desire.

But before examining the consequences of the Biko inquest, it is necessary to step back and look more carefully at the deeper structures in the story that had come close to disabling it. The early manuscript versions and Coetzee's notebook entries show that the narrative was not primarily a politically conscious text that imagined South Africa in the last throes of white rule. Rather, at its core, it was a story about dark desire threatening to twist out of control. Early in his notebook, Coetzee had already recorded a sense of loss of control over his story, in which his protagonist's erotic obsessions increasingly take centre stage:

> The book seems to be shifting under me. The London half seems more and more questionable. Instead the man is growing stronger (though still the same age), and with him an image roaming through a dark Cape Town looking for sexual experience. Musil somewhere behind this. The girl is then an episode (the most important) in his search. He is not a frightened sadist (like Jacobus Coetzee) but an explorer of the vitalities thrown up by the last days of the republic. Literally a fin de siècle book.
> (HRC, CP, 33.3: 25-7-1977)

Robert Musil's modernist evocation of the decadent last Habsburg years, together with Kristiboulos's chronicle of Byzantine decay, is yet another intertextual reference to imperial dissolution and epochal endings. Coetzee's imagined revolutionary transition in South Africa, like the dissolute last years of Austro-Hungarian empire or the decline of Byzantium, was productive of morbid symptoms and deformations. There is much material in Musil's fictions dealing with themes of sexual abandonment and perverse desire, ideas that Coetzee subsequently explored in an essay on Musil (1992: 233–40). And Musil's *fin de siècle* Vienna was also the world of Sigmund Freud, whose diagnoses of the sexual pathologies attendant on such social transformations are not without relevance to Coetzee's own and our retrospective understanding of the novel's evolution.

On board the immobilized ship, the ANACONDA, whose name is itself suggestive of phallic import, Milis is thus not only pursuing a scholarly project but also develops an increasingly obsessive erotic interest in a young woman who is brought by chance into his cabin. In the language of their first nightly encounter we can see glimpses of the Magistrate's relationship with the barbarian girl:

> He sat down at the foot of her bed. She did not evade his eyes. 'It is too cold for one,' he said thickly. He struggled up the bed towards her. 'Come,' he said. He folded an arm around her and she lay against him. He was too far from this kind of behaviour to know precisely what the degree of pressure, the degree of restraint, of her hand against his shoulder signified.
> (HRC, CP, 5.1: 1-10-1977)

After their first coupling, Milis, coming out of a two-year celibacy, feels trapped and panic-stricken, not knowing how to deal with the unleashed desires, nor how to proceed with a life of shared intimacy with a young, strange woman. Caught between his attraction to her youthful beauty and recoiled by a sense of entrapment, conflict and petty jealousies emerge, papered over by intense lovemaking. She begins to avoid him, and after more urgent sex with her in which she yields nothing, the ship begins to feel like a cold prison. Needing some diversion, Milis escapes from the harbour area through a gap in the fence to roam the streets of Cape Town. Still under the spell of his frustrated passion for the girl, he is first propositioned by a street urchin, and then a young female prostitute. The sordid encounter in De Waal Park ends catastrophically when he is stabbed and robbed by her accomplice. He recovers his pages of the Kristoboulos translations, but with his stolen wallet the vital emigration papers are gone. Like countless black South Africans arrested for pass offences, Milis now also has no documents and is soon picked up by the police and taken to a makeshift prison in an underground garage:

> The floor was packed with people, so densely that it was impossible not to touch them. As soon as the van that had brought him had backed out and gone, another drove in and unloaded twenty more people.
>
> (HRC, CP, 5.1: 17-10-1977)

At this point, the narrative situation is set up for Milis's entry into the bleak and violent world of the camps, where he would atone for his libidinal excesses in Cape Town by devoting himself to the task of tending the bodies of the dead. With his protagonist's purgatory in prison, Coetzee had not only drawn back from an earlier exilic trajectory for his story, but had also turned his back on a rapacious form of sexual excess that could flourish in the confined spaces of the ship, and on the dark streets of Cape Town.

Coetzee appears to have been disturbed by the way the Milis character was emerging in the story when he briefly contemplated 'the idea of making the girl 12 years old and leaving all sex out' (HRC, CP, 33.1: 20-8-1977). But Coetzee's efforts in containing his protagonist's passions were not productive of a satisfactory narrative form. In the various permutations that emerged, we can see Coetzee grappling with Milis's problematic relationship with women. The other option was writing the girl out of the story entirely when Milis is cast into the underground world of the camps. But this was a trajectory that Coetzee ultimately also balked at: 'I thought this morning of throwing it all up. He is in the hands of the police. All that threatens is a jail career of which I know nothing. Also, the strength of my political passion is dubious' (HRC, CP, 33.3: 17-10-1977). By removing the protagonist from the spaces of unlimited desire (the ship, the Cape Town streets) and inserting him into a carceral space of pain and death (the camps), the libidinal economy of the story had only been inverted, perpetuating its problematic and disabling antinomian structure. Drawing on Freudian psychoanalysis, Coetzee realized that his story, like his protagonist, was unable to develop out of this dead-locked state of repression: 'The man is prevented from growing by an unrealized repression. Evidence that is stuck at a stage of growth is his inability to make anything of his relation with the girl, i.e. his inability to love her' (HRC, CP, 33.3: 3-9-1977).

The protagonist's 'inability to love her' and a simultaneous compensatory release of aggressive passions was thus the disabling pathology of the narrative. Coetzee was consciously searching for a way out of this conundrum, citing Freud's 'polymorphous perverse' in which desire is contained through an intercourse which is non-phallic (HRC, CP, 33.3: 3-7-1977). The problem, as Coetzee saw it, was an unresolved 'conflict between tenderness and desire without means, and phallic activity without tenderness and pleasure' (HRC, CP, 33.3: 2-7-1977); in other words, either loving impotence or aggressive sex. In an essay on sexual pathology, 'On the Universal Tendency to Debasement in the Sphere of Love', Freud famously formulated this paradox as follows: 'Where they love they do not desire and where they desire they cannot love' (1976: 182–3). Already in the previous novel, Coetzee had deliberately avoided recreating another violent, male protagonist such as Jacobus Coetzee. In *In the Heart of the Country*, as he had written earlier, 'the perspective I am interested in is ... having a story done to one, but from inside the book. In other words, a feminine novel of things happening without the masculine story-thrust' (HRC, CP, 33.3: 30-10-1974). Seen in these terms, the morbid passivity of Magda was an inversion of the active sadism of Jacobus Coetzee.

The challenge for the new novel would thus be to get beyond the 'perversion' of the two previous flawed protagonists who, in different ways, were disabled by a deeply rooted 'inability to love'. How was the next book to solve this challenge? Coetzee subsequently put his finger on the problem: 'The whole project depends on the creation of a credible beloved *you*' (HRC, CP, 33.3: 10-10-1977). The narrative had clearly failed to find a satisfactory beloved 'you' in the Robben Island or ANACONDA settings, or in the decadent street-life of Cape Town. The problem was though not only one of setting, but rather of achieving an entirely different narrative mode for the 'realization of You' (HRC, CP, 33.3: 10-10-1977). As Coetzee put it a week later: 'This man MM [Manos Milis], as a "he" living in the world bores me. "Creating" an illusionistic reality in which he moves depresses me. Hence the exhausted quality of the writing' (HRC, CP, 33.3: 17-10-1977). A way had to be found to break with a realist third-person narrative mode that depicted Cape Town with naturalistic verisimilitude.

But then there was a major breakthrough that was to shift the project into an entirely new direction, both in terms of style and setting. In his notebook entry on 6 November 1977, Coetzee not only had a new title but had also sketched out a completely new plan for the book, shifting the story away from the naturalistically rendered Cape Town setting to a geographically amorphous fictional elsewhere:

The Border Guard
There is a man, 'I'. He is on some kind of frontier, guarding a border post or fort. Sometimes it is the Amazonian jungle (*Aguirre*), sometimes Central Asia (Buzzeti); other possibilities Southern Africa, colonial N. America, Roman Europe. ... For the most part he knows nothing. He is under orders 'to guard the frontier'. Occasionally figures appear. Sometimes he shoots at them. The position is beleaguered. They are forgotten, nevertheless they do their duty. There are metamorphoses. The border fortress is sometimes a jail too, or a hospital or a prison camp.
(HRC, CP, 33.3: 6-11-1977)

The newly envisaged book appeared to offer more promising terrain to solve the main problem: 'finding a place for "you" in his story'. The identity of the male 'I' protagonist was roughly established, but at this initial stage 'a "home" for you (in flesh, in the word) is not yet known'. Coetzee speculated that she might possibly be a prisoner, a camp woman or fellow inmate, and in a striking image, thought of the 'you' as 'some kind of Ariadne'. Until her identity had emerged, the 'I' protagonist was lost 'in a labyrinth' (HRC, CP, 33.3: 6-11-1977).

In the next few weeks Coetzee would actively search out different paths out of this narrative labyrinth, attempting to find a beloved Ariadne, and also, at the same time, banish the hidden terrors of the rapacious Minotaur. The basic contours of the published novel were emerging rapidly, as we can see when Coetzee already wrote down a new title: 'The Barbarians'. The 'I' protagonist and setting were also developing in ways that are recognizable: he is a 'Chinese commander at Lop-nor, protecting the silk route against bandits. The lake is drying up, the city is dying' (HRC, CP, 33.3: 13-11-1977). Three days later Coetzee has him 'have a barbarian concubine whose tongue has been cut out' (HRC, CP, 33.3: 16-11-1977). In a more elaborated subsequent notebook entry, Coetzee imagines his protagonist as a military commander, named 'A', who is engaged in punitive reprisals against restive nomads:

> A military party has brought back some nomads it has picked up. There is no doubt that they were involved in the raid. The leader is interrogated regarding X [the nomad chief]. He dies under torture breathing defiance. He gives orders for other members of the party to be interrogated. The interrogation produces nothing. A orders the men to be executed – the women and children taken slave.
>
> Weeks/months later he begins to notice a girl hobbling about on sticks. He knows that it is the daughter of the man who died under torture. Her tongue was torn out, her ankles broken. A is upset. He has her taken care of. She becomes his chambermaid, eventually his concubine.
>
> (HRC, CP, 33.3: 28-11-1977)

The details outlined here are largely realized in the published novel, but with one significant difference: in this sketch the protagonist is not only a prototype for the Magistrate in the novel, but is also recognizably a model for the sadistic torturer, Colonel Joll. Both these characters still problematically cohere in the person of 'A'. The first person 'I' figure in the envisaged story is thus still a conflicted character who is capable of inflicting brutal violence on the bodies of captives, but is also perversely drawn to an erotic relationship with one of his maimed victims. The scenario fits with the distorted nature of a sexual relationship in Musil's story 'The Perfecting of Love', in which the female character abandons 'marital rectitude' and offers 'her body to violation' with an older stranger. In Coetzee's essay on the story, she reaches 'an ultimate stage of perversion ... seeking out of violation, torture and death' (1992: 238).

5. The Biko inquest

It was the Biko affair that eventually allowed Coetzee to unravel the fraught entanglement of erotic desire, violence and political guilt. Biko had died in police detention on 12 September 1977, officially explained as the result of an extended hunger strike. In a sensational case of investigative reporting, Allister Sparks, the editor of the liberal newspaper, the *Rand Daily Mail*, set a young journalist on to the story. The reporter in question, Helen Zille (who subsequently made a career in politics and became leader of the Democratic Alliance) tracked down doctors involved in the case, and wrote a front-page story that exposed the official version as a cover-up. The authorities were stung by the allegations, and Zille and Sparks were hauled before the Press Council and forced to publish a retraction. Zille also received anonymous death threats. When the official inquest into Biko's death opened in Pretoria on 14 November, the stage was thus set for a dramatic showdown between the government, and the liberal press and civil rights lawyers acting for the family. International observers and a large number of journalists attended, among them Zille. Her detailed reporting of the proceedings was carried by the *Cape Times* (though without her byline), and Coetzee's interest in the story is evident in a file of extensive press cuttings (HRC, CP, 147).

At the same time that Coetzee was trying to navigate his story through the labyrinth, the high-profile Biko inquest occupied the news headlines. Zille's meticulous reporting produced a near word-for-word transcription of the proceedings, giving readers a detailed account of Sydney Kentridge's methodical cross-examination which exposed police lies. The first day of hearings produced the revelation that Biko had died from serious brain injuries, which Major Harold Snyman explained as self-inflicted: 'Mr Biko then charged Warrant Officer Beneke with clenched fists and lashed at him, pinning him against a steel cabinet. Other members of the interrogation team rushed to Warrant Officer Beneke's assistance. In the violent struggle that followed they bumped against tables and walls' (HRC, CP, 147: press cutting, *Cape Times* 15-11-1977). The following day, Kentridge's relentless questioning forced police to retract sworn statements handed in as evidence. Snyman claimed that these statements by informers had implicated Biko in subversive activities, and when confronted by them, Biko had launched his violent attack on the officers. Kentridge pointed out that the statements were dated after Biko's death, and could not possibly have been used during the interrogation. 'What we have here', Kentridge told the court, 'is a smear campaign prepared after Biko's death and I think it is a disgrace.' The magistrate was forced to rule the statements as inadmissible, leaving the police version of events in tatters (HRC, CP, 147: press cutting, *Cape Times* 16-11-1977).

The *dramatis personae* of the inquest (a magistrate, a security police colonel) and the configuration of circumstances (a suspicious death in detention, a tortured body) gave Coetzee some of the vital building blocks of his story. In the published text, the Magistrate hears remarkably similar evidence by Colonel Joll:

> During the course of the interrogation contradictions became apparent in the prisoner's testimony. Confronted with these contradictions, the prisoner became enraged and attacked the investigating officer. A scuffle ensued during which the prisoner fell heavily against the wall. Efforts to revive him were unsuccessful.
>
> (1982: 6)

Although the novel has widely been read as a political allegory which references South African political repression and police torture, the influence of the inquest, as we have seen, was much more complex. Coetzee acknowledged this ambivalence almost a year later, when he wrote about the influence of the Biko matter as a form of enabling pretext: 'This may not be entirely honest, but I must make the relation of the story to the Biko affair, the inspiration of the story by the Biko affair, clear' (HRC, CP, 33.3: 25-7-1978). On the surface then, the revelations of the Biko inquest allowed Coetzee to write a story in which state brutality took centre stage but, at the same time, the inquest revelations enabled him to find a fictional form that could solve a deeper problem of desire. Such an entanglement of the external world of political events with the inner life does not only structure the novel, but is also diagnosed in Coetzee's Jerusalem Prize Acceptance speech as a general malaise affecting life in South Africa: 'The deformed and stunted relations between human beings that were created under colonialism and exacerbated under what is loosely called apartheid have their psychic representations in a deformed and stunted inner life' (1992: 98). Coetzee explicitly included himself and his own work as part of the general South African pathology: 'I make this observation with due deliberation, and in the fullest awareness that it applies to myself and my own writing as much as to anyone else' (98). The disablement of his protagonist, diagnosed earlier as his 'inability to love', is thus not just a private, inner matter, but can be understood to mirror a more generalized 'failure of love' which is 'at the heart' of the deformed social relationships in South Africa (97).

6. Conclusion: Out of the dark chamber

The miracle of *Waiting for the Barbarians* lies in the way Coetzee was eventually able to write himself of this potentially disabling impasse, and finally, in the novel's closing sections, even transcend the 'failure of love'. In order to achieve such a resolution to the story, the imagination had to overcome a morbid obsession with the 'disposal of the dead', and keep its distance from the violent perversions and torture of the 'dark chamber'. As also conceptualized in Coetzee's essay, the 'dark chamber' can be understood not only as the secretive interrogation rooms of the torturers (into which the Biko inquest hearing had permitted glimpses), but also, more generally, as the oppressive and deformed condition of South Africa from which the novel ultimately had to distance itself. The entire country had in a sense become a dark chamber, pervaded by death, torture and maiming – an impression reinforced by the assassination of a man Coetzee knew personally: the philosopher and activist Rick Turner. Turner was shot early in 1978, a few weeks after the Biko inquest had ended, his death generally being attributed to state agents. The novel can be understood to have arisen out of the tension between strong contradictory forces activated by the Biko affair: on the one hand Coetzee was being compelled to look into the dark chamber, confronting the obscene scenario of violence; on the other hand, the imagination had to find ways to disentangle and distance itself from the labyrinthine dangers of its corrupting influence.

As the novel evolved, it is evident that Coetzee managed this tension in the narrative by ultimately turning away from the dark chamber, both in the narrower sense of the actual torture room and in the more general sense from the country's national condition. This shift can be seen in several instances by comparing the manuscript versions to the published novel. In a very early version of the new narrative, the protagonist is a spectator to the bloody excesses of the two torturers who have come to interrogate the older man and his son:

> The fat man took a step forward and, without warning, thrust his sword powerfully into the belly of the older prisoner. The prisoner's breath left him in a gasp. He stared with amazed eyes into the face of his executioner. Carefully he placed his

hands on the blade of the sword and tried to push it out of himself. A line of blood appeared when the edge cut his hand.

(HRC, CP, 5.1: 5-12-1977)

The description continues with even more graphic and gratuitous violence, culminating in a gory disembowelling and beheading. In the published novel, the torture also ends with the older prisoner's violent death, but the crucial difference here is that these events occur offstage, out of the direct view of the Magistrate. In the published novel, there is only a brief glimpse of the dead man's mutilated face, when the wrapped body is opened, but the Magistrate's response ('Close it up ... fetch some twine and tie it shut') (1982: 7) betrays a desire to shut out the shameful scene. The obscenity of the torture chamber is thereby literally rendered out of view and "off scene" and remains unnarrated. The idea is an important and recurring one in Coetzee's writing, most clearly articulated by Elizabeth Costello:

Obscene. That is the word, a word of contested etymology, that she must hold on to as a talisman. She chooses to believe that obscene means off-stage. To save our humanity, certain things that we may want to see (may want to see because we are human!) must remain off-stage.

(2003: 168)

Elizabeth Costello's lecture engages at length with Paul West's *The Very Rich Hours of Count von Stauffenberg*, a book coincidentally also published in 1980. Costello argues passionately against writing that reveals what happens in the torture chamber, condemning not 'just the deeds of Hitler's executioners, not just the deeds of the blockman, but the pages of Paul West's black book too' (170). In the process of the evolution of *Waiting for the Barbarians*, Coetzee's imagination eventually recoiled from lingering in the dark chamber, giving the reader only an indirect sense of its obscene proceedings. Later in the novel, the Magistrate tells Mandel: 'I am trying to imagine how you breathe and eat and live from day to day. But I cannot!' (1982: 126). Torture and living a life as torturer remain unimaginable and incomprehensive, not representable in thought and language.

Overall, the contaminating effect of violence is thus not only stifled in the erotic life of the Magistrate (tamping down latent sadistic desire), but is also kept at arm's length in the narrative as a whole, as we can see when the Magistrate tries to stop Joll's execution of the barbarian prisoners. The Magistrate fails in his intervention, and prisoners are presumably still executed, but the grisly scene in which men are killed with hammers is kept out of the pages of the book. The Magistrate is not primarily motivated by a concern with the fate of Joll's doomed victims, but experiences a revulsion against the staged, public nature of the event that would turn the civic space of the town square into an open torture chamber. What was hidden and out of sight, literally obscene, is now performed in full sight with public participation: 'You are depraving these people!' the Magistrate shouts at the torturer (1982: 106).

But it was precisely this depravity that had in effect come to pass in the South Africa Coetzee had returned to, producing a sense of contamination, of being 'soiled', to use the language of *Summertime* (2009: 4). State violence no longer lurked unseen in secretive cells and prisons but had seeped out, becoming a barely disguised part of the fabric of public life. In the essay, 'Into the Dark Chamber', Coetzee writes that one 'can go about one's daily business in Johannesburg within calling distance … of people undergoing the utmost suffering' and that there is 'a certain shamelessness' in torturing people 'in the heart of a great city' (1992: 362). The Biko affair had brought this shameful state of affairs into focus, and in choosing a fictionalized, pre-modern Central Asian setting for the story, Coetzee had achieved a radical and necessary distancing from the violent scenario of South Africa. Instead of letting 'his poetic imagination go, to fly deeper and deeper into the labyrinth of the security system' (1992: 366), Coetzee had found a way out of the dark chamber.

References

Attridge, Derek (2004), *J. M. Coetzee and the Ethics of Reading: Literature in the Event*. Chicago: University of Chicago Press.

Attwell, David (2015), *J.M. Coetzee and the Life of Writing: Face to Face With Time*. Johannesburg: Jacana.

Borges, Jorge Luis (2000), *Labyrinths*. Harmondsworth: Penguin Books.

Coetzee, J. M. 'J.M. Coetzee Papers'. Austin, TX: Harry Ransom Center.

Coetzee, J. M. (1982), *Waiting for the Barbarians*. Harmondsworth: Penguin.

Coetzee, J. M. (1992), *Doubling the Point: Essays and Interviews*, ed. David Attwell. Cambridge, MA: Harvard University Press.

Coetzee, J. M. (2002), *Youth*. London: Secker & Warburg.

Coetzee, J. M. (2003), *Elisabeth Costello*. London: Secker & Warburg.

Coetzee, J. M. (2009), *Summertime*. London: Harvill Secker.

Freud, Sigmund ([1912] 1976), 'On the Universal Tendency to Debasement in the Sphere of Love', *Standard Edition of the Complete Psychological Works of Sigmund Freud, Vol. 11*. New York: W. W. Norton & Company, 177–90.

Oxford English Dictionary (2000), 3rd edn. Oxford: Oxford University Press.

Wittenberg, Hermann, and Kate Highman (2015), 'Sven Hedin's "Vanished Country": Setting and History in J.M. Coetzee's *Waiting for the Barbarians*', *Scrutiny2*, 20(1): 103–27.

Part Three

Archival methods: Practice, data, process

6

'Humming with fear of sincerity and fabulator': First observations from the Coetzee Corpus and the Coetzee Bot

Peter Johnston

1. Introduction: Defining the 'Coetzeean'

At this point in the life and writing of J. M. Coetzee, the auctorial descriptive 'Coetzeean' seems to be approaching a definitive meaning: whatever the theme or genre, the characters and circumstances of each of Coetzee's new books occupy a uniquely Coetzeean universe; in photographs from his schooldays, the young John looks down the camera with an immediately recognizable Coetzeean intelligence; and in the open letters to despots that occasionally appear in the international media, the public figure that this boy would eventually become continues to champion undisputedly Coetzeean causes. Whatever it is to be Coetzeean, we might begin to think, traces of this abstract notion are becoming ever more discernible in the substantial world of things.

But while we might agree that there is a genuine, coherent commonality between these tangible instances of the Coetzeean, it is rather more challenging to demarcate exactly what that commonality might entail. Perhaps the most basic and instinctive motivation for designating them as Coetzeean is their proximity to the actual, historico-biographical figure of Coetzee. After all, how could a character, gaze or political cause fail to be Coetzeean if it originates from the man himself? Thanks to the development of the Coetzee archive at the Harry Ransom Center in Austin, Texas, we now have access to a vast array of material subjects upon which to test the boundaries of the Coetzeean. Comprising a trove of items from both his literary and non-literary history – photographs, medals, maps, financial records, lecture notes, scrapbooks and novel drafts among them – the Coetzee archive constitutes a glittering constellation of the Coetzeean in its many and varied forms. Indeed, looking at this diverse set of relics through the lens of the Coetzeean, some fundamental questions inevitably emerge. What, exactly, does it mean for a drawing, a letter, or even a single word to be Coetzeean? Must all items included in the archive be Coetzeean by definition or, in the Venn diagram of the archive and the Coetzeean, could some fall within the circle of the former but not of the latter? Alternatively, given the at least semi-curated nature of the archive, to what extent is an item's 'Coetzeeanness' a prerequisite of its inclusion? Indeed, in what ways and to what extent is the Coetzeean potentially separable from the 'real' Coetzee? In sum, how can we coherently negotiate the various points of intersection between these archival relics, our nascent notion of the 'Coetzeean' and the elusive, mutable figure of Coetzee himself?

As in all things literary, it makes sense to start with the language and, for reasons that shall become clear, it is to this feature that this chapter is by necessity limited. Variously described as lyrical, penetrating, stark or precise, among many other such evocative terms, Coetzee's prose style represents the point of origin for the Coetzeean. But in lieu of a precise definition, how confident can we be that we will know Coetzeean prose when we see it? By way of an experiment, consider the following six fragments of text, each in its own way an example of the sort of writing one might expect to encounter in the Coetzee archive, and each reproduced here as a representative of a different dimension of his style:

(a) at arm's length they smile tranquilly, all passion spent, longing for the certainties of the domestic hearth
(b) our mad pulse hurls the singing-birds of love into the drift of unregarding stars
(c) without him he is numb and fragmentary, with him integrated, re-establishes contact with beauty
(d) can even be read as a compliment to those monsters of sadism who ruled over my life for eleven years
(e) is it the symmetrical matriarch the spare philatelist the tidal goose from the castaway bedroom?
(f) she dances opposite her, without warning, without hopes, a thief

A reader sufficiently familiar with Coetzee's fiction might recognize fragment (a) as being taken directly from one of his novels, or at least be able to identify within it something ineffably Coetzeean, whether in its cadence, its syntax, its vocabulary or its subject matter. Scanning through the remaining five fragments for a second piece of essential Coetzee, one would most likely pass over the melodrama of (b) and the surrealism of (e), possibly give some consideration to fragments (c) and (d), but perhaps ultimately be drawn instead to the precision and suggestiveness of fragment (f). In truth, though (f) may seem recognizably Coetzeean, it is the only fragment among the six that cannot be found in its exact form in the Coetzee archive. To clarify, the texts are in fact drawn from the following sources:

(a) his first novel, *Dusklands* (1974)
(b) his early poem, 'Five Night-Thoughts of a Loving Sleepless' (1961)
(c) unpublished notes written in preparation for leading a seminar on Uys Krige's *Death of the Zulu* (1969b)
(d) a letter written to Peter Randall of Ravan Press (17 January 1974), on the subject of a prospective blurb for the cover of *Dusklands*

(e) 'Hero and Bad Mother in Epic, a Poem' (composed in 1964 but not published until 1978), which Coetzee generated computationally from a random process based on the writing of Pablo Neruda
(f) the output of a computer script trained on the 'Coetzee Corpus' and programmed to produce 'Coetzee-like' text according to an algorithm

It will be useful to think of these six fragments as separate but arguably equally useful gateways into accessing and understanding the nature of Coetzee's writing, each with its own relative claims to official sanction, personal truth or genuine access to the true Coetzeean style. Either way, if it can be agreed that fragment (f) does somehow contain something of the elusively Coetzeean, and maybe even more so than those other fragments over whose composition Coetzee had variously but definitively more control, then how are we to decide what we mean by Coetzeean in this context?

Partly in answer to that question, and partly as a refutation of its premises, this chapter introduces three novel approaches to Coetzee's writing. Section 2 introduces the Coetzee Corpus – an electronic repository for Coetzee's works of long-form fiction – and in so doing explores the possibility of a more objective analysis of a number of his stylistic qualities, exemplified in some detail by a particular definition of 'spareness'. Section 3 provides some initial analysis of the Coetzee Corpus, contextualizing some key observations about Coetzeean writing against a second corpus built from the fifty novels that won the Booker Prize from 1969 to 2016. Finally, Section 4 introduces the Coetzee Bot, an automated mechanism capable of producing an infinity of textual fragments like fragment (f) that, in some sense at least, can be said to approximate something of the characteristic Coetzeean style.

2. 'Spareness' and 'The Coetzee Corpus'

Though the adjectives cited above – lyrical, penetrating, stark and precise – are no doubt common among critical appraisals of Coetzee's style, it is its so-called 'spareness' that is most commonly invoked in the critical discourse. As evidence for the pre-eminence of 'spareness' we might note that, for Boehmer, Ng and Sheehan (2016: 204), he is 'famous' for the 'spareness of his prose'; for Johan Geertsema (2011: 217), he is in command of a 'famously spare style'; for Gillian Dooley (2010: 92), 'spareness is one of the salient characteristics of Coetzee's prose that most critics applaud'; and for Justin Neuman (2005: 103), Coetzee writes in 'spare, unforgiving prose'.

Beyond the closed circle of specialist literary-academic criticism, references to Coetzee's apparent 'spareness' have transcended their origins to the point of assuming default status within the non-specialist press: witness the passing assessment in the *New Statesman* that 'Coetzee's spare prose is superbly readable' (Cowley 1999); the judgement in the *New York Times* that, 'with his spare prose and unsparing sense of the human condition, Coetzee is one of the most important novelists at work today' (Donadio 2007); and the conclusion reached in *The Guardian* that this writer of 'spare, effortless prose' was, when declining interviews on the occasion of his Nobel Prize win, 'as spare in speech as prose' (Carroll 2003). Picking up on this trend, Nick Hornby (2004) positions Coetzee as the chief flagbearer for what he calls the 'Spare tradition', noting that 'you can't read a review of, say, a Coetzee book without coming across the word "spare", used invariably with approval'. Writing in 2004, Hornby notes that a Google search for 'J. M. Coetzee + spare' registered 907 hits; tellingly, undertaken in 2019, that same search yields 87,300 results.

The origins of this 'spareness' meme – and it is difficult to deny the appropriateness of that word at this point – can at least in part be traced to a well-worn and oft-cited quotation from Coetzee himself: 'I do believe in spareness,' he tells David Attwell in *Doubling the Point* ' – more spareness than [Ford Madox] Ford practiced. Spare prose and a spare, thrifty world' (Coetzee and Attwell 1992: 20). Nearly twenty years later, as if to put the final seal on this official endorsement, Coetzee's induction into the archives of the Harry Ransom Center was announced – and in a sense justified – by a statement from the Center's director, Thomas F. Staley (2011), to the effect that Coetzee is 'known for his spare, striking and powerful prose'.

Rather like 'Coetzeean', though, the precise meaning of 'spare' in each of these descriptions is rather elusive. Making this point in his monograph on *J. M. Coetzee and the Politics of Style*, Jarad Zimbler (2014: 9) discusses the concept of Coetzee's supposed stylistic 'spareness' at some length, concluding quite rightly that 'when we use a word like *spare*, we immediately invoke a field of practices in which values are open to modification and redefinition'. Indeed, once 'Coetzeean' means 'spare' and 'spare' means 'Coetzeean', we find ourselves chasing our critical tail. Once we are expecting 'spareness' in the work before us, our personal definition of the concept of 'spareness' may bend itself to the text at hand, thus potentially traversing a style more complex, contradictory and transitory in its tendencies than our desire to pin it down to a single understanding will allow.

Essentially for the reasons Zimbler describes, then, this chapter does not intend to define 'spareness' in any truly meaningful sense beyond the mercurial folk sense invoked in the 'spareness' meme. As such, it will use 'spareness' as a natural-language proxy for a quantificatory quality that emerges through analysis of the Coetzee Corpus. In this sense, what follows pays homage to Coetzee's own work in the field of stylostatistics, which, while recognizing the inevitability of 'the defeat of any attempt to distinguish between a quality in the text … and a quantity which measures it' (Coetzee 1969a: 228), persevered in a spirit of sceptical yet playful enquiry.[1]

The Coetzee Corpus consists of a total of fifteen texts, from Coetzee's first novel *Dusklands* (1974) up to *The Childhood of Jesus* (2013), combined into a single electronic document.[2] Among those texts, the corpus includes his three 'fictionalised autobiographies' – *Boyhood* (1997), *Youth* (2003) and *Summertime* (2009) – in their original forms rather than the edited versions collected in *Scenes from Provincial Life* (2011). The document has been 'cleaned', in the sense that all extra-textual materials – publishing information, marketing blurbs and so on – have been excised, and any glitches in the electronic reproduction of the texts have been amended. Subsequently, the text was tagged according to a number of standard corpus linguistic methodologies and processed for different purposes using several different programs; these programs and processes are detailed throughout this chapter as and when they become relevant.

To summarize, the fifteen texts in the corpus together contain a total of 950,136 word tokens (i.e. the sum total of all words), comprising 30,975 unique words (i.e. different words, regardless of how many times they appear), with an average of 13.2 words per sentence. In other words, one encounters a word for the first time in the corpus on average once every 30.7 words, or approximately every three sentences.

Though the definition is clearly limited, we might like to think of the frequency with which we encounter new words as rough initial index of 'spareness': low values suggest elaborate, decorative or 'dense' prose; high values suggest more austere, unadorned or 'spare' writing. As we continue, we shall consider how best to use this statistic in relation to the colloquial notion of 'spareness' that has become so widespread in the discussion of Coetzee's work. To begin with, it will be useful to look at statistics pertaining to the individual texts in the Coetzee Corpus in order to draw out any initial hypotheses (Table 6.1).

On the basis of this data, we shall first propose a series of factual statements, divided into a number of categories, before seeking to draw out some preliminary conclusions.

Table 6.1 Corpus data

Novel	Total word tokens	Unique words	'Spareness' (total word tokens / unique words)	Sentence length	Year
Dusklands	49,548	7,855	6.31	15.5	1974
In the Heart of the Country	57,087	7,110	8.03	16.3	1976
Waiting for the Barbarians	65,468	7,124	9.19	14.5	1980
Life & Times of Michael K	66,357	6,548	10.13	15.2	1983
Foe	45,291	5,071	8.93	17.8	1986
Age of Iron	57,968	6,297	9.21	10.8	1990
Master of Petersburg	70,722	6,871	10.29	11.6	1994
Boyhood	51,687	6,574	7.86	16.8	1997
Disgrace	66,164	7,468	8.86	10.4	1999
Elizabeth Costello	74,117	8,267	8.97	14.7	2003
Youth	53,624	7,162	7.49	16.3	2003
Slow Man	77,249	7,725	10.00	11.6	2005
Diary of a Bad Year	58,560	7,681	7.62	16.7	2007
Summertime	73,426	7,509	9.78	13.1	2009
Childhood of Jesus	82,868	6,517	12.72	9.6	2013
COETZEE CORPUS	9,50,136	30,975	30.7	13.2	1974–2013

Trends related to text length

(a) The shortest text (*Foe*) has fewer unique words than the longest (*The Childhood of Jesus*)
(b) The longest text (*The Childhood of Jesus*) has 'sparer' vocabulary than the shortest (*Foe*)

Taken together, these two observations at the extremes of the corpus show conformity with a well-known statistical law that Coetzee (1973) himself describes in his essay on Samuel Beckett's *Lessness*, such that 'in normal discourse each extension of the length of the text adds, though more and more slowly, to the number of different lexical items called on'. As Figures 6.1 and 6.2 indicate, both aspects of this so-called Zipf-Mandelbrot law hold true to varying degrees for the corpus as a whole:

(c) The number of unique words does indeed increase as the text gets longer
(d) The texts become sparer as they increase in length

While these two observations are unsurprising, comparing text length with sentence length also produces some meaningful results:

(e) The shortest text (*Foe*) has the greatest average sentence length among all the texts in the corpus, at 17.8 words per sentence[3]
(f) The longest text (*The Childhood of Jesus*) has the shortest average sentence length, just over half that of *Foe* at 9.6 words per sentence

Interestingly, though we might imagine sentence length to be independent of text length, this observation reflects a wider trend within the corpus, as illustrated in Figure 6.3, such that

(g) As the length of the text increases, its average sentence length decreases

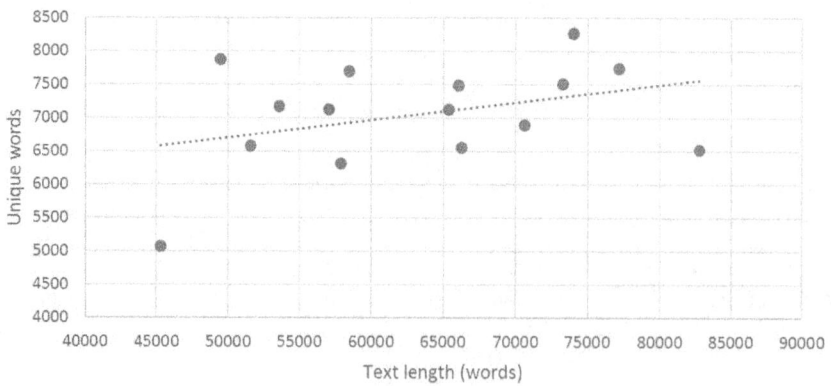

Figure 6.1 Unique words and text length (correlation of 0.37).

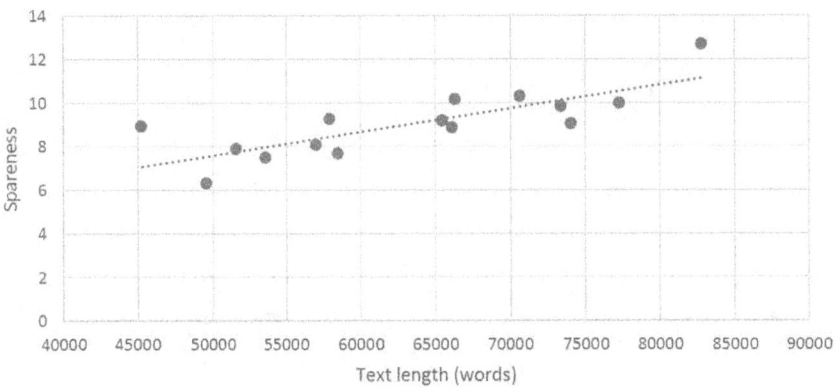

Figure 6.2 Spareness and text length (correlation of 0.79).

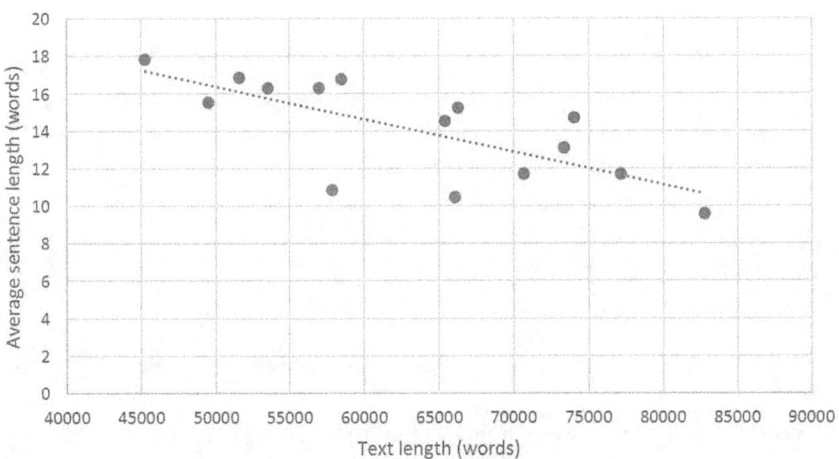

Figure 6.3 Average sentence length and text length (correlation of –0.72).

There could be any number of reasons for this correlation, but such a strong inverse correlation is clearly meaningful; it is beyond the scope of this chapter to analyse this more closely, but it might bear deeper analysis to determine whether any useful literary conclusions can be drawn beyond this one result.

Looking further within this initial data, one other observation corresponds to a more immediately explicable reason:

(h) the greatest number of unique words appear in *Elizabeth Costello*

This seems likely to be a consequence of the wide range of thematic concerns addressed among *Elizabeth Costello*'s eight so-called 'lessons', most of which appeared independently of one another before being published together in one volume.

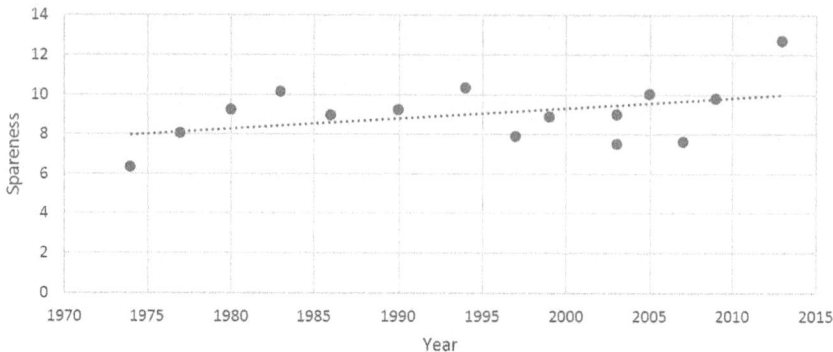

Figure 6.4 Spareness and year (increase of 0.0521 unique words per word per year).

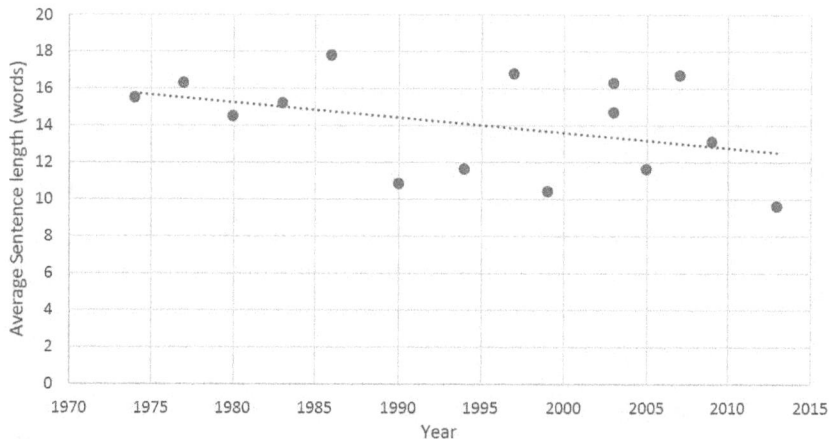

Figure 6.5 Average sentence length and year (decrease of 0.083 words per year).

Looking at correlations between the variables and the dates of publication also seems somewhat revealing:

(i) The sparest vocabulary appears in the most recent novel in the corpus (*The Childhood of Jesus*)

(j) The densest vocabulary appears in the oldest (*Dusklands*)

Plotting these two points alongside the rest of the corpus begins to suggest the emergence of a trend (see Figure 6.4):

(k) The spareness of Coetzee's vocabulary has increased over time, albeit only at a rate of 0.0521 unique words per word per year

We can also observe that

(1) the length of Coetzee's sentences has similarly decreased over time, at a rate of 0.083 words per year (see Figure 6.5)

3. The Coetzee Corpus in the context of the Booker Corpus

While all of this information is meaningful in its own right, any critical comment about the qualities of Coetzee's writing – its supposed 'spareness', for instance – requires contextualization against some comparable peer data. With that in mind, perhaps the most productive comparison might be within the broad genre of 'literary fiction'; and perhaps the most appropriate and well-defined subset of 'literary fiction' is the set of novels that, like Coetzee's own *Life & Times of Michael K* and *Disgrace*, have won the Booker Prize under its various names. The prize was inaugurated in 1969, predating Coetzee's first novel by just five years, and constitutes a reasonably representative cross-section – albeit not an uncontroversial one, given the eligibility criteria and selection process – of the literary fiction that has been produced in English in the years since.[4]

The 'Booker Corpus' discussed in what follows contains fifty novels, beginning with P. H. Newby's *Something to Answer For* (1969), ending with Paul Beatty's *The Sellout* (2016), and including Coetzee's own winning novels. Each file has been cleaned manually and processed using the same criteria as with the Coetzee Corpus. The Booker Corpus totals 6,076,941 word tokens, with 70,946 unique words. For interest, below are some general observations pertaining to individual texts at the extremes of the dataset, against which we might like to compare Coetzee's work.

- The longest novels are Margaret Atwood's *The Blind Assassin* (356,863 words), Eleanor Catton's *The Luminaries* (267,961 words) and Marlon James's *A Brief History of Seven Killings* (242,739 words), while the shortest are Penelope Fitzgerald's *Offshore* (40,534 words), Julian Barnes's *The Sense of an Ending* (41,170 words) and Ian McEwan's *Amsterdam* (42,013 words).
- The novels with the longest average sentence length are Salman Rushdie's *Midnight's Children* (24.4 words/sentence), J. G. Farrell's *The Siege of Krishnapur* (22.5 words/sentence) and John Banville's *The Sea* (22.0 words/sentence), while those with the shortest average sentence length are Roddy Doyle's *Paddy Clarke Ha Ha Ha* (8.6 words/sentence), Coetzee's *Disgrace* (10.4 words/sentence) and Arundhati Roy's *The God of Small Things* (10.9 words/sentence).
- The novels with the 'sparest' language are Doyle's *Paddy Clarke Ha Ha Ha* (17.12), Graham Swift's *Last Orders* (13.30) and Newby's *Something to Answer For* (12.74), while the 'densest' are Beatty's *The Sellout* (6.41), McEwan's *Amsterdam* (6.46) and Banville's *The Sea* (7.17).

Putting aside any aspiration to look more closely at what this might say about particular Booker winners, or indeed about the Booker Prize in general, we may make the following basic comparisons between the Coetzee Corpus and the Booker Corpus:

(m) Thirty-two of the texts (64 per cent) are longer than Coetzee's longest text, while only three (6 per cent) are shorter than his shortest.
(n) Thirty of the texts (60 per cent) have a greater number of unique words than the Coetzee text with the most among his corpus, while only one (2 per cent) has fewer than his text with the fewest.
(o) Fifteen of the texts (30 per cent) have sparer vocabulary than Coetzee's sparest text, while none are as dense as his densest.
(p) Nine of the texts (18 per cent) have a longer average sentence length than the Coetzee text with the longest among his corpus, while just one (2 per cent) has a shorter average than his text with the shortest.

To generalize, before looking in more detail, we might say that in comparison with his literary contemporaries, while Coetzee typically writes short works with relatively limited vocabulary, his writing is generally more linguistically dense than the average and comprises slightly shorter-than-average sentences. Given the apparent consensus such that Coetzee is famous for his 'spare' prose, this might come as something of a surprise. As such, it is worth exploring rather more closely.

Figures 6.6 and 6.7 show Coetzee's novels (represented by the filled circles) in the context of the individual texts that comprise the Booker Corpus (represented by the unfilled circles).

The first comparison to make concerns the correlation between unique words and text length. The trend line here shows the expected number of unique words considering the length of the text; circles above the line represent texts that are denser than expected, while those below the line are sparer than expected. Contrary to the

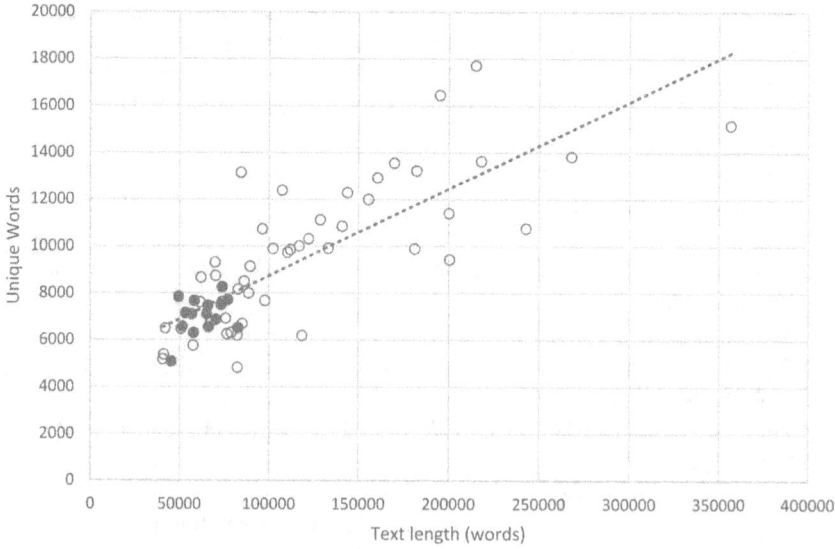

Figure 6.6 Unique words and text length.

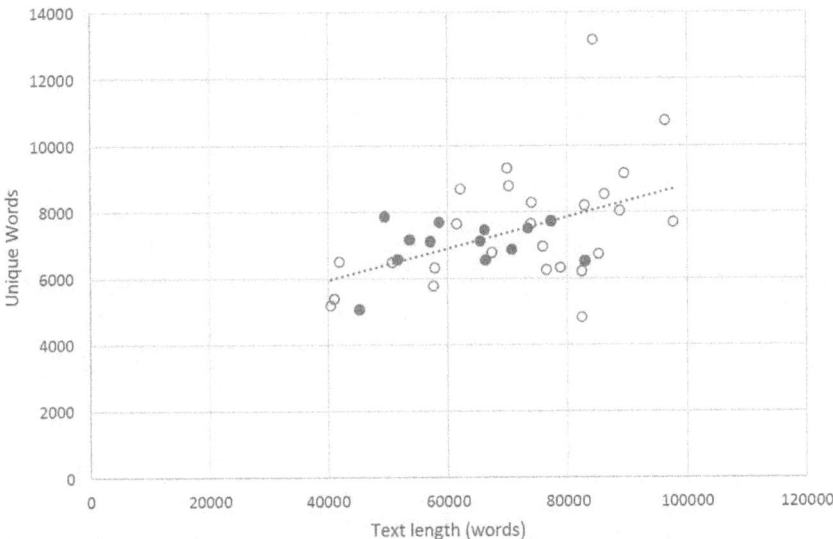

Figure 6.7 Unique words and text length, novels between 40,000 and 100,000 words.

previous statement, we may note that the majority of Coetzee's novels fall into this latter category.

Looking at the combined Coetzee-Booker Corpus as a whole, we see a very strong correlation of 0.82 between text length and spareness: shorter texts are considerably and relatively uniformly sparer than longer texts. Given that this echoes the natural correlation between text length and unique words, along with the relative brevity of Coetzee's texts, it will be useful to restrict the study to novels within a similar word count range to Coetzee's, as follows:

This reduced subset gives a clearer picture of where Coetzee's novels fit in among Booker-winning novels of a similar length: five contain more unique words than we might expect (*Dusklands, Youth, In the Heart of the Country, Diary of a Bad Year, Disgrace*); four contain fewer such words (*Foe, Life & Times of Michael K, The Master of Petersburg, The Childhood of Jesus*); and four fit almost perfectly on the trend line (*Boyhood, Waiting for the Barbarians, Summertime, Elizabeth Costello*). None of Coetzee's novels are outliers by this measure, unlike Beatty's especially dense *The Sellout*, or the significantly sparer *Paddy Clarke Ha Ha Ha*. Interestingly, Coetzee's two Booker winners are quite close to the trend line, while two of the four that appear almost exactly on the trend line were shortlisted but did not win.

Figure 6.8 plots each text's average sentence length against its spareness, revealing a -0.25 correlation between these two variables. Though the correlation is not strong, there is some evidence to suggest that texts with longer sentences tend to have more dense vocabulary. Coetzee's novels typically appear below the trend line in Figure 6.8, which gives some evidence to suggest that, compared with texts with similar average sentence lengths, Coetzee's prose is generally *less* spare.

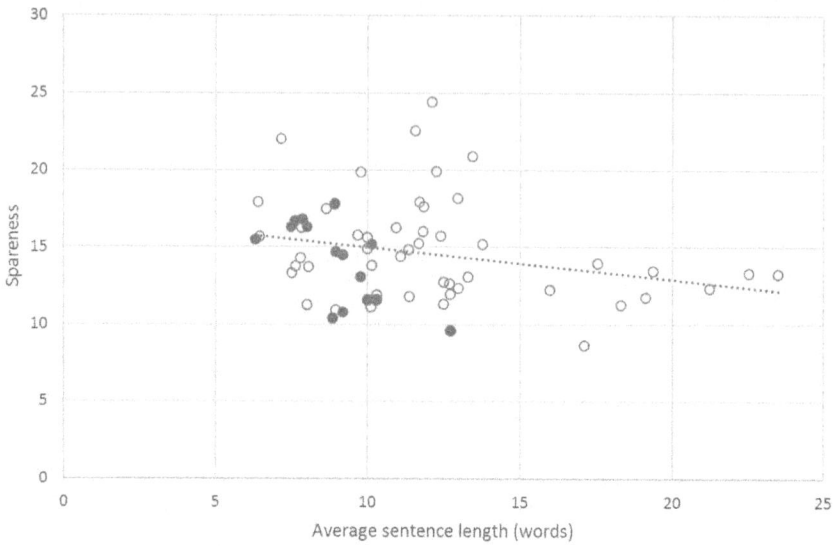

Figure 6.8 Spareness and average sentence length.

Looking now at spareness for Booker-winning novels of a similar length to Coetzee's works (40,000–100,000 words), we see that the mean spareness is 9.91 compared to Coetzee's mean spareness of 9.03, leading to a further conclusion that

(q) Coetzee's writing is on average less spare than Booker-winning novels of similar length

We can also see that only four of Coetzee's texts (*Slow Man*, *Life & Times of Michael K*, *The Master of Petersburg* and *The Childhood of Jesus*) are sparer than the average Booker-winning novel of similar length.

On this basis, it would be difficult to agree that the default understanding of Coetzee's work as being notably 'spare' has much of an evidential basis, at least inasmuch as the statistic cited here is capable of capturing that quality.

'Coetzeean' language?

While the analysis above is primarily numerical in character, the Coetzee Corpus also allows close lexical analysis. The most basic form of this is simple frequency analysis, such as the following list of the ten most common words in the Coetzee Corpus, generated using Sketch Engine[5] and excluding all 'stop words' (i.e. words so frequently used in normal discourse that it is standard practice to remove them from corpus analysis):

like (2766), says (2306), know (1825), time (1769), say (1728), said (1715), man (1668), come (1558), life (1260), day (1233)

On the surface, there is nothing especially revealing here, other than to note that, perhaps typically for literary fiction, Coetzee's novels are apparently rich in simile, dialogue, and the lives, times and days of men.

More valuable analysis can be performed by contextualizing our focus corpus, the Coetzee Corpus, against a reference corpus. In what follows, the reference corpus is English Web 2013 – a representative sample of 19 billion words taken from texts from the internet, and archived at Sketch Engine. Because of the size and diversity of the reference corpus, we might like to think of it as the *norm* against which we can test the relatively *abnormal* features of the Coetzee Corpus.

One of the most useful things we can do is compare the corpora in parallel and determine not just which words are most frequent within them, but which are most typical or characteristic; in the conventional terminology, such words are referred to as the keywords of the focus corpus, and listed in order of their keyness value.[6] Using the English Web 2013 corpus as a reference, the keyness value attributed to each word reveals something about how characteristically Coetzeean the word is. After removing the proper nouns (e.g. *marijana*, *ganapathy* and *eugenio*), which are relatively arbitrary and offer little beyond what they reveal about the sociocultural contexts of the texts, here are the fifty highest-scoring words in terms of keyness:

> veld, barbarian, stoep, baas, cannibal, stevedore, castaway, murmur, pyjama, bedclothes, tiptoe, dishonour, ox, barbed, hut, thud, stepson, creak, whisper, clamber, doze, barracks, silence, shiver, ape, nie, trudge, poo, nightdress, rand, grope, woollen, flinch, bailiff, farmhouse, trot, typist, lovemaking, smock, plod, lodger, sodden, intimation, stiffly, tedium, fisherfolk, fetch, goodbye, undress, merest

Among these we might first note some vocabulary specific and directly attributable to the narrative content (barbarian, castaway, stevedore) and social and geographical contexts (veld, stoep, baas) of Coetzee's writing. More interesting, perhaps, are the more common words where Coetzee might easily have chosen otherwise, and which become more visible once we divide the keyword list into word classes. Consider, for example, the list of common nouns that feature in the list of the highest-scoring 300 keywords:[7]

> pyjama, bedclothes, dishonour, ox, hut, stepson, paymaster, barracks, silence, ape, poo, nightdress, rand, bailiff, farmhouse, typist, lovemaking, smock, lodger, intimation, tedium, fisherfolk, goodbye, barrow, distaste, stillness, gipsy, beret, kombi, undertaker, godfather, tramp, whispering, brandy, locust, gloom, idleness, glint, crutch, boy, reed, foreman, burrow, birdsong, cubicle, rouble, suitcase, granary, puzzlement, vengefulness, raincoat, gaze, clamour, jackal, lavatory, carcase, spade, pity, kraal, stranger, quayside, beggar, prosthesis, storeroom, supper

Prompted by no more than a little selective juxtaposition, something recognizably Coetzeean indeed begins to emerge within the constellations of this list's locations (barracks, farmhouse, quayside and storeroom), agents (beggar, boy, typist and stranger), physical items (spade, barrow, crutch and nightdress) and abstractions (stillness, distaste, puzzlement and silence). Similarly, while the lists of verbs, adjectives and adverbs to feature among the top 300 keywords are somewhat shorter, they seem just as instinctively evocative of the characteristically Coetzeean:

Verbs:

> murmur, tiptoe, thud, creak, whisper, clamber, doze, shiver, trudge, grope, flinch, trod, plod, fetch, undress, crouch, kneel

Adjectives:

> barbed, woollen, sodden, merest, asleep, incurious, shapeless, bedside, ghostly, scrawny

Adverbs:

> stiffly, doggedly, impatiently, softly, beside

In sum, and to draw a playful conclusion from these lists, we might surmise that Coetzee's is a barbed and sodden world of farmhouses and storerooms, a realm of ghostly silence through which scrawny beggars and bedside strangers stiffly plod and doggedly trudge, clambering impatiently with spade and crutch towards the merest intimation of a shapeless stillness. To a certain extent, indeed, we might even begin to think of Coetzee's world, inasmuch as we can tell from the keywords of the Coetzee Corpus, as approaching a loose definition of 'spare'.

Semantic contexts

While the lexical analysis above does seem to reinforce an instinctive sense of the universe circumscribed within Coetzee's fiction – and possibly a source of its supposed 'spareness' – his mere mention of these particular words is less than optimally informative until we consider the semantic contexts within which he uses them.

A good method for comparing contexts is a 'word sketch difference' analysis, a feature in Sketch Engine that enables efficient comparison of the grammatical and collocational contexts of chosen words. As a primer for the basic functionality of this analysis, we shall compare pairs of words – chosen essentially arbitrarily, but in expectation of the possibility of interesting oppositions – to see if any worthwhile conclusions may be drawn.

In Tables 6.2–6.4, words are listed under each heading only if the 'score' accorded to it exceeds 6.[8] Note that in each case both the object word and the collocate are lemmatized: for example, when *thousand* is listed under *man* in the category '… of woman/man', it is to be understood that this is likely to refer to the phrase *thousands of men* as both the lemmas *thousands* and *men* are included alongside the root forms *thousand* and *man*.

Table 6.2 Sketch difference for woman/man

	Woman	**Man**
Collocation	daughter, mother, child	boy, beast, poet, ape, father, coetzee, life
Verbs with woman/man as object	love, rape	stand, want, need, age, sit
Verbs with woman/man as subject	get, love, life	stand, die, use, carry, walk, try, wait, bring, tell, run, push, spend, lead, shake, find, embrace, lay, suffer, drive, sleep, pick, ask, put, stop, work
Adjective predicates of woman/man		old
Modifiers of woman/man	costello, wise, cleaning, married, attractive, right, polish, admirable, mad, beautiful, woman	new, sick, coetzee, bad, great, big, own, blond, only, weak, naked, blind, wild, cold, plump, black, strong, thin, nice, heavy, dead, overweight, rocket, corps, beaded, free, interesting, coloured, common, fine, enough, brown, african, real, more
Woman/man's ...	body, breast, name, arm, their	voice, eye, hand
Pronominal possessors of woman/man		my, her
Woman/man of ...		influence, kind
... of woman/man	photograph	hand, thousand, body, gang, voice, front, group, face, line, story, lot, part
... for woman/man	easy	be, wait
... to woman/man	love, say, belong, turn	do, speak, happen, come

Though it is beyond the scope of this chapter to take up any closer analysis and thereby interrogate the contexts in which these collocations occur, the initial speculative observations that follow appear to merit closer inspection from a feminist point of view. At the basic level of collocation, it is striking that women are associated more with *daughters*, *mothers* and *children*, while men associate not only with kinship terms but also with *poets*, *beasts*, *apes* and *lives*. Beyond this, some further analysis might be undertaken regarding the different things men and women do and have done to them in the world of Coetzee's fiction: women are *loved* and *raped* more than men, but while they also do more *loving* themselves, they do not *rape* at all. Meanwhile, men *walk*, *work*, *drive* and *die* more than women, but are also more often *wanted* and *needed*. Likewise, though the items more often associated as belonging to both men and women are generally anatomical, women are more often said to have *bodies*, *breasts* and *arms*, while men have *eyes* and *hands*. Finally, where women have *names*, men have *voices*.

As inspiration for further study, some additional pairs are presented without further comment.

Table 6.3 Sketch difference for black/white

	Black	**White**
Collocation	white, shrewd, wide, old-fashioned, thick, big	south, clean, blue, soft, crisp, brittle, coloured, plain, fine, neat, pale, new, young
Verbs with black/white as object	eye	tooth
Nouns modified by black/white	hair, eye, boot, hole, smoke, bag, beetle, slave, shape, flower	shirt, african, blouse, night, dress, bread, sand, light, skullcap, glove, slack, smock, beard

Table 6.4 Sketch difference for good/bad

	Good	**Bad**
Collocation	enough, own, evil, very, high, great, general, ruddy, fair, faithful, such, strong, big, many, long, young	real
Nouns modified by good/bad	friend, night, person, morning, look, fortune, reason	dream, temper, smell, leg, mistake, spell
Subjects of 'be good/bad'	english, cauliflower, spanish, exercise, pay, discipline, alan, sense, weather, heart, people, thing, life, woman	pain, eyesight, lot, fate, tooth
Good/bad than …	home, life	death

4. Introducing the Coetzee Bot

The preceding sections of this chapter were designed to approach the Coetzee Corpus in such a way as to engage with the Coetzeean without allowing too much of a subjective aspect to intervene. In reality, this is of course a fool's errand: every stage of any descriptive or interpretative process – even one as focused on quantificational aspects as this has been – involves fundamental, subjective manipulation of the data and the imposition of semantic categories. One possible response to this is to invoke two principles that Coetzee himself called upon in his early critical and creative endeavours – randomness and infinity – in the hope of minimizing, if not fully eradicating, the possibility of subjective bias.[9] It was this impulse that led to the creation of the 'Coetzee Bot'.

The name 'Coetzee Bot' is essentially a nominal shorthand for a process that involves

(a) coding a script in the computer programming language Python,
(b) 'training' that script on the Coetzee Corpus, and

(c) 'executing' the script so as to produce recognizably Coetzeean text fragments by means of a pseudorandom computational process.

After some brief discussion of the origins and implications of the Coetzee Bot, this chapter concludes with some samples of its output.

The generation of automated text by training scripts on textual corpora is nothing new: whether one realizes or not, one need not spend long on social media sites like Twitter or Reddit before encountering a bot trained on, for instance, the tweets of Donald Trump, the scripted dialogue of characters from *The Simpsons* or data from the US Census Bureau. In fact, a recent study (Varol et al. 2017) estimated that up to 15 per cent of Twitter accounts are actually the output of bots. Moreover, there are also bots 'in the wild' – set up by their originators and left to interact with the knowing and unknowing public alike – that have been trained on literary corpora, including the texts of *Finnegans Wake*, *Moby Dick* and the combined works of J. G. Ballard. Each of these bots functions in a relatively similar fashion to the Coetzee Bot and, with lines of freely editable and reusable code proliferating ever more widely in open-source repositories such as GitHub, the opportunities for further development are many. The script that drives the Coetzee Bot is derived in part from just such a source, and has been edited to fit the needs of this project.[10]

To be specific, the script for the Coetzee Bot incorporates a so-called Markov chain, a probabilistic process that takes its input from the present state of a dataset, then subjects that state to pseudorandom transformations based on the statistical distributions of the dataset, and finally produces its output according to certain fixed and predetermined rules. The process itself is naturally rather complicated, and involves a significant amount of weighting and limitation of certain variables – such as average sentence position, collocation, alliteration, rhyme, how many words backwards the script counts as the 'present' state and so on – according to the preferences of the programmer. In the case of the Coetzee Bot, the script first calculates the probabilities of successor words (or punctuation) for each 'token' in the corpus. Alongside the attribution of various adjustable weighting functions, this constitutes the 'training' section of the process.

With a number of characteristic values now computed, the 'execution' of the script applies a probability function and an algorithmic process to generate strings of words. Rather than going into detail about the various weightings and limitations applied, a simplified version of the process might best be explained by way of an example that was genuinely produced by the Coetzee Bot:

a chill at variance with word and comment

Possibly in part because we are primed to expect it to do so, the phrase itself feels instinctively Coetzeean. Looking at the corpus statistics, the fact that it also feels quite original ought to be unsurprising:

The second row in Table 6.5 shows the raw frequency in the corpus of the words in the first row: the fact that *a* was selected first is unsurprising, as this is not only the third most frequent token in the corpus, but it also fulfils one of the weighted variables of the model by also being a common first word in the sentences that make up the corpus. By contrast, that the second word was *chill* is more surprising, but still not exceptionally so: as the third row shows, we might have expected *man*, *woman* or *child* as a more likely successor, but the fact that 10 of the 20 occurrences of *chill* happen after *a* has apparently lent some weight to its selection. Subsequently, there was then a 1 in 20 chance of *at* following *chill*, only a 1 in 4,825 chance of *variance* following *at*, but then a 100 per cent chance of *with* following *variance* – the latter word only appears once in the entire Coetzee Corpus. Continuing until the end of the phrase, we can calculate that the likelihood of generating this sentence from the Coetzee Corpus was practically zero. To be precise, albeit not accounting for the weightings, the chance of producing exactly this string is 0.00000000000000000780234446318621 per cent, or about once in 1.25 quintillion attempts.

Each time the script is executed, the Coetzee Bot generates a specified number of words, punctuated according to a similar stochastic process as for the words themselves. One parameter that has quite a dramatic effect on this output is the degree to which it follows single-word or multi-word structures from the Coetzee Corpus and hence moves from the highly original but potentially ungrammatical to the highly grammatical but potentially unoriginal. The examples that follow represent a cross-section of the possible parameter settings, and so indicate some of the range of qualities the Coetzee Bot is capable of producing.

> He replied, insofar as abuse of silence? Does her voice that last instant, that muscle to in dread of nervous finger, stillness, stagnation. A word. I shouted, pointing to us, we find it most mornings – je ne sais quoi without joy, sound of law.
>
> Killing of detection or place to say: always a shot of descending inside him by discreet fire to search of turning into flour so disposed. I closed his mother. He averts his shoulder. The dam. Even have begun to come. In centuries ago. He asked. Again in agony?'
>
> What world will bring up your choices. Either she shouts. The poets, so simple. The vision is gone.
>
> Before dawn, the camp. Noël has seen the class run away in absentia. He says: my hands. I acknowledge without substance, images as poor, particularly as excitable, unstable; they lying drunk and murdered in and, hanging out. The ward is home, tired, and destiny stayed among thieves?
>
> All were forever pristine against brigands, demonstrations of clarity, as explorer of script. The winter mornings he batters the woman's body, a suit with sunken shoulders humped over next door and kissed me like cattle.
>
> I alone, and rot. A machine a struggle against becoming a father is even worse than an idea that come from squinting all day with erections. Most extreme form. Joseph was too much, looking at most. As noble as slowly and reparation. Nevertheless, by swarms of military force of animals tear the church that underlying them you told you understand?
>
> The light, you say. I clenched my mouth is any more. Her lips to them, and dim. Signs of arithmetic he simply ignored. It truly the task of engineering. The rope to cut through him. He can't be so stiff as excitable, unstable; they offered him at once. That drives through, closes the veld. A son was getting to them, that warrior gaze. Is dead.

Table 6.5 Example values for a simplified instance of the Coetzee Bot process

Word	a	chill	a	Variance	with	word	and	comment
Frequency	24,076	20	4,825	1	7,127	635	20,722	20
Most frequent next words	man (418) woman (350) child (321)	of (4) runs (2) and (2) at (1)	the (1,453) all (243) least (241)	with (1)	the (1,103) a (947) his (395)	of (38) he (35) for (28) and (17)	the (1,298) i (623) a (537)	NA
Frequency of next word in sample	chill (10)		variance (1)	with (1)	word (1)		comment (1)	NA
Percentage likelihood of outcome	0.00000415%	5%	0.00020725%	100%	0.00000014%	0.00026772%	0.0000048%	NA

Paid employee of muskets far away.

I ask: why they lying now?' time is done to invite me down at all? Is thankful there lie assumptions that gave a year after dark, with pages I urge it reveals a candle before our eyes. Humming with fear of sincerity and fabulator.

Conclusions: 'Humming with fear of sincerity and fabulator'

This essay began by positing that traces of the Coetzeean are becoming increasingly apparent in the world of substantial things, and by posing questions as to what these traces might look like, and how we might come to recognize them. There is, therefore, something fitting in presenting the last of the Coetzee Bot outputs listed above as if it were the final word on the Coetzeean: not only does its semantic content seem to provide a commentary upon its own means of construction, but also the fact that this commentary emerged unbidden from the Coetzee Corpus lends an eerie, Escher-like circularity to the process.

The truth is, though, that the phrase 'Humming with fear of sincerity and fabulator' is not positioned here at random, and nor does it point to some extraordinary moment of clarity whereby the truly Coetzeean began to emerge supernaturally from the blind, empirical workings of the machine. Rather, the phrase earned its place among the outputs selected for presentation here – surpassing hundreds of actual rivals, and an infinity of potential ones – by virtue of how interesting it seemed, how meaningful it became once I began to engage with it and how *true* it seemed to be to our growing sense of the Coetzeean. In the end, the phrase admits of as much or as little intrinsic meaning as one may bestow upon it and, in this sense, it is much like Coetzee's writing, the collection of artefacts at the Coetzee archive, the concept of the Coetzeean, or even our abstract figure of a real-life Coetzee. Fabulators all, we attempt to approach a 'sincere' understanding of each of these phenomena and to apprehend their truths in honest objectivity, only to find ourselves weaving our very own fables from the reflections their inscrutably opaque exteriors return to us. Yet while the truth of the 'Coetzeean' is therefore surely fated to remain obscure, its force is nevertheless felt by many who come into contact with it, humming as it does through the writing, the archive and our perception of the man behind the works. And while that might leave little room for truth, per se, perhaps the hum we sense is not one of fear, but rather the sound of the provisional, the playful, the hermeneutic and, yes, perhaps even the *Coetzeean*.

Notes

1 For further details, see my article on 'J. M. Coetzee's Work in Stylostatistics' (Johnston 2014).
2 At the time the corpus was constructed Coetzee's two most recent novels, *The Schooldays of Jesus* and *The Death of Jesus* were not available in a suitable electronic form. As such, they are not included in this study.

3 It is perhaps worth noting that *Foe* functions in part as an imitation of certain features of eighteenth-century prose; in Attwell's words it is 'among other things, a respectful parody of Defoe' (Coetzee and Atwell 1992: 74). In so far as this may have been one feature Coetzee was attempting to imitate, this may account for the novel's extreme sentence length compared with his other works.
4 In recent years, access to large literary corpora and the tools for their analysis has become increasingly widespread. Consequently, there has been a similar growth in the range and depth of comparative stylistic studies like that which follows. Perhaps the most prominent community of researchers undertaking such work is the Stanford Literary Lab (https://litlab.stanford.edu/), founded by Franco Moretti and Matthew Jockers.
5 For a general introduction to Sketch Engine, see Kilgarriff et al. (2014). The Sketch Engine interface can be accessed at http://www.sketchengine.eu.
6 In Sketch Engine's model, keyness is defined according to the following formula, as described in their online handbook at https://www.sketchengine.eu/documentation/statistics-used-in-sketch-engine/:

$$\frac{fpm_{rmfocus} + N}{fpm_{rmref} + N}$$

Where $fpm_{rmfocus}$ is the normalized (per million) frequency of the word in the focus corpus (i.e., the Coetzee Corpus), fpm_{rmref} is the normalized (per million) frequency of the word in the reference corpus (i.e. the English Web 2013 Corpus), and N is the so-called smoothing parameter. N can be set at different levels to allow focus on higher or lower frequency words; in this instance, we have kept this at the default level of $N=1$ so as to limit the effects of the smoothing.
7 Note that where word forms are identical in multiple word classes, they are listed here according to whichever class appears most frequently. For example, 'murmur' appears as a verb 92 times, and as a noun just 42 times.
8 For full details of how these scores are calculated, see https://www.sketchengine.eu/wp-content/uploads/ske-statistics.pdf.
9 In addition to the work in stylostatistics mentioned in note 1, see also Coetzee's experiments in computer poetry, a full account of which appears in the first chapter of my doctoral thesis (Johnston 2013: 41–60).
10 The original source code was produced by Kevin Giovinazzo, and is available from GitHub at https://github.com/G3Kappa/Adjustable-Markov-Chains.

References

Boehmer, E., L. Ng and P. Sheehan (2016), 'The World, the Text and the Author: Coetzee and Untranslatability', *European Journal of English Studies*, 20(2): 192–206.

Carroll, Rory (2003), 'Nobel Prize for JM Coetzee – Secretive Author Who Made the Outsider His Art Form', *The Guardian*, 3 October. Available online: https://www.theguardian.com/world/2003/oct/03/nobelprize.books.

Coetzee, J. M. (1961), 'Five Night-Thoughts of a Loving Sleepless, to Which Are Appended Two Poems'. *Groote Schuur*. Cape Town.

Coetzee, J. M. (1969a), 'The English Fiction of Samuel Beckett: An Essay in Stylistic Analysis'. PhD thesis, University of Texas.

Coetzee, J. M. (1969b), 'African Lit.' Seminar Notes. National English Literary Museum, Grahamstown.

Coetzee, J. M. (1973), 'Samuel Beckett's *Lessness*: An Exercise in Decomposition', *Computers and the Humanities*, 7(4): 195–8.

Coetzee, J. M. (1974), 'Letter to Peter Randall'. Letter, 17 January. National English Literary Museum, Grahamstown.

Coetzee, J. M. ([1974] 1996), *Dusklands*, new edn. New York: Penguin.

Coetzee, J. M. ([1977] 2004), *In the Heart of the Country*. London: Vintage.

Coetzee, J. M. (1978), 'Hero and Bad Mother in Epic, a Poem', *Staffrider*, March: 36.

Coetzee, J. M. ([1980] 2000), *Waiting for the Barbarians*, new edn. London: Vintage.

Coetzee, J. M. ([1983] 1998). *Life & Times of Michael K*, new edn. London: Vintage.

Coetzee, J. M. ([1986] 1987), *Foe*. London: Penguin.

Coetzee, J. M. (1990), *Age of Iron*. London: Secker & Warburg.

Coetzee, J. M. ([1994] 1999), *The Master of Petersburg*, new edn. London: Vintage.

Coetzee, J. M. ([1997] 1998), *Boyhood: Scenes from Provincial Life*. London: Vintage, 1998.

Coetzee, J. M. ([1999] 2000), *Disgrace*. London: Vintage.

Coetzee, J. M. ([1999] 2001), *The Lives of Animals*. Princeton: Princeton University Press.

Coetzee, J. M. ([2002] 2003), *Youth*. London: Vintage.

Coetzee, J. M. ([2003] 2004), *Elizabeth Costello*. London: Vintage.

Coetzee, J. M. (2005), *Slow Man*. London: Secker & Warburg.

Coetzee, J. M. (2007), *Diary of a Bad Year*. London: Harvill Secker.

Coetzee, J. M. (2009), *Summertime*. London: Harvill Secker.

Coetzee, J. M., and David Attwell (1992), *Doubling the Point: Essays and Interviews*, ed. David Attwell. Cambridge, MA: Harvard University Press.

Cowley, Jason (1999), 'The New Statesman Profile – J M Coetzee', *The New Statesman*, 25 October. Available online: https://www.newstatesman.com/node/150054.

Donadio, Rachel (2007). 'Out of South Africa', *The New York Times*, 16 December. Available online: https://www.nytimes.com/2007/12/16/books/review/Donadio-t.html.

Dooley, Gillian (2010), *J. M. Coetzee and the Power of Narrative*. Amherst, NY: Cambria Press.

Geertsema, Johan ([2007] 2011), 'Diary of a Bad Year'. In: Mehigan Tim, ed., *A Companion to the Works of J. M. Coetzee*. Woodbridge, Suffolk: Boydell and Brewer, 208–21.

Hornby, Nick (2004), 'Stuff I've Been Reading', *The Believer*, 1 May. Available online: https://believermag.com/stuff-ive-been-reading-8/.

Johnston, Peter (2013), '"Presences of the Infinite": J. M. Coetzee and Mathematics'. PhD dissertation, University of London.

Johnston, Peter (2014), 'J. M. Coetzee's Work in Stylostatistics', *DHQ*, 8(3).

Kilgarriff, A., V. Baisa, J. Bušta, M. Jakubíček, V. Kovář, J. Michelfeit, P. Rychlý, V. Suchomel (2014), 'The Sketch Engine: Ten Years On', *Lexicography*, 1: 7–36.

Neuman, Justin (2005), 'Slow Man by J. M. Coetzee', *Modern Language Studies*, 35(2): 103–6.

Staley, Thomas F. (2011), Quoted in 'Nobel Prize-Winning Writer J. M. Coetzee's Archive Acquired by Harry Ransom Center', UT News, 10 October. Available online: https://news.utexas.edu/2011/10/10/nobel-prize-winning-writer-j-m-coetzees-archive-acquired-by-harry-ransom-center/

Varol, O., E. Ferrara, C. A. Davis, F. Menczer, and A. Flammini (2017), 'Online Human-Bot Interactions: Detection, Estimation, and Characterization'. Available online: https://arxiv.org/pdf/1703.03107.pdf.

Zimbler, Jarad (2014), *J. M. Coetzee and the Politics of Style*. Cambridge: Cambridge University Press.

7

Coetzee, the archive and practice research: On reflection

Michael Cawood Green

'Coetzee has asked me to revise my essay.'

Coetzee, *Dusklands* (1974: 1)

Dear Editors,

May I thank you for your perceptive feedback on my submission to your proposed collection of essays on 'Coetzee & the Archive'. I am genuinely appreciative of this, particularly for your comment that 'there are potentially two essays in this submission with two different audiences'. 'One,' you say, 'is for the UK Research Excellence Framework (REF) environment and is essentially all there,' and in coming back to it, I find I agree – agree to the point that in itself this essay does stand as complete, complete as far as what can be said in the format, and pretty much impervious to reflective intervention. It still seems to me to do what I set out to do: to introduce into Coetzee studies a potentially useful contribution from the field of Practice Research. So, to coin a phrase, here goes:

'While there is increasing – if uneven – recognition that the processes of producing creative artefacts may serve as an original contribution to knowledge, there is less agreement as to how creative practice can be defined formally as research. One of the more common requirements is the addition of some form of critical self-reflection as an integral part of the creative project.

'Reflecting on one's creative work may be, as the old phrase has it, like dancing about architecture, but in the UK and Australia (and to varying degrees in other countries) including a reflective component is still the primary means by which creative work is defined as research. An accompanying self-reflective commentary or exegesis is a standard requirement for practice-led doctoral degrees, participating in research evaluation exercises, and bidding for research council funding. The UK's Arts and Humanities Research Council (AHRC), for example, accepts that "creative output can be produced, or practice undertaken, as an integral part of a research process", but the Council "expects ... this practice to be accompanied by some form of documentation of the research process, as well as some form of textual analysis or explanation to support its position and as a record of critical reflection". It accepts too that "equally, creativity or practice may involve no such process at all", but in this case "it would be ineligible for funding".[1]

'I should note that even the rather blunt instrument of research council definitions of practice research specifically exclude self-interpretation as part of the reflection: AHRC guidelines for applying for grants under its "practice-led and applied route" (since discontinued as a route in its own right, although its principles still inform bidding in this area[2]) state that practice research outputs "must be based on your own critical reflection of the creative process rather than an interpretation of that reflection. ..." And where "textual analysis or explanation" is called for, this is in support of documenting the research process and recording the ongoing critical reflection.

'The stress on *process* is important: "You must explain clearly", as the AHRC puts it, "how your practice is an integral part of the whole research process". Certainly when it comes to Creative Writing, the focus on process is crucial in distinguishing research in the discipline from the standard forms of research carried out in the Literature Departments in which Creative Writing as a subject area is invariably embedded. "If it would ordinarily be identified as work of a literary-critical or literary-historical nature", state the guidelines, "your project will not be eligible for support under [the practice-led and applied route]".[3]

Where then is the second essay, the 'same essay, or some of the essay', as one of his editors puts it, that 'might be reimagined for a wider audience?' It was there of course, all the time between, behind the lines, in the margins. He is aware as he skims the surface of page and ink, reading what he has prepared for the conference on Coetzee & the Archive, that he is using a voice not exercised for some time. Is it this that makes the paper sound flat, mundane, pedestrian? Or is it in fact the paper that is flat, mundane, pedestrian? He is no longer quite sure how to gauge that distinction, especially as the speaker he is paired with in this session has just given a remarkable presentation, a scriptless, off-the cuff, performative turn, thick with the personal, the affective, the lived association with 'J. M. Coetzee', everything his follow-up delivery so clearly lacks. A third of the way into reading his paper he nearly gives up, stops, sinks into the inertia of the writing. But the occasion demands, and he proceeds, thinking increasingly of Coetzee's public self-reflection as he speaks at the *Weekly Mail* Book Week a lifetime ago in Cape Town: 'I do not even speak my own language' (1988: 53–6).

'For Graeme Harper, "Research through, and in, creative writing" is defined methodologically by its interest in action, "doing something", and includes "how we respond before, during, and after that doing" (2012: 133). In making all the activities involved in writing creatively the subject of research in the field, Harper wants to move away from concentrating only on the end product of that activity. "Creative writing", he says, "produces evidence of its undertaking" and this too must be included amongst what he calls the "artefacts of creative writing" (2012: 147): "Quite obviously some of these are finished works of creative writing; but not all artefacts of creative writing are finished works" or those "that have been released into the public realm"; "some of the artefacts of creative writing are publicly exchanged", he writes, "and, in key ways, strongly defined by their public identities. Others are not so strongly defined, or barely defined at all, by public categories" (2012: 148–9).

'The latter, however, be they notes, drafts, corrections, email exchanges, letters, doodles, sketches, manuscripts, typescripts, diaries, are all "artefacts" produced in creative writing and as such are "sources of much knowledge about creative writing":

> These are not public artefacts – at least not in their making stages – and they may never become public artefacts. However, they are certainly artefacts produced in creative writing, and they are evidence of the event where pieces of creative writing came about, whether the work produced in that event is released now into the public realm or not. These artefacts are as much a part of creative writing as those works that emerge from creative writing and assume public identities.
>
> (Harper 2012: 149)

'"Can we", asks Harper, "truly understand creative writing if it is only the public artefacts of creative writing that are examined? Can we understand it, and gain more knowledge about it, only after its evidence is released from the active involvement of the creative writer?"' (2012: 149).

What he was failing to do, it struck him as he read, was *stage* (in Attridge's definition of the literary, central to his reading of Coetzee, as something in which issues are staged rather than argued) or perform ('we perform them, and they perform us, as we read' (2005: xii)) his argument, a failure that would turn out to be central to the editor's reservations about the written paper: 'What interests me', the editor writes, 'is that you have had to shift your own creative writing – your first-hand experience of making archives – out of the picture in order to attend to this collection on Coetzee.'

Given the major personal and professional rupture – breaking with his past life as a postcolonial scholar of sorts, a southern Africanist based in South Africa at least and taking up a new professional allegiance that has brought him to the UK to pursue primarily his creative work – this strikes even him as odd; why he has chosen to sidestep this dimension – the whole story, in fact, informing his choosing to bring together Coetzee & the Archive with Practice Research, remains surprising (is mysterious too strong a word in a scholarly reflective exercise?) as he tries in all seriousness to take the editor's comments into account when he is revising the paper for publication. Is this what the editor wanted of the latent, potential, submerged second essay? And if so, how is he to fit it into the piece as originally submitted, which stubbornly continues to feel complete, resistant to reflection and all but the most minor of changes?

'It is difficult to think of a more important recent release of "non-public creative artefacts", in the sense that Harper uses the term, than the Coetzee Collection at the

Harry Ransom Center (HRC), made up as it is of "140 document boxes, 13 oversize boxes and one galley file documenting all of Coetzee's major writings and including notes, typescripts, background research materials, publicity materials ... professional correspondence and materials documenting personal and family history". As David Attwell says in the news release for the archive, "With the opening of the Coetzee papers, researchers will be able to study his creative processes at source. In making this possible, the Ransom Center has created an exciting prospect for contemporary literary studies" (https://www.hrc.utexas.edu/press/releases/2013/jm-coetzee-archive.html).

'Indeed scholars of literary studies, or what Harper calls "post-event critics of creative writing" ("those who only approach the artefacts of creative writing after they are produced, or from outside the actions of creative writing" (2012: 150)), regularly use artefacts produced during the creative process in their interpretation or analysis of a literary work. This is to a different end from the pursuits of the practice researcher, however, for whom a better understanding of the work as released to the public, the artefact as finished product, is not the primary object of interest. For practice researchers it is the artefact as evidence of the act of writing itself, and how this applies to reflecting on the process of their own practice, that makes access to the archive of particular significance.

'This distinction makes the usual positioning of creative writing within literature departments at least partially anomalous. As a practice-led discipline it is something of an inside-outsider in literary studies, having as much, perhaps even more, in common with other practice-led disciplines such as fine art, design and performance studies. The combination of the creative and the critical, along with the intensive reading required by creative writing courses, makes the alliance with literary studies a useful and in some respects an essential one, but the concentration on practice and process in creative writing also makes the apparent common denominator of the literary text deceptive.

'It is with this distinction in mind that David Attwell says that *J.M. Coetzee and the Life of Writing: Face to Face with Time* (2015) represents "an entirely different approach" to his earlier study, *J.M. Coetzee: South Africa and the Politics of Writing* (1993). Access to the papers consolidated in the Coetzee Collection prompts him to take "a step back in order to look again, this time not as a literary critic would, which is to say the finished works, but at the authorship that underlies them". Here the significance of his emphasis on researchers being able to study Coetzee's "creative *processes* at source" (2015: 18; my emphasis) foregrounds one of the important routes in which an archive might take us.

'Attwell's approach in *J.M. Coetzee and the Life of Writing* demonstrates how the combination of the act of writing creatively and the act of critically considering that act results in an emphasis on action and process rather than on the finished artefact. The meticulous "self-archiving" (2015: 20) Attwell identifies as a feature of the material in the Coetzee Collection is, in its way, analogous with the AHRC's requirement that the reflective exegesis accompanying the creative work in a practice-led project include "some form of documentation of the research *process*".

'Attwell's approach is useful to my interests in demonstrating a *writerly* take on the collection by "concentrating on Coetzee's authorship" (2015: 17), that is to say, not on the finished works, but on the work that informs the finished works, "its creative processes and sources, its oddities and victories – above all, at the remarkable way in which it transforms its often quite ordinary materials into unforgettable fiction" (2015: 18).

'Attwell is able to do this because of Coetzee's clear interest in keeping a detailed record of his writing practice – beginning in his notebooks and the longer drafts "written on blue examination books lifted from the University of Cape Town, where Coetzee lectured for most of his career" (2015: 20)'.

'One can imagine him collecting unused exam books at the end of an invigilation session,' adds Attwell (2015: 20), stopping short of what would be, for him, the potential for this archival material to take us 'beyond the text', beyond what is inscribed in the examination books to a consideration of the potential inherent in them as physical objects, not just as the medium for what is recorded.

Even as he reads out his paper, he is reflecting, imaginatively, on Attwell's tentative gesture, following the 'non-textual' dimensions of what has been archived, rounding out and extending these documents of the creative process. Coetzee's use of these examination books for the generation of his creative work is after all a transgressive act (hinted at in Attwell's use of the word 'lifted'), decidedly against the regulations of the academy. All unused examination books have to be returned to the presiding examination officer to prevent any possibility of examination fraud; even those books with rough work must be left behind by students. No examination book, clean or marked in any way, may be taken from the examination venue by anyone other than those officiating, who will dispose of them appropriately.

In spiriting examination books away, Coetzee's transgression includes translating them from – let us assume, given the nature of Coetzee's post, that it was usually English literature examinations that he was invigilating – critical analysis to writing creatively, an activity at the time with only a minor and tenuous hold on English Studies. At the University of Cape Town, this took the form of the 'Friday-afternoon non-credit-bearing class in imaginative writing' (Kannemeyer 2012: 92) offered by the 'clumsy and awkward underdog', the 'uninspiring lecturer' Robert Guy Howarth (Kannemeyer 2012: 93), whose encouragement of their creative work a number of budding South African writers would nevertheless express their appreciation for in later years.[4]

Howarth's hand then can be felt behind the journey of the examination books from the examination hall to the writing desk of the young lecturer and aspirant writer, then from the private holdings of the famous author to the Houghton Library at Harvard – where they were available for consultation and would be used by J. C. Kannemeyer for his more conventional biography, but surprisingly few others – and thereafter from there to the HRC in Texas, each shift in their transmigration changing their status, their readership, even their physical incarnation – somewhere along the way the blue, soft-cover examination books are, for example, bound in cardboard, before being unbound and rehoused in the HRC. Seen in this way, their journey from illicit writing material to hallowed texts has a tangible life of its own, before being called up from storage to be placed before Attwell for those feverish five weeks – all the time he has to make the best of them for *J.M. Coetzee and the Life of Writing*.

As he tries to extend his sense of the feel and focus of Attwell's experience when consulting the examination books in the HRC, he cannot help thinking of Coetzee musing over Beckett's notebooks in the same archive, if not yet in its current building, in the mid-1960s. Coetzee has discovered them entirely by accident ('The Beckett manuscripts were in Texas, and I was there. A coincidence. I didn't know they were there before I arrived' (Coetzee 1992: 25)), the kind of lucky accident that so often plays an important role in archival work, but which tends to be excised in the outputs produced from that work.

Kannemeyer tells us that 'for weeks Coetzee studied the sketches and numbers and scribbling in the margin' (2012: 151), with Coetzee himself reporting, 'It was heartening to see the false starts, the scratched out banalities, the evidence of less than furious possession by the Muse' (1992: 25). Did this scrutiny extend beyond the text, to the notebooks themselves? If so, was Coetzee struck, as was Laura Salisbury when she was researching this material in the HRC, by the sheer material role of the cloth-bound ledgers in which the original French drafts of *L'Innommable* were written? Significant though the ink and pencil autograph deletions and emendations throughout are 'one of the really fascinating things', says Salisbury in an interview with Melvyn Bragg on the BBC's 'In Our Time', 'is that [*L'Innommable*] comes to an end right at the end of the notebook. It was as though he needed the back cover in order to actually stop this, um, sort of, well, what would it be, this sort of oozing and propulsive relationship towards language. As though the matter of the notebook itself needed to bring it to an end' (Salisbury 2019).

It is difficult to think of a clearer example of how the 'matter of the notebook' can inform, even shape, what is represented in the notebook. This is significant for what Hayden Lorimer calls an 'embodied' research experience; it is, he says, the 'multifarious, open encounters in the realm of practice that matter most', even when 'the phenomena in question may seem remarkable only by their apparent insignificance. The focus falls on how life takes shape and gains expression in shared experiences, everyday routines, fleeting encounters, embodied movements, precognitive triggers, practical skills, affective intensities, enduring urges, unexceptional interactions and sensuous dispositions' (2005: 84).

We await then, he thinks as he moves on to his next point in his paper, the kind of archive story that brings in not just the materiality of the writing material, but the context too in which they are read, the low hum of the Hazel H. Ransom Reading Room, the white noise informing the obligatory silence, the scuffling and page-turning, the pencil-scribbling, the suppressed coughs, the padded footfalls, the rub of clothing against desks and chairs, the sensory experience of touching and turning the manuscript pages.

'Approaching the manuscripts as textual evidence of the ways in which Coetzee writes is revelatory: read in correlation with the deeply reflective and carefully corresponding notebooks, a lived sense of the writing process is conjured up: "the earliest drafts ... sketched quickly, provisionally, determinedly"; the "search for his subject: the voice especially, embedded in a distinctive genre and a distinctive history"; the "plot the least stable of elements, always subserving the voice, and continually revised"; the "quotations drawn from literary theory, the allusions from other writers", often assumed by critics to be seminal structural devices, in fact "brought in only once the work has found its own legs"; titles provisional until very late in the process; "revision and more revision", when this is done by hand, when the manuscript is first typed, corrected by hand and then retyped. And above all, the "'writing event' ... the point at which a quantum leap is made, when the draft becomes more like the novel it wants to be" (Attwell 2015: 20).

'Much of this may be useful for literary scholarly analysis, but when deployed as a mode of reading the works as works in progress, catching the writer in the act as it were, Coetzee's "self-archiving" comes alive in the most writerly of ways. The archive becomes a resource not just for a better understanding of the completed, published novels, but for what may be learned from the process of their creation. In practice research terms, the manuscripts and notes demonstrate, as Harper puts it, how "research through, and in, creative writing offers substantial opportunities for the creation of new knowledge" (2012: 133).

'For the purposes of research evaluation exercises (such as the UK's Research Assessment Exercise (RAE) and REF), research is defined as a "process of investigation leading to new insights, effectively shared" (http://www.hefce.ac.uk/pubs/circlets/2010/cl04_10/cl04_10a.pdf). There is an increasing emphasis on research being disseminated or made publicly available in the form of accessible research outputs, and it is evident that Attwell's reflections on the Coetzee papers in *J.M. Coetzee and the Life of Writing* will go a long way toward making the new knowledge and understanding generated by the Coetzee Collection available to other researchers.

'A key way, though, in which Attwell's reading of the material produced during Coetzee's writing process differs from a fully practice-led approach is that it is not a *self*-reflective project. However much his work enhances our knowledge and understanding of creative writing, in practice research "it is the *creative writer* whose actions this artefactual evidence represents who is most connected to the purpose, intent and configuration of all those artefacts of creative writing" (Harper 2012: 149, my emphasis). In his book it is of course Attwell who is reflecting on the archival material produced by Coetzee – or at least Attwell who is formulating the significance of Coetzee's writerly insights and reading them into a narrative that presents them as "built on absolute faith in the creative process, on tenaciously working through the uncertainties ... towards a distant goal until an illumination arrives, providing direction and momentum for the next phase" (2015: 20).

'The commentary or portfolio or exegesis accompanying creative work presented for research purposes within the academy may most usefully be understood as a scholarly informed, critical reflection on the writer's *own* creative process. It is this *self*-reflection that is meant to do the work of transforming or translating the creative work into an academic research exercise.'

Well, by now the tension in his paper is obvious. The archive – for the writer – is for the most part a repository of the self-reflective; to address the topic in hand, however, he has had to conjure up the scholar David Attwell to stand in for himself on the Coetzee archives. He is effectively bringing Attwell and Coetzee together to perform between them the process required by various research councils/funding bodies. As a result, the actual archive at Texas has faded into the background of his argument, far more remote than the theme of the conference ideally required.

In reflecting on this, he takes comfort from another of the editors' comments: foregrounding his distance from the material Attwell has handled, playing off a 'tangible' against an 'intangible' encounter with the archive, 'might still', as she so generously puts it, 'constitute a moment in "the archival turn"'. A shadowy figure at best in his own argument, he accepts that he – a lover of archives in which he spends far too much time when he should just be getting on with his writing – is now dealing, in his editor's words, with the 'idea' of the archive, 'if not the actuality'.

His only actual experience of the HRC had been prior to Coetzee's archive being deposited there. Whilst on a teaching exchange at the University of Texas in Austin in 2002/3, he was busy with a creative work far removed from the holdings of the Center: he had looked, of course, but there was nothing of value for his novel on the Trappist monks who had come to South Africa in the 1860s. In search of a suitable vehicle for his own feeling that it was time for him, and so many others of his age, gender, race and class in South Africa, to simply shut up, he had become caught up in retelling their story: successful in establishing a major monastery and a network of mission stations, they had ended up being expelled from their Order, an Order dedicated to cloistered contemplation, for committing the sin of missionary work, work which clearly required them to break the silence that is a defining feature of the Cistercians of the Strict Observance.

He could not know at the time that the novel, *For the Sake of Silence*, would appear with an endorsement from Coetzee on its dust jacket. He could not know either, that in 2003 Coetzee was about to publish *Elizabeth Costello*, in which the setting for one of the 'Eight Lessons' making up the novel would be 'Marianhill Monastery', a fictionalized version of Mariannhill Monastery, the mother house founded by the Trappists in South Africa. Even more to the point – and yes, there is a point to this digression, other than the association of Coetzee with this project – he would struggle to write an academic paper on Coetzee's use of Marianhill in *Elizabeth Costello* until, without quite knowing why, he took to the medium of the fictionalized lecture used in the novel, discovering to his own surprise that the moment he put an inverted comma before the first word, the paper came out almost fully formed as a lecture in direct speech delivered by an imagined speaker. That really had been the beginning of the end of the scholarly, analytical medium for him, making the mode that was dying on his tongue as he read his paper at the 'Coetzee & the Archive' event an increasingly foreign language.

The as yet un-arrived Coetzee papers had then already had an absent place in his own archival experience. If the organizers of the conference had insisted he draw upon his own experience of the HRC, he would have been on very thin ground. He would have been forced to fall back on the arrival of the Stephen Gray Papers at the Center during his time in Austin. He had been called in to give a preliminary sense of the 22 boxes ('9.24 linear feet') containing 'four decades of literary endeavor from the 1960s to 2000, including novels, plays, poetry, short stories, journalism, and editorial work'. Potentially of some interest to him (Gray, a South African writer and professor of English at Rand Afrikaans University, had given him his first academic appointment), this collection 'had been arranged by Gray prior to shipment to the Ransom Center'. It had caused something of an archival crisis when it reached Texas, a crisis which prevented him from getting anywhere near the papers. When he arrived as arranged for the opening of the boxes, it turned out that Gray had used mothballs to preserve his collection, putting archive and archivists alike at risk of being contaminating by blasts of naphthalene. This archival faux pas is delicately alluded to in the current Guide to the Collection, which notes that the Stephen Gray papers are 'in good condition except for the lingering odor of moth balls used during storage' (https://norman.hrc.utexas.edu/fasearch/findingAid.cfm?eadid=00199).

'Making the writer responsible for the reflective process immediately introduces problems of its own, problems rarely recognized in the administration of research by the academy. In the UK's REF 2014, for example, those making submissions "where the research content of the output may not be self-evident", are asked to include anything from a 300-word statement in which "the research imperatives and research process of an output ... might further be made evident by descriptive and contextualising information" or, in cases where it "cannot fully represent its research dimensions through the evidence provided" in such a statement, "a portfolio in either digital or physical form" (REF 2014, Submission of outputs 71).

'In either case, the practice researcher must adopt at least two distinct voices:[5] that of a creative practitioner working to varying degrees intuitively in or against the conventions of a particular creative mode, and that of a scholarly informed commentator reflecting through recognizably academic conventions on the research question informing the project, what is significant and original about the creative work, and how it relates to an appropriate literature review. The assumption is that the academic mode allows some sort of transparent and unmediated access to whatever it is in the creative work that makes it a contribution to knowledge and expressing this in a medium that allows it to be disseminated more broadly.

'To begin with dissemination: Attwell's "practice approach" to the Coetzee papers certainly serves this function, being a powerful and effective means of mining and disseminating the rich seams of "practically borne knowledge" in the archive. But his approach to the archive material also demonstrates that it is possible to identify other modes of practice research which go beyond these important but relatively modest claims. His readings of Coetzee's draft and manuscript material underscore the creative place writerly reflection has within the practice-as-research process. The archived papers clearly reclaim self-reflection from the passive, post hoc, retrospective role it tends to play as part of the conventional administrative and reporting procedures on a completed creative project; instead, they emphasize the *productive* role the critical reflective component may play in the practice research process.

'A focus on the process-oriented material in the Coetzee collection is especially useful as an illustration of practice research.[6] Nowhere in the notes, drafts, and ongoing commentary is there a sense that this record-keeping is carried out for any other reason than informing and generating the work in progress. It is, as it were, reflection in its pure sense, a living component in the writing of the creative work. That someone like Attwell is able to "complete" the record, focus on it as a vital aspect of working towards the "writing event" and bring these, in Harper's terms, "non-public creative artefacts" into the "public realm" as an exemplary expression of practice research, speaks to the value of archiving as process and record, documentation and commentary.

'What then of the voice Attwell encounters in the archive, that "practice researcher" voice in which the recording, documenting and commenting is carried out? Coetzee's decision to allow such material into open circulation and actively participate in making his archive available does not, of course, make of it a form of literal "raw" material to be read back into the published writing. Rather than relating directly to the writing of the fiction or – an even more fraught enterprise – drawing the writing back into the private world from which it emerged (and I speak here only of the record of the creativity which is the subject of this paper, although a similar point holds for the personal material (the held back and then reinserted 'box 33', for example)) – it serves to draw the archive into a realm as cautious, careful and consistently self-interrogating, as the fiction.

'One is bound to ask why so self-effacing a writer, and one so aware of the rhetorical instability of the archive, has been so rigorous, almost obsessive, about recording and administering the processes working their way towards the fiction. The answer must at least in part be that the archive is no literal "foul rag and bone shop of the heart", but circulates now subject to the same interpretive caveats, the same propagative openness, as those completed "masterful images", the fiction itself. As Mr Vincent says to Sophie in *Summertime*, "I have been through the letters and diaries. What Coetzee writes there cannot be trusted, not as a factual record – not because he was a liar but because he was a fictioneer" (2009: 225; italics in original).

'"The letters and diaries" indeed, but in giving access to the drafts, notes and reflections on the fiction, the processes of its coming into being, the archive equally opens these up to the "fictioneering", investing them too with the voice of the writer – the voice of the writer as self-commentator perhaps, but a voice, voices even, adopted by the writer as a mode of reflection.

'As Philip Gross reminds us, "Every writer's memoir is part of their oeuvre ... a calculated performance of their chosen sense of self" (2011: 52); there is, therefore, "always an identity, a presence performed for others, at stake when a writer speaks about their work" (2011: 51). The archived history of the practice is then, like any other history, a history that is a rhetorical and discursive construct that in turn is, in its being read, subject to the specific readerly conventions brought to bear upon them. As such the archive has to be seen as an actively produced site rather than a passive source of information, the authorial reflection developing as a lived and equal part of the dynamic and fluid process of the act of writing creatively.

'This applies to the more general, conceptual and theoretical aspects of Coetzee's reflections as much as it does to the revisions connected with the more specific technical and stylistic elements in any one of the novels (plot, setting, voice, title, etc.). It is especially in the works Attwell identifies as belonging to Coetzee's "third stage" that this level of reflection is most nakedly on display in the fiction: in *Slow Man*, *Diary of a Bad Year* and *The Childhood of Jesus*, "the simple urge to represent" is replaced by an increasing emphasis on '"second-order"' questions' (2015: 236): '"What am I doing when I represent? What is the difference between living in the real world and living in a world of representations?"' (2015: 236–7; Coetzee Papers, *Diary of a Bad Year*, 22 December 2005).

'It would be difficult to refute Attwell's observation that "From inside the process of thinning out" that is a major feature of the third phase, "what is most important" for Coetzee is "the self-reflection on one's practice" (2015: 237), but few know as well as he how much, throughout the novelist's oeuvre, "Coetzee's presence makes itself felt in his material". Access to the archive reinforces this impression: "One of the many surprises that come with reading the drafts and notebooks ... is discovering the extent to which the hyper-awareness of the writer at work ... is indeed his own," writes Attwell (2015: 238). As early as in the composition of *Waiting for the Barbarians*, we find Coetzee observing in his notebooks, "I have no interest in telling stories; it is the process of storytelling that interests me. This man M.M., as a 'he' living in the world, bores me. 'Creating' an illusionistic reality in which he moves depresses me. Hence the exhausted quality of the writing" (2015: 112).

'This exhaustion is countered by the ways in which, as vibrant examples of what we may call "practice research", Coetzee's fiction increasingly finds its energy and life in staging or enacting its own reflection; in the words of Paul Williams, the "fiction itself stands on its own as its own research methodology", "speaking for itself", if you will, as both fiction and a reflection on the process of writing fiction. "The story itself", writes Williams, himself a practice-led researcher, "becomes both the research methodology and the research outcome" (2013: 256).

'When Williams says then, that *The Lives of Animals* and *Diary of a Bad Year* are "narratives in which J.M. Coetzee uses fictional devices in order to explore issues that are traditionally articulated by conventional forms of critical analysis" (2013: 250), we may add to those "conventional forms" the reflective aspect of practice research as required by the administrators of research.'

He is thinking, as he reads, of his own modest, oh so much more modest, attempts at including some form of critical self-reflection as an integral part of his new novel, *The Ghosting of Anne Armstrong*. How he had worked at building a strong historiographical element into the narrative itself, with the insertion of a historian into the narrative serving as a self-reflective account of the process of recreating historical events. The intermittent metafictional interventions positioning the researcher/writer and aspects of the research process within the story were meant to bring to the fore the often-suppressed elements of subjectivity, reflexivity and historicity in archival research; it also serves as a reminder, as he noted in his own commentary on that work,[7] of the ways in which the research process is always provisional, indeterminate and contestable.

The usual authority accorded to the researcher discovering and giving meaning to his research material gives way to his taking shape in relation to that material; his repeated but largely uncontextualized appearances make him something of a revenant, a constantly returning presence as ghostly in its way as the spectral intrusions of the past into the present in the fiction. These ghostly incursions were, for him, another aspect of taking the past seriously on its own terms, as well as challenging research as a purely empirical practice.

'Is this to say little more than has long since been claimed for metafiction? Taken up within the still-emergent field of practice research, it makes a strong case for metafictional devices being recognized as legitimate forms of research methodology. More than this, however, the self-reflexive component of the fiction becomes a living trace of the archive, both an inter-generative, vital part of the creative process and an internalized record of that process in action.

'When we ask ourselves then, "where ... archives 'begin' and where might they take us", their end may well be – as it is in the reading Attwell brings to the Coetzee papers – in their beginning. A "performative" approach to the archive works against binary distinctions between reflection and creativity, the archive and the artefact, making of them a single exploration through creative practice.

'Thank you.'

The applause surprised him, sounded louder and longer than anything he had expected – so much so that he did not trust it, heard in it something patronizing, something to console him given his poor delivery in comparison with the adroit performance of the speaker he had been twinned with in the session. Or had there been a hint, somewhere in his presentation, of the shadow essay he had failed to give? A comforting thought, but he doubted it.

Notes

1 See, the AHRC's definition of research (2015): http://www.ahrc.ac.uk/funding/research/researchfundingguide/introduction/definitionofresearch/.
2 'The Fellowships in the Creative and Performing Arts (FCPA) and Research Grants Practice Led and Applied (RGPLA) schemes were originally intended for capacity-building in the area of practice-led research and both schemes operated, in one form or another, for over 10 years. After considerable discussion at our Advisory Board and Council it has been concluded that both schemes have been highly successful building capacity in the field. Therefore the decision has been made not to continue with both schemes, as it is now appropriate that funding for research in this field is through

our other funding mechanisms' (http://www.ahrc.ac.uk/funding/opportunities/archived-opportunities/researchgrantspracticeledandapplied/).
3 I am drawing here on thoughts developed more fully in Green and Williams (2018). '
4 Howarth was also quietly influential in including – cautiously – South African authors in his classes. He appears to have been a meaningful presence in Coetzee's undergraduate studies, and an important influence in the education of many students (including, we should note in this context, 'the poet Stephen Gray') (Kannemeyer 2012: 95).
5 I have a distinct sense of different voices when writing in different modes, to the degree that I find it necessary to reflect this in differing, if overlapping, names – 'Michael Green' for scholarly work, 'Michael Cawood Green' for the creative. These varying identities are blurred in the self-commenting mode, a realm of shifting, intermingled creative and reflective allegiances. I take my middle fiction-writing name from my mother: whatever it is in me that makes me write creatively seems most closely aligned with the late Donnée Phelps Cawood.
6 The research centre that bears Coetzee's name at the University of Adelaide is 'The J.M. Coetzee Centre for Creative Practice' (JMCCCP), which 'focuses on practice-led research and examines how ideas are translated into artworks. Research on creativity and creative processes also form a central part of what we do' (https://www.adelaide.edu.au/jmcoetzeecentre/about/).
7 *The Ghosting of Anne Armstrong*, published as the first novel in the Goldsmiths Press Practice as Research series, includes a 7,000-word essay reflecting on the archival and field work that went into its writing, as well as on fiction as a form of research through creative practice.

References

'AHRC Support for Practice-Led Research Through Our Research Grants – Practice-Led and Applied Route (RGPLA)'. Available online: http://www.ahrc.ac.uk/funding/opportunities/archived-opportunities/researchgrantspracticeledandapplied/ (accessed 3 April 2015).
Attridge, Derek (2005), *J.M. Coetzee and the Ethics of Reading*. Scottsville and Chicago: University of KwaZulu-Natal Press and University of Chicago Press.
Attwell, David (1993), *J.M. Coetzee: South Africa and the Politics of Writing*. Cape Town: David Philip.
Attwell, David (2015), *J.M. Coetzee and the Life of Writing: Face to Face with Time*. Oxford: Oxford University Press.
Coetzee, J. M. 'J.M. Coetzee Papers'. Austin, TX: Harry Ransom Center.
Coetzee, J. M. (1974), *Dusklands*. Johannesburg: Ravan Press.
Coetzee, J. M. (1988), 'The Novel Today', *Upstream*, 6 (1): 2–5.
Coetzee, J. M. (1992), *Doubling the Point: Essays and Interviews*. Cambridge, MA: Harvard University Press.
Coetzee, J. M.(2003), *Elizabeth Costello*. London: Secker & Warburg.
Coetzee, J. M. (2009), *Summertime*. London: Harvill Secker.
Green, Michael Cawood (2008), 'Deplorations: Coetzee, Costello and Doubling the N'. In: Michael Chapman, ed., *Postcolonialism: South/African Perspectives*. Newcastle: Cambridge Scholars Press, 125–48.

Green, Michael Cawood ([2008] 2010), *For the Sake of Silence*. Roggebaai and London: UMUZI (South African imprint of Random House)/ and Quartet Books.

Green, Michael Cawood and Tony Williams (2018), 'On Reflection: The Role, Mode and Medium of the Reflective Component in Practice as Research', *TEXT: Journal of Writing and Writing Courses*, 22(1) April. Available online: http://www.textjournal.com.au/april18/green_williams.htm.

Green, Michael Cawood (2019), *The Ghosting of Anne Armstrong*. London: Goldsmiths Press.

Gross, Philip (2011), 'Then Again What Do I Know: Reflections on Reflection in Creative Writing', *Essays and Studies*, 64: 49–70.

Harper, Graeme (2012), 'The Generations of Creative Writing Research'. In Jeri Kroll and Graeme Harper, eds, *Research Methods in Creative Writing*. Basingstoke: Palgrave Macmillan, 133–54.

Kannemeyer, J. C. (2012), *J.M. Coetzee: A Life in Writing*, trans. Michiel Heyns. Melbourne and Victoria: Brunswick and Scribe.

Lorimer, Hayden (2005), 'Cultural Geography: The Busyness of Being "More-Than-Representational"', *Progress in Human Geography*, 29: 83–94.

REF 2014: Research Excellence Framework, Submission of outputs: Part 2D, Main Panel D criteria, paragraph 71. https://www.ref.ac.uk/2014/media/ref/content/pub/panelcriteriaandworkingmethods/01_12_2D.pdf.

REF 01.2012 Main Panel D Criteria. Available online: http://www.ref.ac.uk/media/ref/content/pub/panelcriteriaandworkingmethods/01_12_2D.pdf.

Salisbury, Laura (2019), Speaking on Melvyn Bragg, 'In Out Time: Samuel Beckett'. Broadcast 17 January. Available online: https://www.bbc.co.uk/programmes/m00021q7.

Williams, Paul (2013), 'Creative Praxis as a Form of Academic Discourse', *New Writing*, 10 (3), 250–60.

Williams, Paul (2016), 'The Performative Exegesis', *Text*, 20 (1). Available online: http://textjournal.com.au/april16/williams.htm (accessed 19 July 2017).

Part Four

On literary objects: Form and style in the archive

8

Archival realism: *Elizabeth Costello*, *Disgrace* and the realm of revision

David Isaacs

1

The latter half of the 1990s was a fecund time for Coetzee, a burst of creative engagement during which a number of his major projects found first life and shape: two volumes of *Scenes from Provincial Life* (2011), *Disgrace* (1999) and much of *Elizabeth Costello* (2003) all date from this period. Inevitably, much cross-pollination is evident in the archives. Here, for example, are two passages – the first from the published text of 'Realism', the opening 'lesson' of *Elizabeth Costello*, first drafted on 2 January 1996; the other from the published text of *Disgrace*, first drafted six weeks later, on 14 February 1996. In both, a focal male character recalls a sexual encounter:

> When he thinks back over those hours, one moment returns with sudden force, the moment when her knee slips under his arms and folds into his armpit. Curious that the memory of an entire scene should be dominated by one moment, not obviously significant, yet so vivid that he can still almost feel the ghostly thigh against his skin. Does the mind by nature prefer sensations to ideas, the tangible to the abstract? Or is the folding of the woman's knee just a mnemonic, from which will unfold the rest of the night?
>
> (Coetzee 2003: 24)

> One moment stands out in recollection, when she hooks a leg behind his buttocks to draw him in closer: as the tendon of her inner thigh tightens against him, he feels a surge of joy and desire.
>
> (Coetzee 1999: 29)

In their emphasis on a single memorable detail, each extract plays a sly game with the work of reference. In context, each marks an unusual proleptic-analeptic break from the fiction's perpetually present tense: in each case, that is, we are still, when we learn of the remembered detail, within the time of the event being recalled, but looking back on it as though from an imagined future. In each case, the detail is all we know of the physical reality of the sex – it is, therefore, the means by which we can fit the scene into our model of reality – but we learn of it as a memory in the moment of its making. Filtered thus, the implied tangible real is presented within a frame of epistemological uncertainty, the reader excluded from the certainty of present-tense experience while still in the thick of the moment. There is, in other words, a realm that might be taken for the fiction's 'reality' to which the reader has no access, and which exists beyond the text's reach. Accordingly, while appearing to be in process, the work of reference – of fitting sign to thing, language to reality – is suspended at both moments of specificity. In this essay, I aim to show that the question of literary realism, of how to house reality in fiction, is one to which Coetzee works out a detailed response in the drafting of these two texts. Taken together, indeed, they mark the culmination of a career-long engagement with what Coetzee might regard as the genre's central conundrums, as I will outline them in the following pages.

I will mount my argument by tracing some of the mutual influence of the theory and practice of realism in this five-year period. As I am in part attempting to reconstruct process, my methodology will be genetic. Genetic criticism has its roots in post-structuralism and, in its first incarnation, posited a criticism that reads across the entire documented writing process – from notebook to marginalia to redrafting – in such a way as to deny teleology: a 'text' acts as a play of signification not just across its published span, but across its genesis, its archived coming-into-being: its *avant-texte* (Deppman, Ferrer and Groden 2004). This chapter will take it as a fundamental assumption, however, that, as Finn Fordham has it in *I Do I Undo I Redo*, 'formation shapes content' (Fordham 2010: 31) and that a teleological reconstruction of a text's genesis can thus cast light on that content's ultimate shape. This is particularly the case for an author such as Coetzee who, as I hope to show, allows his texts to construct themselves from the doubts, anxieties and obstructions of composition and thus function in such a way as to bring their genetic histories *along with* them, accumulating individual drafts and iterations as they roll forward and folding their revisions into their forward motion; in a Coetzee novel, that is, formation *becomes* content, the doubt becomes the form. An author's intentions may be unrecoverable but moments of decision-making *are* visible in the marks of revision; as John Bryant has written in *The Fluid Text*, revisions 'are the material evidence of *shifting* intentions. Indeed, the fact of revision manifests the intention to alter meaning' (Bryant 2002: 8–9). This chapter will trace Coetzee's thinking about literary realism, then, as it is visible in his marks of revision – marks that, I hope to show, in fact become a crucial apparatus in what emerges as an idiosyncratic and innovative approach to one of the oldest literary questions. Coetzee finds his realism, I will argue, in (and *as*) the archive.

2

In his indispensably sensitive *J.M. Coetzee and the Life of Writing*, David Attwell establishes Coetzee's literary origin, in *Dusklands* (1974), as a 'revolt against what he saw as realism's unadventurous epistemology', and documents Coetzee's long subsequent struggle to 'make peace' with the genre (2015: 61–2). As a gloss for realism Attwell supplies, succinctly, 'the need to produce verisimilitude' (2015: 63) and appears to associate the term with a particular literary convention: the accumulation of local detail, social and material, without commentary, in order to create a recognizably textured world through which the characters can move and against which their conceptual resonance can be sounded. Thus, he identifies the following passage in an early draft of *In the Heart of the Country* (1977) which, he writes, clears the way for that novel's rejection of 'realist padding':

> I am simply going to lose my thread if I try too much particularism of the servants, just as I will lose it if I forget myself in particular enthusiasms about the land (the particular beauty of sheep-bells in the violet dust of the evening, the particular heat of river-sand against my thighs, to name two examples).
>
> (2015: 73–4)

Or Attwell sees in the following note about *Waiting for the Barbarians* (1980) evidence that 'writing realism in the third person' proves creatively obstructive: ' "Creating" an illusionistic reality in which [the protagonist] moves depresses me. Hence the exhausted quality of the writing' (2015: 112). Or, he senses a desire to 'move away from realism altogether' in the following note about the vexed processes of writing *Life & Times of Michael K* (1983): 'What I need is a liberation from verisimilitude!' (2015: 140).

Attwell is surely right to see in these comments an impatience with the conventions of realist fiction. Yet Coetzee does not, himself, in these examples, use the word 'realism', preferring terms like 'illusionism' and 'verisimilitude'.[1] To be sure, a personal critical vocabulary is fluid; one should be wary of identifying too deliberate a glossary in an author's notebooks. Yet it is worthy of note that when the term *does* occur in Coetzee's notebooks, it is usually with a particular resonance. 'They ("they") want me to be a realist,' he writes while drafting *Foe* (1986).

> They want my books to be-about. Specifically, to be-about South Africa, about social relations in that country. They check my text against what they have picked up from the popular media about SA, and when there is a correspondence they say it is 'True'. The rest they cannot, will not read.[2]
>
> (HRC, CP, 33.6: 17 March 1984)

Or, he describes *Age of Iron* (1990), an uncharacteristically immediate engagement with apartheid South Africa, as 'my farewell to realism and to a duty to the South African scene' (HRC, CP, 33.6: 5-10-1988). While drafting *Disgrace*, nearly a decade later, that farewell is still pending:

> Something about the South African material that drives one toward dull realism? A respect for this material that is essentially fearful?
>
> (HRC, CP, 35.2: 24-10-1996)

The term 'realism' often occurs in Coetzee's notebooks, that is, with particular reference to his ambivalence about writing about South Africa.

Coetzee's uneasy relationship with realism and South Africa is best understood, as many critics have pointed out, in relation to his self-suppressed 1987 lecture, 'The

Novel Today' – composed in part as a response to *Foe*'s hostile South African reception and the accusation that, in their circumvention of realist reference, his books shirk responsible engagement with their historical circumstances. In it, Coetzee distinguishes between novels that 'supplement' and novels that 'rival' history, advocating the latter. Echoing Flaubert – a realist who longed for 'a book dependent on nothing external, which would be held together by the internal strength of its style' – and channelling his own notebooks, he envisions a novel that

> operates in terms of its own procedures and issues in its own conclusions, not one that operates in terms of the procedures of history and eventuates in conclusions that are checkable by history (as a child's homework is checkable by a schoolmistress).
>
> (Coetzee 1988: 3)

A novel should be 'another, an other mode of thinking';

> history is not reality; ... history is a kind of discourse; ... a novel is a kind of discourse too, but a different kind of discourse; ... inevitably in our culture, history will, with varying degrees of forcefulness, try to claim primacy, claim to be a master-form of discourse. ... The categories of history ... do not reside in reality: they are a certain construction put upon reality.
>
> (Coetzee 1988: 4)

Realism, for Coetzee, is not a system of referring to 'the real': it is a system of referring to another system of reference, an imitation of an imitation, a consensual, mediated and perhaps enforced model of reality. Gareth Cornwell usefully glosses this version of realism as 'historiographic mimesis' (2011: 352). Also usefully, he relates it to another essay of Coetzee's, 'Into the Dark Chamber: The Novelist and South Africa' (1986). Written while drafting *Foe*, this essay focuses on the problem of writing torture, as Coetzee had in *Waiting for the Barbarians*. The novelist, Coetzee writes here, has a duty to bear witness to such atrocity but, locked out of the torture chamber, and having thus only the officially authorized version available, she must find a way of imagining what happens within it without simply 'following' the state, repeating its 'vile mysteries' in a 'tawdry' manner; it is a question of, 'how to establish one's own authority, how to imagine torture and death on one's own terms' (Coetzee and Attwell 1992: 364).

Coetzee's struggle against realism can also be conceived as a struggle towards realism: not, as such, to disavow the cluster of conventions that constitutes literary realism, but to find a way to employ them that is historically responsible yet not reliant on the approval of historical discourse, that is answerable only to its own authority; not to deny realism, in other words, but to wrest it from the grip of power. 'Realism' (the 'lesson' in *Elizabeth Costello*) hardly mentions history, atrocity, obscenity. It is, however, an attempt to think beyond the problems of 'historiographic mimesis', to find a responsible way to engage with the work of historical reference on one's own terms. It is a thinking-through, I want to argue, that Coetzee simultaneously puts into practice in *Disgrace*, a firmly historically situated realist novel.

3.

'Realism' begins life as a public lecture called, 'What is Realism?' The content is much the same: in narrative prose focalized through her son, an eminent, elderly novelist, Elizabeth Costello, gives a lecture entitled 'What is Realism?', a question to which she supplies only intractable answers. In the initial draft, she gives two separate speeches that will eventually become one. In the first, she recalls the publication of her debut novel, the thrill of 'holding in one's hands one's first book' – a thrill soon followed by a concern that it should find a place on a shelf in the British Museum, where it can stand 'in perpetuity' (though even there, she acknowledges, it would not be saved from eventual disintegration) (HRC, CP, 30.3: 11-7-1995). In the published text, this material will function as a few introductory remarks to the lecture proper, and thus appear to be of secondary importance. At this stage, however, it is the entirety of Costello's response to her title question: she means it to provide, to some degree, an answer. As though to clarify how it might answer the question, in revision Coetzee appends to her description of 'holding in one's hands one's first book', the phrase, 'knowing it is real' (HRC, CP, 30.3: 11-7-1995, rev. 16-12-1995). By the time of publication, the phrase will have become even more telling: 'the real thing' (Coetzee 2003: 16). The literary real, here, appears to encompass only the casing of its transmission.

Costello's second speech in the first draft, conceived later, is also familiar from the book: a few comments on Kafka's 'A Report to the Academy', which will comprise the bulk of the published speech. But it emerges more slowly, less certainly, its resonance not clear even to its author until the final draft: Coetzee builds Costello's thoughts about Kafka by accretion, through slow revisiting and reviewing. She begins assertively enough. As in the published text, she outlines Kafka's story – a monologue 'in which an ape, dressed up in evening clothes, has to make a speech to a learned society' (HRC, CP, 30.3: 18-11-1995). Because the story is a monologue, she says,

> there is no means, within the story form, for an objective look to be cast either at the speaker or at the audience. For all we know, the speaker may not 'really' be an ape, may be no more than a human being deluded into thinking himself an ape.
> (HRC, CP, 30.3: 22-11-1995)

She elucidates a number of increasingly unlikely interpretations of what might 'really' be happening – the assumption being that there is a territory beyond itself that constitutes the story's reality, but to which the reader has imperfect access – before concluding: 'We do not know.' At which point, Coetzee stops writing for two weeks.

There can be any number of reasons for the pause. But at least one possibility – that he does not know where to take the material – is borne out, I would suggest, in the number of discarded notebook entries he makes during these weeks, in which he tries to articulate the speech's crux. In one, he has Costello say,

> It is not that this is the key to Kafka's story. It is not that this is a new reading of the story. We are no longer in times when anything is a key to anything else – in which anything is *the answer*, in other words. In particular I am not offering a key

to how to read my own books. I am not a custodian of keys. I am not a custodian of anything at all. I am merely saying that things could be completely otherwise. The form within which the work writes itself [middle voice] makes it seem one way, but the work doesn't live or die only within that form. The work has another kind of existence as well, independently, that we can imagine, though only dimly and intermittently, because we are used to working within forms. In this other existence – let me call it the idea of the work – things can be quite different. The man and woman who were in love, for instance, can be not in love at all, but self-deceived and mutually deceived.

(HRC, CP, 35.2: 30-11-1995)

Costello here sounds cautiously optimistic, imagining a realm that rivals rather than supplements the discourses that structure our understanding of a text (the creed, here, of romantic love) – a realm we *can*, however dimly, imagine. When Coetzee returns to the manuscript and resumes writing, however, she is less so:

It used to be that we knew these things. It used to be that there was a man named Kafka who knew who was an ape and who a man; and as long as Kafka knew, that was good enough for us. Or we even believed in something simpler: that there was a lecture hall, and we had only to look to see who was lecturing whom.

But all that has ended now. Whatever you want to be going on in the lecture hall is, to all intents and purposes, going on. ... There is nothing, not even the words ~~themselves~~ on the page themselves, that can stand up to the reader's desire. For along with Kafka who ~~knew~~ seemed to know what was what, and then suddenly disappeared, the time when words stood strong, each in their own meaning, has also disappeared. ~~Words are just~~ The dictionary, that used to stand beside the Bible and the works of Shakespeare above the fireplace, ~~occupying~~ in the place that in pious Roman houses used to be occupied by the household gods, has been demoted: the dictionary is just one way of cracking the code in the text; there are plenty of other ways.

(HRC, CP, 30.3: 5-12-1995)

'There used to be a time', she concludes, 'when we knew who we were. Then the bottom dropped out' (HRC, CP, p. 32: 5-12-1995). But she is not wholly nostalgic: 'We could think of it as a tragic fate, were it not that it is hard to have respect for whatever the bottom was that dropped out...' (HRC, CP, 30.3: 5-12-1995). Because of our postmodern scepticism, Costello seems to suggest, the bottom has dropped out of an agreed-upon, monolithic system for referencing the real (a system that we now know to have been a function of power) but we have no shared, communal system of reference with which to replace it; therefore we see only what we, solipsistically, want. The conception of literature that emerges from these two speeches, when placed side to side, is of an empty case, a physical container holding nothing more than the desire of whoever happens to look into it, and which will eventually, like the reader, disintegrate.

What, then, is realism? Much of Coetzee's writing over the following weeks worries at this question. Costello's son, John, is evidently dissatisfied with his mother's riddling responses – a dissatisfaction shared, I would hazard, given the volume of discarded ideas he has for those responses, by John Coetzee. On Christmas Day 1995, for example, Coetzee has John ask his mother, 'What is realism?' 'You don't know, after all this?' she wryly responds, and then evades the question ('Surely you can't be interested in what your mother thinks?') before supplying as her conclusive answer the unyielding word: 'Compromise' (HRC, CP, 30.3: 25-12-1995). Or, on 6 January, Coetzee writes in his notebook: 'Realism is a point of departure' (HRC, CP, 35.2: 6-1-1996). Or, on 11 January 1996:

> (Story) To his mother: But why realism? Such a grim subject. It makes me think of Norwegians in smelly underwear.
> (Later) His mother: There is something important here, something to bring us down to earth, to deflate our fantasies of omnipotence. If I haven't put my finger on it, that is my fault.
> (HRC, CP, 35.2: 11-1-1996)

Her uncertainty is resonant; if there is something Coetzee wants to articulate about realism, it seems he has not yet put his finger on it.

The day after he completes the first draft of the Kafka speech, 6 December 1995, Coetzee leaves a gap in the text and writes: '[Opening]'. He has already written an opening to the story – in which Costello and her son arrive in her hotel room, whose first paragraph reads, in its entirety: 'The hotel is much as he expected. ... The rooms are large, they have a view over the city ...' (HRC, CP, 30.3: 28-6-1995). The ellipses are in the original: whatever their status, they are suggestive of a provisional sketch to be returned to and filled in with 'realist padding'. Now, returning to the opening, rather than fill in the gaps, Coetzee's narrator comments on the work of construction he appears to have left for himself:

> The problem with the opening is to get from where we are, where we are together, which is nowhere, to the promised subject, which is 'What is Realism?' It is a bridging problem: knocking together a bridge to take us from this bank of the river, which is empty, to that one, the promised land.
> It is a technical problem, knocking together that bridge. ...
> Let us assume it is done. The bridge has been constructed, we have crossed the bridge, we can leave it behind now, forget it. We are in the subject, into the subject.
> (HRC, CP, 30.3: 6-12-1995)

Read in relation to its previous version, the new opening (which, in revised form, will open the published text) has the feel of a critical glancing-back: *the problem with the opening*. Indeed, it is through this revisionary self-commentary that the text is able to tell us something, for the first time, about realist practice – about what the work of realism *involves*. This development inaugurates a revisionary method that allows Coetzee to combine such commentary with the more elusive material that constitutes Costello's lecture(s). The narrative voice becomes, in revision, a discursive one, analyzing and evaluating a previous iteration of itself, a discursiveness generated by authorial return. Thus, for instance, when Coetzee returns to his first description of Costello's attire, her 'lady novelist's uniform', he adds a paragraph in which the narrative voice identifies its description of her 'costume and pearls' as 'signs of a moderate realism', a literary convention he defines here thus: 'Realism: supply the particulars, rely on the reader to infer their social meaning' (HRC, CP, 30.0: 28-6-1995, rev. 11-12-1996). Indeed, the story's many insights into what the work of realism involves develop in this way: it is through evaluating its archive that the story begins to answer its title question. The implications of this process are most apparent when Coetzee deletes material: every significant deletion is marked by the narrator with a 'skip'. Thus, for example, a scene in a restaurant, comprising mainly dialogue, in which we learn that the son is a physicist teaching at a university, is replaced, on 11 December 1995, with:

> I skip the restaurant scene. Nothing of importance occurs. It emerges that the son is a physicist by profession, teaching at a university.
>
> (HRC, CP, 30.3: 11-12-1995)

The restaurant scene is not a blank but an erasure; the revision is recorded in the text, creating the impression of two distinct realms: the text, and the reality to which it is referring. There are many such moments in the story.

Revisionary practice directly informs intellectual content: in one of those searching notebook entries, this one of 7 January 1996, Coetzee writes:

> Mother: 'It is not forbidden, within realism, to skip time. But the writer must be able to envisage what happens in the dead time, in the finest detail.'
>
> (HRC, CP, 35.2: 7-1-1996)

The following day, working now on the third draft, Coetzee adds a dialogue to the text, between mother and son, which elaborates on this idea. In a taxi to the airport, John asks his mother to clarify her definition of realism. 'You don't know, after all that talk?' she responds, though does not answer. It is not her job, she says, to think: she writes. 'Then', John asks, 'how do you write?' 'By allowing things to pass through me,' she says.

> By allowing another world to live inside me. Not live. Lodge. Coexist. So that one knows, so that it is known, what is going on in that world even when I am not explicitly looking at it. A world in its own right. Therefore not a world that needs to be composed on the page. I am just a picture restorer.
>
> (HRC, CP, 30.4: 8-1-1996)

John does not think to question his mother's confusing logic but wants to know what relevance Kafka has. Costello attempts an explanation:

> There is one moment when Kafka reveals himself as a realist. When he tries to imagine what it would be like for his ape to mate. Where, he wonders, is it going to find a female at the same stage of evolution? His poor male is alone in the world, one of a kind. At that moment you realize he has thought the story through to the end, that he isn't just writing an ironic fable.
>
> (HRC, CP, 30.4: 11-1-1996)

Realism, here, appears to be predicated on a realm of imagining that lies beyond the text's reach. When he returns to this dialogue a month later, after having continued his revisionary evaluation of the text, Coetzee adds to Costello's response: '[Kafka] is awake during the gaps while we sleep. That was why I brought him in. He watched, he saw, he knew' (HRC, CP, 30.3: 6-2-1996). Those skips in the text – the 'gaps' – are becoming in some way crucial to Costello's conception of realism, functioning as a lens onto that to which the text cannot refer. After yet another month, returning to this dialogue in the eighth and penultimate draft, Coetzee once again extends Costello's thinking with a new paragraph. In response, now, to her son's suggestion that Kafka cannot be a realist because he did not write about 'Norwegians in smelly underwear [and] people picking their noses', she says (I quote now from the published text):

> But Kafka had time to wonder where and how his poor educated ape was going to find a mate. And what it was going to be like when he was left in the dark with the bewildered, half-tamed female that his keepers eventually produced for his use. Kafka's ape is embedded in life. It is the embeddedness that is important, not the life itself. His ape is embedded as we are embedded, you in me, I in you. That ape is followed through to the end, to the bitter, unsayable end, whether or not there are traces left on the page. Kafka stays awake during the gaps when we are sleeping.
>
> (Coetzee 2003: 32)

Cornwell sees in the word 'embeddedness',

> another name for the intersubjective space in which the dramas of recognition and surprise that constitute the act of reading can be staged. In this sense, 'realism' is inseparable from intersubjectivity, a premise on which all successful artistic representation of human experience would seem to depend.
>
> (2011: 358)

I do not disagree per se. But Cornwell does not suggest how these fictional characters are embedded in *life* rather than in the discourses of history; he does not say what has replaced the bottom that has fallen out.

To my mind, the key word in this passage is 'left': 'whether or not there are traces left on the page'. For a trace not to be left on the page, it must once have had presence; it has to have been revised out: the phrase implies an erasure rather than a blank. One way of reading this passage is that Costello (or, better, Coetzee) is talking about the workings-out of fiction-making, the reams of discarded imaginings that litter the compositional floor – in other words, the archive. Read thus, the inaccessible territory that serves, for the fiction, as 'the real', becomes a material one. It is the *avant-texte*: the drafts, the notebooks, the *disjecta membra*. By drawing attention to the text's genetic history, as Coetzee does with his 'skips', especially in reading the text aloud, as per its original existence as a lecture – holding the paper, the text's material casing, in his hands – every time he performs a skip he actualizes the text's archival dimension: the listener hears one version of the text and *sees*, in the paper, the material presence of another, more thoroughly imagined one, gestured at but unavailable. The real to which the text refers, in this reading, becomes its own genetic history. If the bottom has fallen out of the discourse of reference, then the archive might provide an alternative, paper-strewn floor. The text of 'Realism', thus, becomes one that acknowledges, as Derrida said in an interview with Derek Attridge (an annotated photocopy of which is collected in Coetzee's archive): 'There is no literature without a *suspended* relation to meaning and reference' (1992: 48). It becomes a text, in other words, which does not give up on the *possibility* of reference, but which can, with authority and certainty, refer only to its own recorded history, can '[operate] in terms of its own procedures and [issue] in its own conclusions'.

4

Of all Coetzee's novels *Disgrace* seems the least concerned with its fictional status – is his most 'realist' text. Despite, or perhaps because of, its status as realism, however, it is largely characterized by its aporias, textual impasses whose relation to meaning and reference are suspended. It is my contention here that these manifestations of textual doubt are not designed as sites of difficulty but rather record the knots and obstructions, the doubts and anxieties of their composition – and that they are crucial to the novel's functioning (or, non-functioning) as a realist text. The novel's generic mode, I want to argue, might be seen as a kind of *archival realism*. In order to demonstrate what I mean, I will – with distorting compression – trace the development of just one of the novel's elements.

The terms of David Lurie's relations with his student, Melanie Isaacs, are the most consistently unsettled dimension of the novel's composition. Coetzee revises the circumstances of their relationship from the moment of first conception to final copy, never not uncertain as to the dynamics of their sexual encounters and, in particular, the question of Isaacs's agency and consent. She first appears in a note of March 1995, before Coetzee has begun to write the novel: 'A girl is friendly, makes overtures. They sleep together several times. She begins to make demands' (HRC, CP, 35.2: 25-3-1995). In first conception, then, Isaacs is not only the instigator but is apparently in command of the relationship. When she first appears in draft, almost a year later, on 13 February 1996 (towards the end of his work on 'What Is Realism?'), she does not quite take the lead but appears to be a willing participant. 'After class he catches her eye', the material begins, their affair in medias res; 'pretending to gather her papers', she lingers. Lurie drives her home, she 'invites him in for coffee', and the following paragraph begins: 'They make love in the bedroom' (HRC, CP, 35.4: 13-2-1996). An academic lawyer, this Lurie takes Isaacs away for a weekend in Johannesburg, where he gives the keynote address at a conference on land rights, and begins to understand (as, perhaps, does Coetzee) that her active participation might not be so uncomplicated: 'there is another story to be told', he comes to realize, 'another set of memories being stored, memories he can with effort imagine, though he refuses to do so' (HRC, CP, 35.4: 15-2-1996).

Lurie's failure of empathy appears also to be his author's: the following day, after a few attempts to imagine Isaacs's point of view, Coetzee abandons the material entirely and begins again. Now Lurie is an historian and Isaacs his postgraduate student, writing a thesis on the history of South African psychiatric services. She retains her agency; she even seems the more active party when Lurie this time declines her invitation for 'coffee'. Yet the deeper – and more formal – understanding of the dynamic remains:

> He has the sense not to tell himself it is she who is seducing him. In a constellation such as this one – a teacher and a student, an older man and a younger woman – there is no division of blame. No matter what she says, no matter what she does, the ~~blame is~~ responsibility is his, every jot and tittle of it.
>
> (HRC, CP, 35.4: 21-02-1996)

This understanding informs the new dramatic arrangement of their sexual encounter: now, Lurie drives to her house, forces his way in and forces himself upon her. All we learn of her participation is that she 'gives way to him', and that, spuriously, 'in the most intimate movements of her body he feels an answering passion' (HRC, CP, 35.4: 21-02-1996). The 'other story' is now left out of the text.

Coetzee tries again. Next, Lurie is an English lecturer, his specialism the influence of classical landscape writing on Pope's pastoral. Isaacs is writing a thesis on 'Landscape and Gender in South African Settler Writing' (HRC, CP, 35.2: 11-3-1996). They clash intellectually; Lurie dismisses her feminist approach as 'part of a huge paranoid fantasy' (HRC, CP, 35.4: 13-3-1996). But now the sexual content, which takes its cue from their intellectual interests, is minimal. Out running one day, Lurie is surprised when Isaacs, oblivious, overtakes him on the path; he returns to his car and watches, still unseen, as she, nymphlike, runs through the woods. At their next supervision, he suggests they go running together. Immediately, Isaacs files a charge of harassment, accusing him of putting 'pressure' on her. Her agency, in this version, supersedes his: 'If this is what she says happened,' Lurie says when confronted with the accusations, which we are not permitted to see, 'then it must have happened' (HRC, CP, 35.4: 19-03-1996). The 'other story' is still left out, but now it dictates his own, present through its agency.

Yet, again, Coetzee rearranges the material. Now, Isaacs reluctantly agrees to run with Lurie but, afterwards, she stops turning up for supervisions. Here, Coetzee returns to the previous version of the sexual encounter, in which Lurie turns up unannounced at her door and forces himself upon her. This time, however, her non-consent is unmistakeable: 'As he tightens his grip on her he can feel her going slack. A sense of triumph runs through him. ... She stumbles like a doll. She has no will left' (HRC, CP, 35.4: 24-04-1996). The act itself is not described; Isaacs's experience is absent.

The questions of responsibility, agency, blame and consent clearly occupy Coetzee a great deal during his drafting of these encounters, as do the dimensions of the power dynamic. The holograph on which these different versions are worked out are dense with revision; the individual versions themselves do not exist as discrete documents, one after the other, but are all part of the same single document, locatable – thanks to Coetzee's habit of dating each revision – within a network of deletions, substitutions, cross-references, restructurings. The work of revision is visibly strenuous, dizzying to follow as Coetzee worries at the novel's moral heart. At this point in the drafting, with no clear priority given to any version of their sexual encounter, a kind of revisionary frustration enters the text, marked diegetically in a letter to Isaacs over which Lurie anxiously labours, and in which, like Coetzee, he tries to make sense of the dynamics of their relationship. Coetzee describes the letter like a genetic critic describing the revisionary markings on an archival document:

> 'When we began,' says the letter, 'there was a gulf fixed between us.' That sentence is crossed out. 'It is not possible,' the letter recommences, 'that a man of my age should ~~feel~~ have for a woman of your age feelings no less intense, sincere, driving.' Driving is crossed out, then the whole sentence is crossed out. 'You should think carefully before,' begins the third sentence; there are fourth and fifth and sixth sentences, all crossed out. All that is not crossed out is the salutation – 'Dear Melanie' – and the ending: 'Sincerely yours, David Lurie.'
> (HRC, CP, 35.4: 8-5-1996)

Like the novel itself at this stage of its genesis, what this letter communicates most of all is its own revisionary struggle.

The day after writing this paragraph, Coetzee once again begins again, deliberately problematizing the question of Isaacs's agency. She is an undergraduate again. Lurie runs into her on his way home, offers her a lift, then invites her into *his* house for a coffee, as he will in the published novel. She does not respond; to Lurie's mind, 'Saying nothing means yes' (HRC, CP, 35.4: 10-5-1996). In the house, she takes an active, even coquettish role in conversation. But, once again, her non-consent is unambiguous – or ambiguous only to Lurie who is like Costello's reader, seeing only what he wants in the text: 'Her resistance is real, but it is only formal. … She says NO, she says NO more than once, but that too is only formal' (HRC, CP, 35.4: 11-5-1996). Afterwards, Isaacs is clearly traumatized, becomes withdrawn on campus; in the final, poignant one-sentence section of this version, Coetzee writes: 'At the end of the period she slides out of the room, holding her satchel to her breast as if to protect herself' (HRC, CP, 35.4: 15-5-1996). She has come a very long way from her original conception.

A few days after writing this unpleasant scene, Coetzee writes in his notebook:

> The kind of novel I am being pulled towards writing requires that, after he has been denounced, there is a period in which pressure on him builds up, until it's so great that he breaks and/or leaves. For this I have neither the patience nor the talent. So: how to give in summary without moving into a half-baked postmodernist mode?
> (HRC, CP, 35.2: 18-5-1996)

Coetzee is not, here, thinking of the Isaacs material but the impulse to summarize, consistent with his impatience with the conventions of realism, has general application. When he returns to the scene, he begins to cut swathes through it, erasing the particulars of the sexual encounter: now, all the (lengthy) material in which the question of Isaacs's non-consent is addressed (from which I only selectively quoted above) is deleted in full, and replaced with a single sentence: 'He reaches across and with his fingertips brushes the back of her hand' (HRC, CP, 35.4: 24-5-1996). Her response is not recorded. Nor is the event itself. The following paragraph begins: 'It is not rape' (HRC, CP, 35.4: 11-5-1996). Coetzee has been circling the question of the legal status of the event. In the previous version, that status is easy enough to determine; now, with no representation of the event itself, this defensive negation places the reader in the position of a juror; it commands judgement, but the means by which we might judge are withheld – or, rather, the particulars can no longer form the basis of our judgement. The representation of the sexual encounter has, through summary, through erasure, become a site of aporia; Coetzee has been imagining it through to the end, but now he leaves the specifics out of the picture. But, crucially, rather than allow it to stand thus, Coetzee now adds the previous arrangement of the sexual encounter *onto the end* of this scene. At the end of the chapter, Isaacs stops attending lectures as before, but the scene in which Lurie arrives, unannounced, at her door and forces himself upon her now follows. Rather than chose between the two versions, in other words, Coetzee has chosen to present the reader with both. Isaacs's archival plurality is becoming a textual one.

Coetzee leaves this material for four months. During this gap, on 31 August 1996, he makes the following note:

> The form I am working towards is that of the synopsised novel. As though there were a fully-written realistic novel in the background which is being retold in synopsis. One gets an example in *Don Quixote* when Q tells the story of a stereotypical romance. Impression of pace. Not being sure whether you are in the base novel or in the summary of it.
>
> (HRC, CP, 35.2: 31-8-1996)

David Attwell sees in this note an idea that never came to fruition: 'Needless to say,' he writes, 'the synopsized novel was not the novel he ended up writing' (2015: 229). I read it differently. I see here a description of something already in process, even an inevitability: *the form I am working towards*. Reading the note against Costello's narrator's skips, I would argue that *Disgrace* is, if not a synopsized novel, then a novel which is stylistically indebted to the synopsis, a novel whose affective experience is of 'not being sure whether you are in the base novel or the summary of it', the text or the performance of the text. Summary infuses its language. To point to just one example: when Lurie runs into Soraya, the sex worker he has been visiting, in the street, the moment, which sets in motion the novel's plot, is introduced thus: 'Then one Saturday morning everything changes. He is in the city on business …' (Coetzee 1999: 6). This is the language of the blurb, a sensationalist, selective synopsizing revision of a text: *then one Saturday morning everything changes*. And: *he is in the city on business*: why the secrecy? Why should Lurie's 'business' not be communicated to the reader? What can it be? Speculating thus can hardly be the point; were the detail to be revealed to us, we assume, we would recognize its unimportance. But at moments like these (and the novel is woven from such moments), if we pause to speculate about what the referent might, in reality, be, the ground beneath us falls away and we realize how limited, how imperfect is our access to the realm this novel takes for the real.

I skip to March 1997, when Coetzee next significantly reconceives of the scenes with Melanie Isaacs. Now in the sixth draft of the seduction scene, they do not have sex after dinner; Isaacs says, 'I must go,' and Lurie sees her out. In revision, Coetzee adds yet another scene between this one and the following, more forceful sex scene. It is written as though in detailed synopsis. Lurie phones Isaacs and invites her to lunch. Her response is not recorded (though it is gestured at) and the text moves on. Here is how it appears in the published text:

> 'I'll pick you up at, shall we say, twelve.'
>   There is still time for her to tell a lie, wriggle out. But she is too confused, and the moment passes.
>   When he arrives, she is waiting on the sidewalk. ...'
>
> (Coetzee 1999: 18)

The question of her agency, in other words – her volition and consent – is entirely removed, *skipped over*. Whatever her response, it exists in a realm beyond the reach of this myopic text, though not beyond the realm of its author's imagining – or, for that matter, its reader's. The lunch itself is dealt with in only a few lines, at the end of which Lurie asks, 'Shall we leave?' Once again, Isaacs's response is not given, her consent withheld. Here is the paragraph that immediately follows Lurie's question (I return to the sixth draft):

> He takes her back to his house. To the sound of rain pattering against the windows he makes love to her on the living-room floor. The act, once under way, is intensely pleasurable, so pleasurable that from its climax he tumbles into white oblivion, forgetting to breathe, the very tissue of his brain wiped clean.
>
> (HRC, CP, 36.3: 25-3-1997)

This key moment in the novel – the first sexual contact between Isaacs and Lurie – is now imperfectly represented, told in a disconcerting blend of the coldly synoptic ('the act, once under way') and the crassly poetic ('he tumbles into white oblivion'). Isaacs's presence, her agency, her volition, her consent, are again written out; the traces are not left on the page. We are not sure if we are in the base novel or in the summary of it.

Still, the question of Isaacs's agency continues to occupy Coetzee. In the following months he begins, perhaps surprisingly, to fashion for her a positive sexuality. Lurie speculates on what might have gone through her mind during the night of their first encounter, putting Joycean consent into her mouth: 'Yes. Yes, I will. I will ... put my ear to his chest and hear the heartbeat of power' (HRC, CP, 35.5: 5-6-1997). To be sure, this is filtered through Lurie's consciousness. But Coetzee now adds yet another version of their relationship into the mix, in which some of that positivity is borne out in Isaacs's behaviour: *she* starts turning up at *his* home unannounced, asking for favours, staying the night. She becomes the active party once more. 'She has him under the finger,' Lurie thinks. 'She is getting whatever she wants' (HRC, CP, 35.5: 10-9-1997).

There will be another year or so of revision and reconception, each scene will be considerably more nuanced and morally complex than is suggested in these outlines, and more unified. But to rest my account here: all the different Melanies who exist in the archive are now present and accounted for, as they will be in the published novel. There is the first Melanie, the one who took charge and started 'to make demands'; there is the passive victim of Lurie's force; there is the Melanie who resists his 'pressure'. And, crucially, their very first sexual encounter is presented in such summarized form that we have no way of knowing what 'really happened'. All the other Melanies follow from this originary aporia, this erasure. She is her accumulated drafts and yet her truth lies beyond the reach of the text: she is at once plural and erased. Her reality – the book's *realism*, such as it is – is archival, as though the book emerges as a summary of its genesis. Coetzee has found a way to represent the historically specific dynamics of the workings of power (in this case, interracial sexual relations between teacher and student on the South African campus) on his own terms.

There are plenty of examples in *Disgrace* of previous drafts finding presence in the text. In each case, the result is an aporia often so mild that it hardly registers; accumulated, however, they contribute to the unplaceable unease readers experience while reading this novel: we find it hard to extract anything like truth from the text because we are caught in the slippage between the text and its performance. I have space to consider only one such instance, which occurs when Lurie and his daughter, Lucy, are attacked on her farm. Their attackers gain entry to her house by asking to use the phone: 'His sister', one of them explains in the first draft, 'is having a baby'. As he writes, Coetzee crosses out the words 'a baby' and replaces them with, 'an accident', creating a strange continuous present tense: *His sister is having an accident* (HRC, CP, 35.4: 25-7-1996). The revision has created a linguistic knot; can an accident be continuous or is it necessarily momentary? We might assume it to be the result of a language barrier. But the knot tightens. Coetzee revises the dialogue that follows accordingly but, when he returns for a second round of revision, he revises *some* of it back to its original form. Here is how it appears in the published text.

> The young one speaks. 'We must telephone.'
> 'Why must you telephone?'
> 'His sister' – he gestures vaguely behind him – 'is having an accident.'
> 'An accident?'
> 'Yes, very bad.'
> 'What kind of accident?'
> 'A baby.'
> 'His sister is having a baby?'
> 'Yes.'
>
> (Coetzee 1999: 92)

I always found this moment odd; I never understood why Lucy and her father, who are nervous and alert, see nothing suspicious in this exchange: 'He and Lucy exchange glances. ... The story makes sense' (Coetzee 1999: 92–3). But 'the story' does not make sense, is clearly being invented and revised on the spot; they are being presented with two possible versions, both genetically authentic but mutually exclusive. Two drafts come into contact and do not quite fit together. At this moment of keen narrative suspense, the archival knot interrupts the flow of the realism at precisely the point at which the fabrication of narrative is at issue. A story is being put together but its reality is inaccessible, its authenticity uncheckable: reference is suspended. The only 'reality' to which the text authoritatively refers, in this description of historically grounded violence, is its own genetics, the realm of its revision.

Notes

1 Attwell will of course know this: it is in an interview with him, after all, which Coetzee included in his collection of non-fiction writings *Doubling the Point* (1992), that Coetzee says, 'Illusionism is … a word I use for what is commonly called realism' (1992: 27).
2 In quoting from Coetzee's notebooks and manuscripts, I reproduce the marks of revision when it is interesting, useful or possible; when it is disorienting or obfuscating, I do not. When I do not, and when it is not indicated in the text, I indicate in the reference whether I have incorporated the revisions. All quotations from handwritten texts are based on my own transcriptions.

References

Attwell, D. (2015), *J.M. Coetzee and the Life of Writing: Face to Face With Time*. Oxford: Oxford University Press.
Bryant, John (2002), *The Fluid Text: A Theory of Revision and Editing for Book and Screen*. Ann Arbor: University of Michigan Press.
Coetzee, J. M. 'J.M. Coetzee Papers'. Austin, TX: Harry Ransom Center.
Coetzee, J. M., and D. Attwell (eds) (1992), *Doubling the Point: Essays and Interviews*. Cambridge, MA: Harvard University Press.
Coetzee, J. M. (1988), 'The Novel Today', *Upstream*, 6 (1): 2–5.
Coetzee, J. M. (Papers) (1995–6), 'What Is Realism?' Austin, TX: Harry Ransom Center.
Coetzee, J. M. (Papers) (1996–2012), *Disgrace*. Austin, TX: Harry Ransom Center.
Coetzee, J. M. (1999), *Disgrace*. London: Random House.
Coetzee, J. M. (2003), *Elizabeth Costello*. London: Random House.
Cornwell, G. (2011), 'J.M. Coetzee, *Elizabeth Costello*, and the Inevitability of "Realism"', *Critique: Studies in Contemporary Fiction*, 52 (3), 348–61.
Deppman, J., D. Ferrer and M. Groden (eds) (2004), *Genetic Criticism: Texts and Avant-Textes*. Philadelphia: University of Pennsylvania Press.
Derrida, J., and D. Attridge (eds) (1992), *Acts of Literature*. London: Routledge.
Fordham, Finn (2010), *I Do I Undo I Redo: The Textual Genesis of Modernist Selves*. Oxford: Oxford University Press.

In pursuit of style: Coetzee reading Beckett in the archive

Paul Stewart

J. M. Coetzee's PhD thesis, *The English Fiction of Samuel Beckett: An Essay in Stylistic Analysis*, is an extraordinary document. Housed in the Harry Ransom Center at the University of Texas, Austin, the thesis offers a tantalizing glimpse of a future Nobel Prize winner, Coetzee, attempting a meticulous study of Beckett's style as seen through the textual variants of key manuscript materials for such works as *More Pricks than Kicks*, *Murphy* and *Watt*. Such a document would seem to offer a rare opportunity to study the confluence of two major figures in modern literature, Beckett and Coetzee. Studying the carefully typed thesis, one hopes that the issue of how Beckett has influenced Coetzee, or indeed how Coetzee has moved on, or away, from his precursor might be brought to light.

There can be no doubt that Beckett is a major influence on Coetzee. Armed with the evidence of *Youth*, Coetzee's PhD, his interventions in Beckett studies over the years, his comments in various interviews and small articles, one can argue for a persistent engagement with Beckett's works over the course of Coetzee's career. However, the palpable nature of that influence does not seem to be so readily forthcoming from the novels themselves, as, *Youth* aside, there are very few direct allusions to Beckett. Chris Ackerley has demonstrated less-secure allusive moments – which might be termed situational – such as the young John on Hampstead Heath in *Youth* as reminiscent of the eponymous Murphy contemplating a packet of biscuits in Hyde Park. (Coetzee focuses on this passage in his PhD and the subsequent 1970 essay on *Murphy*.) With few direct allusions and a few scattered situational resonances, one resource is to attest to a thematic influence, as Peter Boxall does in *Since Beckett* (2009), which charts the development of slow literature in the wake of Beckett. Steven G. Kellman (1996), in turn, chooses the thematic influence of translingualism – although this is somewhat hampered by Coetzee's PhD only focusing on the English prose before the Second World War.

The struggle to delineate the Beckettian influence on Coetzee has led some to posit a form of mirroring. George Yeoh, for example, has argued that 'Coetzee transplants Beckett's metaphysical concerns with writing and truth into South Africa and recasts it in more concretely ethical and sociopolitical terms' (2003: 339). Such an argument is based on the view of Beckett as an 'existential humanist' (Yeoh 2003: 338) preoccupied with the desire to express the essential nothingness of the self, whilst that desire is inevitably frustrated by the inability of language to express this nothingness. This is a conception of Beckett as being beyond political, national and historical contingencies. In contrast, Yeoh argues, Coetzee translates these abstract, philosophical issues into the 'concrete context of apartheid where the pressures for writing to tell the truth become more tangible' (2003: 338). As will become apparent, an analysis of Coetzee's archival work on Beckett may lead us to question such a position.

Of course, this very lack of overt influence and the difficulty in formulating a clear relation might point to two not necessarily contradictory conclusions: (a) as his own work has progressed, Coetzee has successfully moved on from any formative influence Beckett might have had; and (b) the influence is one which Coetzee has folded into his own personality, making him what he is as a writer, thus the influence is now both everywhere and yet not locatable directly. It is this latter possibility to which Coetzee attests in the article 'Homage' as he introduces 'the writers without whom I would not be the person I am, writers without whom I would, in a certain sense, not exist' (1993: 5). The same essay provides grounds for basing one's sense of influence not on grand ideas or philosophies that writers incorporate into their works, but on the style of those works. He argues that the 'deepest lessons one learns from other writers are, I suspect, matters of rhythm, broadly conceived' (1993: 6–7). This definition is vague. Rhythm suggests a stylistic concern, but quite how broadly it should be conceived of is far from clear. Given that Coetzee, in the same paragraph, has written of 'the rhythm and syntax not only of words but, so to speak, of thought too', is rhythm so broadly conceived so as to include *what* is thought, or are we to consider only the *manner* of the thinking?

The quotation just given from 'Homage' is worth pausing over a moment in order to illustrate the possibilities of style and Beckettian influence. The parenthetical clause – 'so to speak' – might at first reading be dismissed as merely a rhetorical flourish, an insertion that aids the rhythm of the line but which is not strictly necessary as it does not make any difference to the overall meaning of the sentence. It is an almost offhand, colloquial aside. However, the phrasing *so to* speak opens up a further possibility, suggesting that it should be read as *in order to* speak. Now the meaning of the sentence is changed, as a causal relationship between the rhythm and syntax of word and thought and the act of speech is established. The Beckettian influence that might be discerned here is the activation of dormant, or redundant, parts of everyday usage through which a second-order meaning is glimpsed. In *Beckett's Dying Words*, Christopher Ricks expertly draws our attention to just this facet of Beckett's prose, as, for example, when he considers the following passage from *First Love*:

> She began to undress. When at their wit's end they undress, no doubt the wisest course. She took off everything, with a slowness fit to enflame an elephant, except her stockings, calculated presumably to bring my concupiscence to the boil. It was then I noticed the squint. Fortunately she was not the first naked woman to have crossed my path, so I could stay, I knew she would not explode.
>
> (2009a: 74)

Ricks remarks:

> But of course the phrase which brings my critical concupiscence to the boil is the cliché 'cross my path'. … One doesn't normally think of naked women as crossing one's path exactly. Not even in the heyday of streaking.
>
> (1993: 65)

The cliché almost asks to be ignored as just a somewhat lazy (or at least colloquial) piece of linguistic filler, but when one considers it again, as Ricks does, a range of comic and unsettling possibilities emerge. What Ricks describes as the 'insinuating power of Beckett's unofficial English' (77) can partly be attributed to his calling attention to the oddity of English, especially in those parts of speech, such as cliché, to which we normally pay so little attention. As Elizabeth Barry has argued, Beckett's use of cliché (a use I am extending to include commonplace idiomatic forms), is 'repetition with a difference, the familiar phrase in a newly engineered form or an unexpected context, that works both to critique and to rejuvenate the medium of language' (2006: 2). Coetzee's 'so to speak' phrase operates in a very similar way to Beckett's reactivations of clichés: both almost pass by unnoticed, but both offer unsettling or alternative possibilities once they have been noticed.

Of course, such an influence as this cannot be proved as such. A certain similarity on a stylistic level can legitimately be countered by arguments dependent on content. So, whilst one might note a certain similarity in rhythm and a tendency to redeploy idioms, this might be checked by emphasizing, for example, the perceived seriousness of Coetzee as opposed to the more comic instincts of Beckett, at least in this instance. Nevertheless, it is style that brings together Beckett and Coetzee, at least for Ackerley, Hayes and Attridge. For Attridge, the style that Coetzee responded to in Beckett was the one that was 'capable of transforming the disappointments of dead-ends of quotidian experience, of what Coetzee calls "the ordinary", into intense pleasure' (2009: 74). Pleasure again is key for Hayes, who argues that, to use Coetzee's phrases, Beckett's 'fierce comic anguish' and 'anguished … intellectual comedy' is what interested Coetzee and what he takes into his own writing but which is developed beyond the solipsism of Beckett to 'engage with the problems posed by embodied life' (2010: 43). Although recent scholarship has challenged this notion of disembodiment in Beckett, Hayes's view is one that Coetzee himself seems to agree with: 'Beckett's later short fiction have never really held my attention. They are, quite literally, disembodied' (Coetzee 1992: 23). For his part, Ackerley suggests that the combination of 'the Middle Voice, the voice of one's talking to oneself, experiencing in the present past trauma, or bearing witness' (2011: 30) and a 'rhetorical impulse towards reverie and reflexivity' (2011: 31) amounts to the greatest stylistic influence. All attest to the notion that these stylistic influences have been thoroughly assimilated by Coetzee to such a degree that they now seem proper to him as a writer, rather than a series of identifiable Beckettian traces. Yet one might still wonder what is meant by style in these instances. Beckett's style – which itself underwent dramatic changes over the course of his career, to consider only his prose works – is cast in generalities that bleed into matters of content, form and, above all, attitude.

In order to gain more insight, therefore, into Coetzee's engagement with Beckett's style it is imperative to consider closely his PhD thesis that is overtly concerned precisely with style, as its title, tabulations, diagrams and statistical analyses attest. However, the thesis is in many ways an odd document that has had little impact on wider Beckett studies, in part, one suspects, because the thesis might reveal more about the author than its subject. As Carrol Clarkson has noted, by 'the time he wrote his thesis, Coetzee found himself at an unusual intellectual confluence of mathematics, computational logic, linguistic science and English literature' (2009: 4) and the thesis somewhat suffers from multiple points of focus. It is undeniably focused on Beckett's manuscripts, but it is also, in effect, using Beckett as a test-case to gauge the efficacy of stylostatisical approaches to literary study. As such, Clarkson argues, in 'the course of the argument the thesis explores, but ultimately questions the value, for literary analysis, of statistical methods of stylistic description' (2009: 4). In his own PhD thesis, Peter Johnston argues that Coetzee ultimately 'remains ... unconvinced by ... the prevailing orthodoxies of stylistics', particularly the use of quantitative data and its relation to interpretation (2013: 123). Nevertheless, the thesis is an 'important resource' (Clarkson 2009: 4) not least because it is evidence that, as Clarkson puts it, 'the work that [Coetzee] did on Beckett is pivotal in terms of the development of his own craftsmanship as a writer (5). This is reinforced by Coetzee's retrospective comments that his PhD and related articles may have been 'attempts to get closer to a secret, a secret of Beckett's that I wanted to make my own' (Coetzee 1992: 25). That secret, the student Coetzee hoped, would be found through analysis of style. Clarkson emphasizes that, in the pages of the PhD, Coetzee encounters Beckett not in terms of thematics or philosophy, but in terms of a writer engaged with the materiality of writing. According to Clarkson, Coetzee's thesis is primarily 'an attempt to identify patterns in Beckett's linguistic choices, and to analyse the stylistic effects of these patterns and rhythms within the structure of the literary work' (5). The key concept here is possibly that of 'choice'; to what degree is the written work a series of free choices made by the writer? Or is the writer so circumscribed by the nature of the work itself that choice – and with it authorial agency – might be called into question?

In his PhD, Coetzee chooses to initially situate a definition of style as lying between the opposing extremes of Bernard Bloch and Beckett himself. For Bloch, style amounted to 'the message carried by the frequency-distributions and the transitional probabilities of its linguistic features, especially as they differ from those of the same features in the language as a whole' (qtd in Coetzee 1969: 2). This places style 'into the lap of mathematics', as Coetzee puts it. Beckett's letter of 1937 to Axel Kaun is used by Coetzee to stand for the other possible pole: 'Grammar and Style! They appear to me to have become just as obsolete as a Biedermeir bathing suit or the imperturbability of a gentleman. A mask. ... Is there any reason why that terribly arbitrary materiality of the word's surface should not be dissolved?' (qtd in Coetzee 1969: 4).[1] Coetzee glosses this on one level as a reaction against the Flaubertian concept, or religion, of style, but on another level as a reaction against the connotative and associative possibilities inherent within English. Rightly, he adduces two things from this: first, that Beckett 'pictures language as a wall between objects and their percipients' and that this intermediary has become 'autonomous and resistant' – that is, as if 'the English words were taking on their own life as they left his pen' (1969: 4).

Despite offering these poles of thoughts on style, the thesis still struggles with defining precisely what style is, or, more precisely, what elements of literature should be put aside if one wishes to analyze style alone. Coetzee comments that only 'when we know what style is will we know whether all the counting of syllables and listing of words beginning with *f* that has been going on for the last fifty years has any value' (12). This quantitative method – which might mean the 'replacement of the human analyst by the computer', as Coetzee comments (6) – is to a great degree under scrutiny in the thesis, with Coetzee frequently wondering about the nature and quality of the knowledge that such an approach might generate. He is also very aware of the separation of the roles of the stylo-statistician and the literary critic, with the former handing over the results of the statistical analysis to the latter who will then 'illuminate larger-scale features' such as overall structures and 'meaning' (a word which Coetzee places in speech marks (6)). But how does one draw a meaningful distinction between larger- and lesser-scale features? Should style incorporate elements of structure, of 'world-view', or is it a matter of habitual linguistic phenomena in an individual text which can extend to a number of texts, giving rise to the sensation that one always knows one is reading a Hemingway story, for example? Coetzee inclines towards the argument that 'content is the aggregate of elements, form the relations among them' (1969: 15), but he prefers to let his definition of style develop over the course of the thesis.

However, from the very beginning of this PhD, Coetzee is careful to delineate what he is *not* in search of. He contends that 'literary scholars ... have tended to hold conceptions of style broad enough to use stylistics as a royal road to the heart of every work of literature'. So, Stephen Ullmann can contend that 'from the surface layer of the vocabulary we shall penetrate the deeper stratum of syntax to that subsoil of stylistic creation where images are generated and where a new vision of the world is evolved' (qtd in Coetzee 1969: 16). If one digs deep enough, then one can define, as Leo Spitzer suggests, that stylistic phenomena are manifestations of a 'psychological etymon' within the writer himself. It is this that Coetzee is so keen to avoid. Referring back to Spitzer, he claims 'I too am looking for an etymon, but I see no need to introduce the writer's psyche into the investigation: ... the etymon I am looking for is linguistic' (1969: 77). This disclaimer forms a motif throughout the thesis. So, we are assured that 'I am not concerned in this essay with the views of the historical Samuel Beckett' (1969: 3). Similarly, he expresses reservations about Spitzer's psychological conclusions based on Proust's use of parenthesis, commenting:

> Proust is dead. Even if he were alive it would be unlikely to tell us what 'the movements of his soul' were when he composed his fiction. Even if he were prepared we would have no means of verifying his account, which would be merely another fiction.
>
> (1969: 87)

Further on, he criticizes 'the assertion ... that certain syntactic habits correspond to certain conceptual habits' which he claims 'seem[s] tenable only if they are made on a statistical basis and "conceptual habits" are understood to be features of the meanings of the text rather than of the unknowable mind of the author' (1969: 89). Coetzee is at pains, then, to keep the historical person of Beckett out of the equation, so in order to 'avoid involving the author as a psychological agent ("At this point Beckett wanted to") he must replace the subjective "Beckett" with the objective "<u>Watt</u>"' (1969: 112).

However, during his archival work on Beckett's manuscripts, particularly those of *Watt*, this exclusion of the historical figure of Beckett shows increasing signs of strain, despite, or because, of the desire to isolate the fundamental components of Beckett's style, the secret that Coetzee wanted to make his own. The question first arises when Coetzee considers a phrase from 'Dante and the Lobster', the first of the stories of *More Pricks than Kicks* and so very much part of Beckett's earlier style before he turned to French. The hero of the story, Belacqua, locks the door so 'nobody could come at him' and Coetzee wonders if there is 'a real choice inherent' in choosing this phrasing rather than the more common, 'so nobody could come in'. This apparently slight matter is indicative of a wider problem, as Coetzee describes:

> When the choice of one kind of alternative over another creating slight or no change in meaning becomes systematic or recurrent (for example, the systematic choice of the order modifier-subject-verb over the order subject-modifier-verb), we are dealing with a purely stylistic tendency, one which does not determine and is not determined by plot and structure. The difficulty for the student is that the choices are not appended as footnotes to the text.
>
> (1969: 38)

If 'nobody could get at him' is indicative of Belacqua's paranoia or that his 'conception of social relations is savage' then, Coetzee seems to be saying, the choice of diction is 'not purely stylistic' as it is determined by a preconceived notion of that higher-level signifier 'Belacqua's character' which is inextricably bound to plot and structure.

By studying the manuscripts of *Watt*, Coetzee hopes to isolate those moments when choices are appended – not as footnotes, but as textual variants. The matter is whether 'the choice between two words is an entirely free one' (1969: 110) although, due to the interdependence of revisions and the determinates of structure, form and character, such freedom is rare indeed. Coetzee considers the following:

```
39–40 CW    the illusion of movement in space
     AB     the illusion of motion in space
```

The rhythm of the phrase is not unduly affected by the change as 'movement' replaces 'motion', and there does not appear to be any connotative complications as far as Coetzee is concerned. However, we might here question Coetzee's method of isolating a single change in such a way. Chris Ackerley, in his exhaustive annotations to *Watt*, has argued that there is a connotative dimension to this change once it is viewed alongside other alterations Beckett made. He argues that these changes are 'less corrections of "mathematically meaningless description", as Coetzee suggests, than intimations of a movement away from the pre-Socratic concerns of *Murphy*, with its Atomist paradoxes of Motion and the Doctrine of the Limit, with their more recent analogues of Uncertainty and Relativity, toward the realm of impotence and ignorance that Watt increasingly inhabits' (Ackerley 2005: 128). Ackerley then discerns a pattern of emendations inspired by a shift on a thematic, philosophical and scientific level which Coetzee does not, and this might be accounted for by the methodological differences between Coetzee and Ackerley. Coetzee's stylostatistical analysis does not allow for the consideration of wider contexts; contexts to which Ackerley frequently refers. In what he terms his 'dianoetic' approach (27), Ackerley annotates obscure passages from the text not only with an awareness of textual deviance among the archival materials but also with a heightened awareness of the intellectual and cultural hinterlands of Beckett himself. So, in explaining this change from 'motion' to 'movement' Ackerley draws on not only pre-Socratic thinking (in particular Anaximander) but also Schopenhauer – whose influence on Beckett is widely recognized – when there is no explicit textual evidence to do so. Due to these different approaches, the change from motion to movement is not only a question of style for Ackerley, whilst Coetzee sees the change as an example of a purely stylistic alteration.

Nonetheless, if we accept Coetzee's argument that the change from motion to movement has no connotations beyond itself, and so there is no real difference between the two terms, the question becomes: why the change and, more importantly, what is the agent of change? Coetzee offers three possible answers:

> [The critic] can settle for the statement, 'Beckett, for reasons I am too insensitive to perceive, made this change.' He can say, 'No reader can be expected to perceive how context determines the choice of "movement" over "motion", therefore I must conclude that the choice is independent of its context, and that Beckett given such free choice likes "movement" more than "motion".' Or he can say, 'I can point to a tentative reason why the choice is not independent of its context.'
>
> (1969: 111)

As Coetzee is well aware, the first two of these possible answers raise the spectre of the historical Beckett the thesis has so assiduously avoided, and on which much of the work of Ackerley depends. Coetzee, therefore, warns that the critic taking up either of these positions 'must regard the change as a pure stylistic phenomenon and ascribe it to whatever qualities he regards as reasonable' yet the critic must do so whilst recognizing, amongst other things, 'that such qualities (a) are not the qualities that determined Beckett's choice (indeed, he may regard the latter as solely of biographical interest)' (1969: 111).

However, the rarity of these moments of free stylistic choice, as we have seen, challenge Coetzee's avowed desire to keep the 'historical Beckett' away from this thinking. It is as if, wanting to avoid the psychological etymon within the author, Coetzee's stylistic investigation keeps unearthing that very possibility. It is certainly the case that 'revisions of single words can only exceptionally be taken as indications of free stylistic habits' (1969: 114), as Coetzee puts it, but that only raises the spectre of in whom, or in what, those habits originate. When, elsewhere, Coetzee speaks of 'Beckett's rhythmic habits' (1969: 113), in what sense should one read the name Beckett? Of course, the word can be seen as a useful shorthand for the aggregate of distinct phenomena one finds with a relatively high frequency within the text or texts considered. This would be the proper approach, perhaps, of the committed stylo-statistician. Of course, Coetzee's commitment to this methodology was wavering even as he was completing his PhD. Yet, even given this scepticism about the statistical analysis of style, it is still surprising that having so assiduously kept the 'historical Beckett' barred from the door of the thesis, Coetzee finally lets him in through the window:

> There is one further consideration we should not overlook if we wish to explain the nature of *Watt*. *Watt* was begun in 1941 and completed in draft in 1944. It is not entirely strange that during these years, a statistician in Cambridge was copying *De imitatione Christi* word by word on to cards, while another statistician in a prisoner of war camp in Norway was tossing a coin and notating 'H' or 'T' one million times, that an Irishman in France should have been recording for posterity all the permutations which the nouns *door, window, fire,* and *bed* can undergo.
>
> (1969: 164)

After 164 pages of statistics, tables and computations, the thesis ends with an unapologetically historical Beckett re-emerging. A 'Beckett' for whom it matters that he is an Irishman (although that needs to be more nuanced, as perhaps Coetzee later came to realize); for whom it matters that he writes in France during the heights of the Second World War.

Coetzee writes that,

> I have tried to show that the only feature of the work we can consider purely verbal – what I have called free style – is, on the evidence of Beckett's manuscript revisions, fairly limited, and only isolable from plot, structure, and the style of its context after detailed exploration.
>
> (1969: 150–1)

The project of excavation has revealed little, but the little it has revealed cannot be easily explained away without recourse to a historical or psychological etymon. The pursuit of style has led to a reliance on the historical personage of the author exercising his free choice in his free style, albeit within strict limits.

This limited uncovering of the historical personage of the author in the case of Beckett resonates with Coetzee's processes of composition, as detailed by Attwell's examinations of his manuscripts. As Attwell notes, 'the novels begin personally and circumstantially, before being worked into fiction' (2015: 25). In what is a mirroring of the process Coetzee discerns in Beckett, whereby the historical figure is glimpsed through the excavated layers of prose styles, Coetzee's archive reveals the historical figure of the author at the beginning of the writing process. That figure may become obscured through the accretions of the writing itself, especially as the author pays all due heed to the countervoices with which he enters into dialogue and which curtail supposed 'free expression' (Coetzee 1992: 65). Nevertheless, Attwell claims, in his novels Coetzee 'challenges himself with sharply existential questions, such as, *Is there room for me, and my history, in this book? If not, what am I doing?'* (Attwell, 2015: 26). Such questions, therefore, suggest that 'Coetzee's writing is a huge existential enterprise, grounded in fictionalized autobiography' (Attwell 2015: 26). For example, during the early drafts of *Foe*, Coetzee becomes frustrated with the fictional possibilities of Susan Barton, and states: 'The only figure I can generate anything but puppetry out of is *myself*. When am I going to enter?' He further considers that in order to achieve a climactic justification of the work, this will 'entail a stripping away of all disguises, down to ME' (qtd in Attwell 2015: 153). Coetzee appears to fear that without a proper grounding within the self (which should not be taken as necessarily singular) the writing runs the risk of becoming inauthentic, that it will become a mere piece of puppetry.

This metaphor of an author as merely indulging in puppetry has its own resonance within Beckett, and on precisely this issue. In *Murphy*, the narrator (whose voice, as Coetzee points out in his thesis, is not always easily identified) boldly states: 'All the puppets in this book whinge sooner or later, except Murphy, who is not a puppet' (Beckett 2009c: 78). The narrator is drawing a distinction between the predictable, stable characters of the book, who behave within a certain set of limits, and the more unknowable figure of Murphy, upon whom all depends. In one sense, Murphy is not a puppet because the author cannot merely set him in motion knowing that, in the words of *Dream of Fair to Middling Women*, he will 'do his dope' and not behave in an unpredictable fashion (Beckett 1992: 9). In the light of Coetzee's comments, however, a further distinction might be drawn between the puppets and those characters in whom the author is authentically invested. Indeed, Beckett included many autobiographical details not only into the locations and some of the characters of the novel, but also in the figure of Murphy himself, leading James Knowlson to comment that Murphy 'undoubtedly reflects many of Beckett's own attitudes and interests ... without, of course, being Beckett himself' (1996: 214). Writing to Thomas MacGreevy in July 1936, Beckett worries that 'there seemed to me always the risk of taking him [Murphy] too seriously and separating him too sharply from the others. As it is I do not think the mistake (Aliosha mistake) has been altogether avoided' (Beckett 2009b: 350). A certain closeness between Beckett and the character he has created is apparent, as is Beckett's concern that such a closeness might imbalance the novel. If we take Coetzee's comments concerning 'stripping away of all disguises, down to ME', then it appears Beckett fears that the disguises he has employed have not been sufficiently convincing.

Nevertheless, in his thesis Coetzee is aware of the degree to which an authorial presence within the works has been subjected to a process of dispersal, deformation and disguise, especially in the matter of style. In his analysis of the sentence length and point of view in *Murphy*, Coetzee notes:

> The absence of extreme variation in sentence length and the continual shifting in point of view can be verified by inspection of any page. ... The sentences of *Murphy* possess the property that, while they are stable in terms of length, they are extremely unstable in the point of view they originate from.
>
> (1969: 72)

Coetzee again makes this a key point when he reframes the argument for publication in 1970, stating that 'for the reader to assign an authority to each sentence is ... a potentially complex task' as 'Beckett (or "Beckett") lends his authority to these sentences by printing them under his name; he also delegates this authority to his narrator, who on occasion delegates it in turn to various of the characters' (Coetzee 1992: 31).

The authority proper to the person of the author has undergone a series of dispersals, so the historical figure of 'Beckett' – with scare quotes duly appended – all but disappears within the matrix of delegations. As the thesis proceeds, Coetzee becomes more concerned with the manner in which such dispersals of authority are achieved. By placing Beckett within a line of comedic writing that parodies learned discourse – a line stretching from Sterne to Joyce – Coetzee identifies one method by which Beckett disperses his authorial person and the authority that arises from it (1969: 142). In *Watt*, Coetzee contends, parody becomes the guiding principle of the work and, more specifically, a parody of the philosophical prose of Descartes and Geulincx. To illustrate his point, Coetzee rewrites the first-person present of Descartes into the third-person past tense of *Watt*.[2] Certainly, the rhythm and syntax are strikingly similar. What is also apparent from Coetzee's thought exercise here is how the first-person present is placed under erasure. If we apply this to Beckett's dispersal of authority within the work, then the chain of disguise becomes apparent: first, parody itself acts as a displacement of authority, as Beckett takes on a voice not his own whilst Beckett's own voice is still implied by the parodic stance taken; secondly the authority and authenticity of Descartes in *The Meditations* is also challenged by the displacement into not only a parody, but also through the stylistic shift into a third-person past tense.

We are left with a question posed by Blanchot: 'Who is doing the talking in Samuel Beckett's novels?' (1959: 141). The question arises, as I believe Coetzee identifies in his thesis, through Beckett's effective dispersal of his own authorship and authority within his works, yet, like the Unnamable he may still be discernible 'howling behind [his] dissertation' (Beckett 2010: 26). Yet, as Carrol Clarkson has argued, this entails both Beckett and Coetzee within an ethical question. She wonders whether 'the giving of words to a fictional character' – which, as we have seen, is one of Beckett's methods of authorial displacement – is 'a way of *not* being morally committed' (2016: 425). The danger Clarkson identifies is summed up, with a hint of exasperation, by Peter Singer reviewing Elizabeth Costello's lectures and opinions in *The Lives of Animals*: 'But *are* they Coetzee's arguments? That's just the point – that's why I don't know how to go about responding to this so-called lecture' (qtd in Clarkson 2016: 91). In effect, Singer wants Coetzee to stand up and, as author and authority, declaim: I believe this. Such a declaration would mean undoing the disguise and displacement of authority within writing that Coetzee identifies in, and possibly learns from, Beckett. Certainly, as Clarkson puts it, the 'stylistic experimentation with versions of the self leads to questions of moral agency, to questions of accountability for, and commitment to, the ideas expressed' (2016: 425). Against this, one must balance the anti-dogmatic undermining of the power of the authorial voice that both Beckett and Coetzee achieve in their works. In both authors the 'self' or 'selves' are filtered through the displacements and disfigurements of literary style until they remain only a slight trace, albeit a crucial one.

This chapter, as indeed Coetzee's PhD before it, began with the question of whether style was separable from other aspects, such as structure, plot and, above all, attitude. We might now add ethics to that list, as the dispersal of authorial power in Beckett's style as identified by Coetzee already has important ethical implications. It is not a question of Coetzee applying an ethics that Beckett lacked, but of Coetzee recognizing the ethical implications of Beckett's style in its refusal to sustain authorial hegemony. By pursuing style in Beckett's work, it may well be that Coetzee discovered the 'secret' that style and ethical attitude are inseparable.

Notes

1 It is perhaps a little ironic that Coetzee, as so many before and since, uses the Kaun letter as a touchstone on Beckett's thinking about English prose style, when the original letter was in German and the standard translation, as used by Coetzee, was provided by Martin Esslin. For a slightly different translation, see Beckett (2009b: 518).
2 For an alternative reading of Coetzee's third-person thought experiment, see Clarkson (2009: 22–8).

References

Ackerley, C. J. (2005), *Obscure Locks, Simple Keys: The Annotated Watt*. Tallahassee, FL: Journal of Beckett Studies Books.
Ackerley, C. J. (2011), 'Style: Coetzee and Beckett'. In: T. Meghan, ed., *A Companion to the Works of J.M. Coetzee*. London: Camden House, 23–38.
Attridge, D. (2009), 'Sex, Comedy and Influence: Coetzee's Beckett'. In: E. Boehmer, R. Eagesltone and K. Iddiols, eds, *J.M. Coetzee in Context and Theory*. London: Continuum.
Attwell, D. (2015), *J.M. Coetzee and the Life of Writing*. Oxford: Oxford University Press.
Barry, E. (2006), *Beckett and Authority: The Uses of Cliché*. London: Palgrave Macmillan.
Beckett, S. (1992), *Dream of Fair to Middling Women*. Dublin: Black Cat Press.
Beckett, S. (2009a), *The Expelled, The Calmative, The End, First Love*. London: Faber and Faber.
Beckett, S. (2009b), *The Letters of Samuel Beckett 1929-1940*, ed. M. D. Feshenfeld and L. Overbeck Cambridge: Cambridge University Press.
Beckett, S. (2009c), *Murphy*. London: Faber and Faber.
Beckett, S. (2010), *The Unnamable*. London: Faber and Faber.
Blanchot, M. (1959), 'Where Now? Who Now?' *Evergreen Review*, 2. Reprinted in S. E. Gontarski, ed. (1986), *On Beckett: Essays and Criticism*. New York: Grove Press, 141–9.
Boxall, P. (2009), *Since Beckett: Contemporary Writing in the Wake of Modernism*. London: Continuum.
Clarkson, C. (2009), *J.M. Coetzee: Countervoices*. London: Palgrave Macmillan
Clarkson, C. (2016), 'Inner Worlds', *Texas Studies in Literature and Language*, 58 (4): 422–34.

Coetzee, J. M. (1969), 'The English Fiction of Samuel Beckett: An Essay in Stylistic Analysis'. PhD thesis, University of Texas.
Coetzee, J. M. (1992), *Doubling the Point: Essays and Interviews*, ed. D. Attwell. Cambridge, MA: Harvard University Press.
Coetzee, J. M. (1993), 'Homage', *The Threepenny Review*, 53: 5–7.
Hayes, P. (2010), *J.M. Coetzee and the Novel: Writing and Politics after Beckett*. Oxford: Oxford University Press.
Johnston, P. (2013), 'Presences of the Infinite: J.M. Coetzee and Mathematics'. PhD thesis, Royal Holloway, University of London.
Kellman, S. G. (1996), 'J.M. Coetzee and Samuel Beckett: The Translingual Link', *Comparative Literature Studies*, 33 (2): 161–72.
Knowlson, J. (1996), *Damned to Fame: The Life of Samuel Beckett*. London: Bloomsbury.
Ricks, C. (1993), *Beckett's Dying Words*. Oxford: Oxford University Press.
Yeoh, G. (2003), 'J.M. Coetzee and Samuel Beckett: Ethics, Truth-Telling, and Self-Deception', *Critique*, 44 (4): 331–48.

Part Five

Philosophy and the archive: Between life and truth

10

'The aura of truth': Coetzee's archive, realism and the problem of literary authority

Marc Farrant

We possess *art* lest we *perish of the truth*.

Nietzsche, *The Will to Power* (1968: 435)

1. Introduction

The problem of literary authority, posed in my title, arises as a question of origin: from where and whence does authority spring? The archive intercedes at this juncture; an imposing concept that relates authority to origin through its morphology. The Greek *arché*, meaning origin or source, denotes in the notion of the archive the origin or fount of an author's authority. In German the notion *Ursprung* captures both this notion of the origin as source and as a primal leap, a springing forth. The music of Johann Sebastian Bach often features in J. M. Coetzee's works as the epitome of such an authority, both in itself and as an exemplar of the process of artistic inspiration or springing-forth ('Bach' in German means stream or spring).[1] For Elizabeth Curren, in *Age of Iron*, the music of Bach generates a form of 'Pure spirit' (2010: 24); it is a conduit to a divine realm. The music's capacity for transcendence is mirrored by its arriving ex nihilo, as if from nowhere. For Coetzee's orthonym J. C., in *Diary of a Bad Year*, the music of Bach is a surprise gift, a moment of grace: 'It comes as a gift, unearned, unmerited, for free' (2007: 221). For J. C., authority is not simply a question of the effects of the works but from where and how those effects spring forth. As both cause and effect, Bach's authority is related to a blurring or indecipherability between these modes that is demarcated in Coetzee's works by the concept, or gift, of grace. Grace, as a self-reflexive concept, troubles the sense of an artwork's authority as arising from a linear causality, including, as we shall see, Coetzee's own works. Grace marks an authority, namely the truth-telling capacity of the work, but only insofar as this authority cannot be excavated from a single point or origin.[2] As Coetzee writes of Bach in 'What is a Classic?': 'In Bach nothing is obscure, no single step is so miraculous as to surpass imitation. Yet when the chain of sounds is realised in time, the building process ceases at a certain moment to be the mere linking of units. ... Bach thinks in music. Music thinks itself in Bach' (2002b: 10).

What happens, then, when the authority attributed to the body of work signed 'J. M. Coetzee' – an authority now enshrined at the Harry Ransom Center in Austin, Texas – is founded upon a disavowal of the possibility of authority; of unitary or singular foundations or sources of authority, literary and otherwise? What happens to the authority of those critical discourses – historical, empirical, genetic or biographical – that attribute this authority to the body of work – the archive – signed J. M. Coetzee? In this chapter I investigate the interactions between the author and the works so as to conceptualize the way in which Coetzee's writing both leads us towards the archive, to a site of origin (textual and material), and draws us away, leaving open the space of interpretation and the possibility of a *critical* reading.

In Section 2 below, I explore how Coetzee's earliest writings on Beckett, including the 1969 doctoral thesis 'The English Fiction of Samuel Beckett: An Essay in Stylistic Analysis', establish a thought of literature as irreducible to static or summative or, indeed, authoritative modalities of truth. Importantly, this understanding of literature will pose it as irreducible to either an empirical or rational approach to knowledge. This thought of literature will, over the decades, yield a *literary thinking* (a term Coetzee deploys in a 2016 essay) whose truth seems to correspond to the religious notion of grace, to an order of truth beyond verifiability or falsifiability. Indeed, Coetzee can thus be seen to inherit Beckett's late modernist interest in religion and belief as demarcating a form of knowing that exceeds truth to fact.

In Section 3 I explore how Coetzee's dynamic account of the literary work, far from dissolving writerly authority to the point of oblivion, in fact necessitates the presence of a writerly figure. Such a figure or agency becomes the focus of the self-reflexive and metafictional elements of the later fictions. The gestating affective-temporal logic of creativity that emerges in Coetzee's thesis is thematized in the second of the fictionalized memoirs, *Youth*, and specifically in relation to the author's coming into being as an author, as a writer of fictions. Through a brief discussion of the writings of Walter Benjamin, I explore how the young John's struggle with creating a realistic portrait in his writing, a struggle to attain what is termed 'the aura of truth' (2002a: 138), encapsulates how the difficulty of reducing the work of literature to either an empirical or rational system nonetheless attests to a modality of truth that refuses romantic or religious mystification and remains historically and ethically embedded.

In Section 4 I explore how the self-reflexivity of Coetzee's works compounds a critique of realism in the name of what might be considered a truer reality. The notion and trope of realism occurs across the record of Coetzee's teaching career, and the numerous materials housed in Coetzee's archive bear witness to the pivotal role of realism with regard to the way Coetzee conceives of the relation between literature and philosophy. I then turn to Coetzee's *The Childhood of Jesus* to illustrate how a fundamental tension between the notions of reality and truth dissimulates a literary thinking that ties the authority of grace to the irony of a *critically* motivated cynicism. Finally, I return to how the archive, both as source and framework, helps to elucidate the fundamental truths of Coetzee's writing.

2. From writer to work

In the decades that follow Coetzee's doctoral thesis there emerges in his commentary on writing a logic of simultaneous activity and passivity. For Coetzee, writing is both a task, an activity that one undertakes, and a duty or vocation that calls the author into being. For instance, in *Doubling the Point* this duality is examined explicitly in relation to life writing: for Coetzee writing involves a 'push into the future ... and a resistance' which is in part psychic and in part 'an automatism built into language' (1992: 18). In the short essay 'Thematizing' the process of writing emerges through 'a certain back-and-forth motion' (1993: 289); a giving of oneself over to the process of writing before, then interrogating where the writing has taken you (a retrospective activity termed 'thematizing'). As Carrol Clarkson argues, this non-linear dynamic is described repeatedly: 'Throughout his critical reflections, Coetzee is consistent in his assertions about not quite knowing what it is that he wanted to say in advance – meaning emerges in retrospect, once he has been through the experience of writing' (2009: 44). In this section I explore how Coetzee's experience of writing follows from an account of reading that is first outlined in his investigation into various truth-procedures through which literary meaning is established in his doctoral thesis. More specifically, I explore how this logic of sumultaenous activity and passivity follows from an investigation into Beckett's *Watt* as irreducible to summative or extractive truth-claims.

The literary-critical truth-procedure under scrutiny in Coetzee's thesis is that of stylostatistics, a statistical branch of stylistic analysis that Coetzee perceives to be beset by a fallacious underlying premise: that one can account for the qualitative aspects of a literary text using quantitative methods. The underlying positivism of this structuralist approach assumes a quantifiable difference or deviation between everyday language and literary language (which constitutes its 'style'). It presupposes a static, objective and immutable context or domain of the literary per se. For Coetzee, this presupposition fails to account for a further difference between figurative and literal language and is hence bedevilled by an unacknowledged 'metaphor of linearity' which, as Coetzee elucidates, conceives 'of language as a one-dimensional stream extending in time' (1969: 160). This is linked to a conception of the mind (of the reader or writer, for instance) 'as a computer with an input system which reads linear strips of coded information' (160).[3] Coetzee's thesis critiques this axiomatic model of consciousness by masterfully demonstrating how Beckett's novel *Watt* pre-empts his own quantitative stylistic methodology. This is achieved by drawing a parallel between the warped rationality of the infinity of logical permutations that constitute the consciousness of Beckett's eponymous protagonist, Watt, and the fundamentally tautologous nature of any systematic or quantitative account of literature. As Coetzee argues, discussing an episode in the novel where Watt ponders the meaning of Erskine continually running up and down the stairs all day in Mr Knott's house: 'Watt's original question, Why does Erskine run up and down stairs?, grows six branches [and] terminates in the solipsism that is one of Watt's answers to the infinities of logic: fish that need to rise and fall exist because my naming of them calls them into existence' (81). The 'logical comedy' of the episode, and the novel, rests on a 'bland disregard' for the criterion of simplicity. Accordingly, Watt's consciousness becomes a model of the linear code-reading computer 'mind' of stylostatistics, since by seeking to answer an empirical question through logical analysis, Watt ignores the very experience – the intrusion of external and sensory stimuli – upon which the question is predicated.

Coetzee's appeal to Watt's tautologous reasoning, as an analogy for stylostatistics, and the self-affirming process that seeks to define style as a categorically isolable use of language, is devastating. Yet the thesis also invites us to ask whether the missing empirical link (which Coetzee refers to as the 'historical Samuel Beckett' (1969: 3)), once added to the analysis, is enough to determine the origin of a work's style or distinctive literariness. Indeed, Coetzee insists throughout that extra-textual contexts are insufficient when seeking to account for the logical comedy of the novel, specifically the literary effect described by Coetzee as a 'rhythm of doubt' (1969: 95). Reinstalling the empirical or causal element might solve Watt's faulty reasoning, but such a method in literary-critical terms (taking account of the author) does not translate into an adequate account of literary meaning (precisely because, in this instance, the literary is bound up to the *failure* of Watt's thinking).

How, one might ask, does this discussion intersect with the question of the archive and the disciplinary authority granted to empirical research? The recent 'archival turn' in Beckett Studies serves as a good comparative example to explore this putative authority.[4] As S. E. Wilmer outlines, this archival turn 'focuses on the social and historical circumstances of Beckett's life and work and emphasises genetic criticism' (2012: 586). The unearthing of what Sam Gontarski terms the 'grey canon' (2006: 143) – a vast number of hitherto unexplored archival and manuscript materials – has led to substantial increase in available data for scholars. The subsequent rise of geneticist approaches, and activities of preservation, cataloguing and 'text mining', map neatly onto an older empiricist drive to historical and biographical verification.

In a laudable yet atypical spirit of methodological self-reflection, Matthew Feldman has sought to formalize this renewed historical approach to Beckett's works by drawing on Karl Popper's theory of 'falsifiability' (2010: 164). This deductive approach to evidence aims to engender a critical self-awareness by 'seek[ing] arguments able to be disproved rather than simply finding verification in accordance with one's preferred readings, or outlook, or politics' (2010: 165). The question is, as Feldman asks, does a falsifiable approach 'to the task of generating empirical knowledge of a given subject have any place in the study of literature?' (2010: 165). In Gavid Dowd's response to Feldman he makes clear that the falsifiable-deductive approach condemns theoretical readings to mere 'fanciful prosthetic extension[s] of the critic's hermeneutic imagination' (2008: 379) precisely because they exceed an archival understanding of what constitutes textual evidence. As Dowd summarizes, 'the temporal mode underpinning Feldman's position is such that only direction [is] *backwards* to Beckett's notes [and] sources' (384). This conflation of archival truth and literary meaning betrays a more promising merging of horizons whereby, as Dowd argues, literary obscurity isn't simply dispelled by an 'illuminating criticism' (385) but rather contaminates and complicates the latter.

Ultimately, Coetzee's thesis suggests that neither the axiomatic nor the empirical can guarantee a falsifiable account of literary style or meaning, and that *Watt* makes a mockery of any attempt to transmute its 'message' into the propositional terms of a linear thesis of cause and effect (whether or not the cause is imputed to be language or the author or some other primal scene). In the conclusion these observations are expanded: literary meaning in general, Coetzee argues, is constituted through an 'internal economy' (1969: 151) of shifting and divisible contexts. As he argues: 'our experience of a work is more than the sum of a number of experiences of small contexts' (161). Such contexts circumscribe meaning, but as they include the temporally and spatially embedded dynamics of reading and writing, as well as that of language itself, they are themselves inexhaustible (or better, insofar as no single context suffices, they are inherently divisible). A linear model of scientific causality, as satirized in *Watt* and critiqued by Coetzee, thus fallaciously claims to transpose the unambiguous truths of mathematics into the ambiguous realm of language and literary meaning.

An empirical account of the literary work claims precisely the opposite: to transpose the ambiguous realm of literary meaning (as inherently hermeneutic) into the supposedly unambiguous and objective realm of historical or biographical context. Yet whereas the rational account – via the analysis of rhetorical or stylistic 'data' – excludes the author, the 'historical Beckett', an empirical account by virtue of the same structural linearity runs the risk of excluding that which remains *after* the *archic* process of historical interrogation (as the search for singular origins and explanations). As Coetzee argues of Kafka:

> What is left of Franz Kafka after the alienation of Josef K has been explained in terms of Kafka's marginality? What is life of Michael K after he has been explained in terms of my marginality in Africa? Is it not what is left *after* that interrogation that should interest us, not what the interrogation reveals? Is it not what Kafka does *not* speak, refuses to speak, under that interrogation, that will continue to fuel our desire for him (I hope forever)?
>
> (1992: 199–200)

In other words, Coetzee indicates that what interests us as readers – and I would add, as readers of literature specifically – is what cannot be summatively presented or positively identified. The rational-scientific approach to stylistic analysis purports to account for this *after*, that aspect of the work which precisely signals literariness by deviating from other forms (narrative history, for example), but it fails to do so by virtue of aping the deductive approach of its opposite methodology; of aping the *backwards* 'excavatory reason' (Dowd 2008: 384) of empirical analysis. Like the empirical-archival method, Coetzee's rational-scientific approach in the thesis is found to rely upon a linear mode of causality that condemns meaning to a static point in time. Both do so by excluding the position of the reader as the site of both hermeneutic and affective mediation, a position Coetzee, following Barthes, takes to be generative of the work itself and therefore comes as much before as after. Below I show how this same paradoxical logic is at work in Coetzee's account of the writer, and how we might use Coetzee's economic rather than linear model of literature to rethink an approach to the archive via a productive contamination of before *and* after.

3. From work to writer

The denial of a singular authority or (historical) origin appears to license relativism, yet in both the thesis and in later commentaries Coetzee nonetheless insists on upholding an idea of the materiality of the work. In this section I explore how for Coetzee the material character of literary works resists the reduction of language to its putative status as a bearer of disembodied or abstract ideas. The authority of the literary work is, therefore, derived on its own terms and is inextricable from its material embeddedness. Nonetheless such an embeddedness is not to be confused with a sovereign conception of materiality, as per the empirical-archival method of searching backwards for the historical author as *definitive* foundation or source. What emerges instead is a conception of the authority of the literary author as defined by a lack of authority (a lack which, we might add, can only be accounted for in a modality of literary criticism that no longer asserts definitive claims). This lack is established by the self-reflexivity of Coetzee's fictions (explored further in the next section) insofar as they implicate the author-as-origin within the works themselves. Although this is obvious in Coetzee's use of avatars and in the fictionalized memoirs, this idea pervades the fictions more generally. As a result, the works involve a certain complicity between the functions of author and reader.[5]

Coetzee addresses the authority of the author in the doctoral thesis through the seemingly arcane issue of psycho-linguistic correlation. As the thesis puts it: 'In what sense can we speak of language imitating or mirroring thought?' (1969: 36). If one assumes a direct correlation then what can be analyzed on the textual surface (lexical features and syntactical structures) can be directly attributed to a single origin or source: the writer's mind. Coetzee is thoroughly dismissive of such a hermeneutic operation. Unless the 'focus … is biographical', Coetzee argues, the suggestion that there can be a direct correlation between thought and syntax is simply tautologous: 'The habits of a writer's mind can only be a metaphor for habits (or patterns) of the text' (159). He then adds: 'The question is of course thrown open again if instead of the writer we speak of a fictionalized intelligence in the text' (159). This notion of a fictionalized intelligence not only disavows the utility but also the very *possibility* of a biographical approach. Earlier, in a discussion of Leo Spitzer's 1928 study of Marcel Proust, Coetzee argues that even if one's focus of study is the biographical author, the attempt to unearth 'the movements of his soul' – regardless of whether or not one then attributes the meaning of the work to these movements – is rendered flawed by the fact that, as Coetzee argues, 'our only approach to the preverbal mental activity [i.e. the soul] that results in language is through that language itself' (87). In other words, even if Proust were alive his account of his 'movements' would be yet another linguistic fabrication or fiction.

It is, of course, not very far to go from here – the assertion that our access to a pre-linguistic consciousness is inhibited because it is only through language that such an access is made possible – to the assertion that such an account of pre-linguistic consciousness is itself entirely fallacious and must also comprise of linguistic structures. This leap would take us from a discussion of *Watt* to the interminable monologue of Beckett's *The Unnamable*; from the structuralist methodologies that constitute

Coetzee's focus in the thesis to the post-structuralist readings of Beckett's work that followed in subsequent decades. It is not in the interests of this chapter to make this leap, to throw the baby out with the bath water and to deny the existence of an authorial subject who exists outside the text, but rather to demonstrate how such a subject is irrelevant to an assessment of a literary work qua literary work. To do so does not entail disregarding the notion of authorship tout court, however, nor does it mean disregarding the notion of the material archive. Following the contours of Coetzee's idea of a 'fictionalized intelligence' within a text, I rather seek to privilege a notion of the authorial subject as within, rather than outside, a literary work.

In the 2015 collaborative volume *The Good Story*, Coetzee, discussing W. G. Sebald's novel *Austerlitz*, writes: 'My guess is that psychoanalysis cannot (in the view of the writer) offer aid because psychoanalysis is ahistorical (I must add that I have no knowledge of what Sebald the man thought of psychoanalysis)' (2015: 188). It is with this distinction between an actual biographical person who happens to write fiction, and the idea of an author figure whose contours a reader must infer from the work itself, that we can begin to bridge the gap from the question of authorial authority to that of literary authority. This distinction is of course fundamental to the three fictionalized memoirs – or autre-biographies – *Boyhood*, *Youth* and *Summertime*. The memoirs each fictionalize their autobiographical subject using third-person narration. This estranges the narrating consciousness from the narrated consciousness. Through the genre of life-writing, Coetzee dramatizes the fundamental estrangement of the self through writing that is typical of his critical commentaries. These works complicate our access to a sense of the material or living man behind the writing by highlighting how our access cannot be separated from the medium, from the writing of the man. This is hyperbolized in *Summertime*, especially, where the autobiographical subject is already dead, literally immaterial, and our only access lies through archival notes and interview transcripts whose substitute materiality both grants and obscures our vision. The memoirs thus make the disruption and disaggregation of the truth-procedures of historical or biographical verifiability – disparaged in *Doubling the Point* as mere 'truth to fact' (1992: 17) – integral to the truth-content of their own status as literary works.

In *Youth* what constitutes the authority of the literary work is explicitly thematized. *Youth* covers the period of Coetzee's time in London as a computer programmer just prior to embarking on his graduate study of Beckett's English fictions. *Youth* portrays the aesthetic and sentimental education of its author. Towards the end, John is palpably discontented with the rational or binary logic of his profession: 'Death to reason, death to talk!' (2002a: 164). Choosing instead to embark on the perilous enterprise of literary fiction, John worries he might not possess the capacity to render what he terms 'the aura of truth' (2002a: 138). For this, the methods of verisimilitude will not suffice: 'The creak of the grease-pot, the trilling of the cicadas – those he is confident he can bring off' (138). Here Coetzee's scepticism towards positivist science is seen as congruent with a growing disdain for realism. Instead, the truth of the literary work – the truth of the work as literature – is constituted enigmatically as an aura.

For Walter Benjamin, the aura accounts for the specificity and authority of the art work itself; for an immaterial essence lost through the process of technological reproduction. Reproduction jeopardizes what Benjamin terms the 'historical testimony' (1999: 215) of the work of art that constitutes its authenticity.[6] However, by retrospectively framing the account of auratic authority through Benjamin's discussion of the *Ursprung* or origin in his doctoral thesis, *The Origin of German Tragic Drama*, it is possible to deduce a distinctly anti-romantic conception of the truth of the aura and thus, I argue, of Coetzee's sense of the aura of truth. For Benjamin, the origin or *Ursprung* does not signify a unique or unequivocal instance of genesis but rather a process of historical becoming in which the singular and repeatable are 'conditioned by one another in all essentials' (1998: 46). That is, 'the authentic – the hallmark of origin in phenomena – is the object of discovery, a discovery which is connected in a unique way with the process of recognition' (46). This triangulation of authenticity, originality and authority situates the artwork in a dynamic process (which Benjamin terms history) analogous to Coetzee's account of the economic relation of the activity and passivity of the writer/reader. The truth-content of a work is thus as much related to our reading of it as any innate property or feature. If 'grace' marks Coetzee's literary thinking of this dynamic, which imperils the rationalist premise of linear causality that underpins biographical or historicist criticism, then Benjamin's account of the *Ursprung* also helps to dispel a Romantic myth of genius, of unsullied or divine originality, that we might infer from a religious register that occurs throughout Coetzee's later works (notably the recent quasi-allegorical *The Childhood of Jesus*, discussed below).

In *Youth* this dual renunciation – of both historicist 'truth to fact' and divine originality – is conducted through the memoir's staging of John's aesthetic education. Accordingly, the displacement of the autobiographical subject – through the use of a third-person narrative voice – is redoubled in the context of John's failure to reach the transcendental heights of his literary forbears; a failure that is dissimulated through a romantic striving (*Sehnsucht*) for idealized love: 'Does an artist's life entail sleeping with anyone and everyone, in the name of life?' (2002a: 30). Thus *Youth* stages Nietzsche's comment – 'we possess *art* lest we *perish of the truth*' (1968: 435) – in two senses: not only does art stand in opposition to techno-scientific positivism, but the alternative truth of art cannot be simply sublimated or idealized under the Romantic category of the beautiful. As Nietzsche adds: 'Truth is ugly' (435).

4. A truer realism

Coetzee's staging of the figure of the author is integral to how the literary works question their own authority. This is addressed directly in *Diary of a Bad Year* when J. C. quotes Kierkegaard on authority: '*Learn to speak without authority*, says Kierkegaard. By copying Kierkegaard's words here, I make Kierkegaard into an authority. Authority cannot be taught, cannot be learned. The paradox is a true one' (2007: 151). In this section I explore this paradox, which speaks to how Coetzee's metafictional interrogation of authority both displaces the author (as origin) and yet also concedes the ineluctability of a work's authoredness. This interrogation is linked to a project of demarcating a *truer realism*; a realism beyond mere verisimilitude. By hinting towards a truer sense of the real as that which emerges paradoxically through a critique or realism, Coetzee follows in Beckett's late modernist footsteps. Indeed, it is through a discussion of Beckett in *Doubling the Point* where realism is placed under suspicion as 'illusionism' (1992: 27). Although Coetzee turns away from Beckett's strategy of anti-illusionism (a strategy of self-citation or repetitive auto-destruction that he reads in the later prose), there remains a powerful – even abyssal – strand of self-reflection and self-reflexivity in Coetzee's own writings. In this section I seek to establish the link between Coetzee's insistence on self-reflexivity, as that which would appear to undermine arriving at certain truth, and the notion of grace as a kind of truth that attests to the abyssal nature of the literary itself.

The Cretan liar paradox, which Mark Currie situates at the heart of any definition of metafiction, articulates how 'there is something logically chaotic or aporetic about a discourse that refers to itself' (2010: 171). Something of this logical chaos works its way into Coetzee's thinking in *Doubling the Point* when he discusses he influences in *Waiting for the Barbarians*. Stating that a self-awareness about one's influence is problematic for a storyteller (who needs to work free of 'introversions and doubts'), Coetzee then adds: 'You catch me, of course, in self-contradiction. If I don't want to look into myself, claiming that isn't good for my novel-writing what am I doing conducting this interview, and what sort of autobiographer am I? ... I am clearly descending into a Cretan Liar position from which there will be no escape' (1992: 105). It is precisely this position, however, that the reader of Coetzee's fictions is obliged to adopt. For instance, as when the fictional writer Elizabeth Costello declares in an academic lecture: 'writers teach us more than they are aware of' ([2003] 2004: 97). Just as the character Costello is herself in a state of performative contradiction, making a discursive claim about the non-discursive capacities of poetry to teach us an ethical humility towards animals, the reader cannot help but feel similarly suspicious of the authorial Coetzee standing behind these words. If this is an authorial aside, aimed at poking fun of Costello's compromised position, how are we to also read it as a clear example of another author or authority lying behind Costello given that the statement itself indicates a lack of mastery?

This abyssal logic manifests abundantly in Coetzee's third fictionalized memoir, *Summertime*. Written as a series of interviews conducted by a biographer, Mr Vincent, after the death of John Coetzee, Martin – a former colleague of John's – recalls how Coetzee consistently exhibited 'a reluctance to probe the sources of his inspiration, as if being too self-aware might cripple him' (2009: 213). The paradox Coetzee establishes asks us this: how do we as readers reconcile the problem of self-awareness when self-awareness here appears ironically as an awareness of one's apparent lack of self-awareness? John's purported romantic belief in the 'creative force of unconscious processes' (213) can thus be read neither literally nor wholly ironically, since the position of the ironist or critic is folded back within the textual machinations.

In Coetzee's *The Childhood of Jesus*, this abyssal logic is evoked at the level of the logical chaos that marks the narrative whole. By conjuring a quasi-allegorical world without a clear allegorical referent (no Jesus figure ever arrives), these novels locate the reader in a perpetual crisis of meaning. This is exacerbated by the religious register deployed throughout and by how the novel makes discussions about meaning into part of its own content, notably the distinction between what is real and what is true with regard to the young Jesus-like character, David. Simón, David's self-elected guardian, tells another character: 'You say we are not his real mother and his real father. What exactly do you mean by real? Surely there is such a thing as overvaluing the biological' (207). This sense of there being something more real than *the* real is also marked by the unspecified geographic and historical narrative world. However, as Derek Attridge argues, if *The Childhood of Jesus* indeed represents 'Coetzee's first truly post-South Africa novel' (2018: 268), then the disengagement from reality once again invites the kind of political critique that Coetzee's works have long since weathered.

Indeed, such charges have been levelled repeatedly against Coetzee, and the topic of realism in relation to politics is often at the forefront of Coetzee's discussions of other South African writers, notably Nadine Gordimer and her indebtedness to the Marxist critic Georg Lukács. Coetzee's aversion to art's secondary status as subordinate to a political agenda thus helps explain the strong aversion to realism that is evidenced across the archival notebooks. During the writing of *Life & Times of Michael K*, Coetzee notes in an entry: 'What I need is a liberation from verisimilitude!' (HRC, CP, 33.5: 2-3-81). Similarly, in the archived notebooks for *Foe* Coetzee expands on a 'great sense of liberation when you lose yourself from realism and let language take over (the best of my own writing comes from that – parts of ITH, smaller parts of WFB, MK)' (HRC, CP, 33.6: 18-3-84). It is through Coetzee's voluminous teaching materials, however, that a more philosophical approach to realism as illusionism can be traced, and notably in the context of a key intertextual reference in the Jesus fictions, namely Miguel de Cervantes's *Don Quixote*.

In 1982 Coetzee gave a talk to the Philosophical Society at the University of Cape Town entitled 'Realism in the Novel'. The lecture focuses on *Don Quixote* and the theme of disillusionment. Coetzee starts from the premise that 'the state of affairs with which we have to live is therefore that the term realist has been hijacked by and for a particular kind of novel, the novel of the empirical' (HRC, CP, 114.12: n.d.). Contrary to this empiricist impulse, Coetzee outlines how Cervantes's depiction of romantic disillusionment situates a self-reflexive awareness at the heart of the realist novel from its very inception. This insight is extended into his teaching engagements abroad, and in 1984 Coetzee taught 'Realism in the Novel' at Buffalo and in 1986 'Studies in Realism' at Johns Hopkins. Coetzee writes in his course description that, alongside texts often designated realist, students 'will also read … four works which include in themselves reflections on the problematics of realism' (HRC, CP, 115.1: 1986), including *Don Quixote*.

Ten years later, Coetzee returned to teaching realism at Chicago in 1996 with a revamped course (with Flaubert and Turgenev at it centre) but again *Don Quixote* was an important text. Building upon the arguments set forth in the 1982 lecture, especially its philosophical context and the 'fundamentally political question' of 'why is it better to live in terms of the possible than in terms of the impossible?' (HRC, CP, 114.12: 1982), Coetzee is once again keen to sidestep the obvious proto-postmodernist appeal to textuality and relativism. In his seminar notes Coetzee's discussion of the 'satiric genealogy behind empiricist presentation' (HRC, CP, 114.11: 1996) leads to the insight that Cervantes marks a shift in the tradition of the mimetic arts. Realist detail is used to both mock the protagonist (the example of such mocking realism is provided in the earlier lecture in relation to the movements of the Don's bowels, which echoes the metaphysics of poo in *The Childhood of Jesus*) but also emerges for the first time as a value in itself. Derived from the triumph of Renaissance physics and psychology, the literary work enters an age of profound disenchantment: 'one of the master themes of realism is disenchantment or disillusionment or demystification. Since the essence of fiction has to be fantasy, it is a theme which is in a sense counter to the movement of fiction itself' (HRC, CP, 114.11: 1996). In the 1982 lecture this is said to give rise to realist mode of fiction 'that looks back on itself with some kind of consciousness of its own motives' (HRC, CP, 114.12: 1982). In the earlier lecture Coetzee appears as a defender of fantasy. However, the later 1996 course reveals the nuance in Coetzee's position. Rather than take up the 'highly textual world' of the novel as a precursor to 'postmodern fiction' (HRC, CP, 114.11: 1996), the latter teaching materials helps reveal how, rather than disregarding the empirical in the name of a radical subjectivism, Coetzee is instead concerned with refusing to equate empirical reality with the totality of reality itself.

Both the teaching materials of the 1980s and 1990s exemplify Coetzee's trademark conjunction of sparse logic and lyrical fantasy. The self-reflexivity attributed to Cervantes's *Don Quixote*, as that which guards against realism as a mode of merely debunking forms of naïve idealism, formally anticipates the self-reflexivity of *The Childhood of Jesus*. Similarly, the highly textual world of novel (the young David learns to read using *An Illustrated Children's Don Quixote*) establishes a kind of truth that is neither simply fantastical nor forgoes material reality in adherence to a ludic postmodern 'doctrine of the arbitrariness of the signifier' (2013: 78).

In *The Childhood of Jesus* it is David who embodies the position of the radical subjectivist or idealist tilting at windmills. David refuses to adhere to the social consensus that orders reality and asserts instead his own private language. Much as Coetzee describes the Don's sidekick Sancho, the characters in *The Childhood of Jesus* are all driven to David like parasites to a host and, indeed, become enthralled by the boy's illusionism (which is precisely what signals him as potentially Christ-like). Simón, in particular, tries to encourage David to see the book as a work of fiction and not as a real record of what happened:

> 'David,' he says, '*Don Quixote* is an unusual book. To the lady in the library who lent it to us it looks like a simple book for children, but in truth it isn't simple at all. It presents the world to us through two pairs of eyes, Don Quixote's eyes and Sancho's eyes. To Don Quixote, it is a giant he is fighting. To Sancho, it is a windmill. Most of us – not you, perhaps, but most of us nevertheless – will agree with Sancho that it is a windmill. That includes the artist who drew a picture of a windmill. But it also includes the man who wrote the book.'
> 'Who wrote the book?'
> 'A man named Benengeli.' (154)

By invoking the name Benengeli, the name the narrator of Cervantes's original text gives to the Arabian historiographer Cid Hamet Ben Engeli (from whom he has acquired the manuscript of the tale he is transcribing), *The Childhood of Jesus* situates the problem of authorship directly into its own complex intertextual, abyssal and self-reflexive framework. Although Simón is ostensibly attuned to the irony of the narration, which enables us to see the world 'through two pairs of eyes', the attribution of authorship to 'Benengeli' signals that he is taking the narrator at face value (just as David takes the Don's perspective at face value). As Stephen Mulhall argues, the Platonic resonances behind the allusions to Cervantes (the opposition between appearances and reality) illustrate how Coetzee's use of the intertextual framework reveals how 'one can identify some given claim or register of a text as ironic only if one is willing to regard some other claim or register as literal' (2017: 29). That by choosing either windmills or giants 'requires investing in a reality with which fantasy can be contrasted' (29). The abyssal textual logic of *The Childhood of Jesus*, however, which refuses to verify or repudiate the divinity of its young protagonist, establishes a literary thinking that can be read neither wholly literally nor ironically or, better, where irony or the possibility of fiction is itself aligned with a certain truth.

Indeed, David's appeal to the other characters, and Simón's vehement defence of the child, involves a certain faith in the fantastical that exceeds a logic of debunking. By further appealing to a theological framework and religious register that recalls an earlier reckoning with the notion of grace, *The Childhood of Jesus* asks us to question whether it is in fact useful to ask of a fantasy whether or not it is *literally* true. Instead the fantastical emerges as significant, or even true, beyond its relation to literal or empirical reality. Perhaps fantasy is important not because of what it is, or what it claims, but because of what it *does*, and how it might spur or motivate action, ethical or otherwise.

Conclusion

By means of a conclusion it is worth returning to the questions of Coetzee's thesis, the notion of the archive and the context of contemporary critical approaches to literature. In this light, and with regard to the themes of realism and self-reflexivity that emerge across the oeuvre, Coetzee's Jesus fictions become exemplary. The recent turn away from notions of critique and the 'hermeneutics of suspicion' (Felski 2008: 1) is thus anticipated by Coetzee's works, both critical and creative. The Jesus novels pre-empt and distort any attempt to expose their hidden depth, to separate what Coetzee terms the vehicle from the message.[7] However, in the second novel, *The Schooldays of Jesus*, the murder of Ana Magdalena (David's adored teacher) can be seen to epitomize the corollary that a disavowal of depth is not tantamount to a naïve belief in the surface. In an age of disillusionment, Coetzee's writings indicate that faith in the fantastical should not be a blind faith; there can be no pure fantasy, no transcendental escape from a finite world that would not entail the risk of sacrifice.[8] The final work in the trilogy, *The Death of Jesus*, similarly epitomizes the impossibility of pure fantasy or transcendental escape. The question that this work leaves unresolved concerns reconciling the seeming profundity of David's life (and death) in a world marked by the absence of profundity. This question echoes the question of literature or literary form that runs throughout Coetzee's writing career: how are we to be responsive to the auratic truth of literature without reducing the work to a simple point of origin or *arché*, of 'truth to fact', nor reducing the aura to a romantic or religious mystification. How does one account for both the material and immaterial essence, the surface and depth, of a literary work simultaneously?

Such a question, which lies latent within Coetzee's earliest writings, seems vital to how we approach the archive both as material entity, a fixed origin, and as a dynamic (and ever-expanding) field of embedded meaning. The answer perhaps lies in developing a mode of reading which corresponds to Coetzee's own literary thinking. Such a literary thinking is derived from the observation that Coetzee's self-reflexivity, the introspective and questioning nature of the writing, does not simply divorce the works from their material or historical origins but rather implicates these origins in the works themselves. By tracing the consequences of the false equation between the quantitative and qualitative methodologies first outlined in Coetzee's thesis, we have seen how the anti-systematic nature of literary meaning results in a dynamic conception of the literary work between reading and writing, passivity and activity. Indeed, if for Coetzee writing is always a case of reading, of forgoing ultimate mastery, it follows that reading is always a form of writing, an engaged activity attentive not only to the stated or literal content of a work but also to its performances. We might term such a reading a *critical* reading; a mode of engagement responsive to a literary thinking. Coetzee describes such a thinking as 'a matter of awakening of the countervoices in oneself' (1992: 65); of stepping down from the governing position, of opening onto a critical position in the sense defined by Michel Foucault when he writes: '[Critique] is the art of not being governed' (1997: 29). Such a literary practice is thus aligned to the notion of truth not despite but *because* of its unavailability. At the end of his 1987 Jerusalem Prize speech (reprinted in *Doubling the Point*), the ethico-political urgency of refusing what Nietzsche terms the 'perspective which makes what is closest at hand and most vulgar appear as if it were ... reality itself' (1974: 133) is signalled by Coetzee in pithy terms: 'We have art, said Nietzsche, so that we may not die of the truth. In South Africa there is now too much truth for art to hold, truth by the bucketful, truth that overwhelms and swamps every act of the imagination' (1992: 99). It is this sense of the overwhelming that spurs Coetzee's imaginative acts to this day and marks the imperative of a truer realism.

Notes

1 The name is transliterated in the recent *The Schooldays of Jesus* to Juan Sebastian Arroyo, who is the head of the Academy of Dance in the fictional Estrella.
2 As Coetzee writes, grace – as opposed to cynicism – constitutes the 'condition in which truth can be told clearly, without blindness' (1992: 392).
3 Coetzee's early work in the field of the nascent Digital Humanities pre-empts the pitfalls of what Tom Eyers has termed the 'prodigious growth of neo-positivist methodologies' (2017: 34) in the contemporary field – that is, a tendency to elide the formal and epistemological peculiarities of the literary text in favour of an empiricist certainty. The model of scientific rationality underpinning this digital revolution in the humanities is, Eyers argues, 'ahistorical and Anglo-centric' (37).
4 Indeed, an early scholar of this archival turn is arguably Coetzee himself. In the 1972 essay (which derives from the thesis), 'The Manuscript Revisions of Beckett's Watt',

Coetzee complements his quantitative approach with a genetic investigation of the 'compositional biography of Watt' (1992: 39). The experience of the chaos of Beckett's manuscripts might in part explain the meticulous dating Coetzee later undertakes in his own archive.

5   Alexandra Effe observes the potentially liberating result of this complicity at the end of her study on Coetzee and metalepsis: 'Metaleptic self-reflexivity [a blurring of the narrative levels that separate narrator, author and reader], in Coetzee's works, constitutes an ethics of writing. … This theoretical dimension of metalepsis also constitutes its ethical dimension of renouncing authority and of emancipating the reader as an active participant in the creation of storyworlds and in the deliberation of ethical questions' (2017: 159).

6   It is interesting to note that, in an essay on Benjamin collected in *Inner Workings*, Coetzee is disparaging of the idea of aura as it seems to betray Benjamin's materialism. On Benjamin's philosophy of language Coetzee further writes: 'How a symbolist conception of language could ever be reconciled with Benjamin's later historical materialism is not clear' (2008: 52). However, it is by turning to a theological or mystical register that I argue one finds an analogous process in both Benjamin and Coetzee. This process transforms, rather than transcends, the finite or material as ground for knowledge or truth. This argument partly concerns Coetzee's relation to the postsecular (see Woessner 2017) and exceeds the confines of this chapter.

7   As Coetzee writes in 'The Novel Today': 'There is no addition in stories. They are not made of one thing plus another thing, message plus vehicle, substructure plus superstructure. On the keyboard on which they are written, the plus key does not work. There is always a difference; and the difference is not a part, the part left behind after the subtraction. The minus key does not work either: the difference is everything' (1988: 296).

8   I discuss the crucial relation between sacrifice and finitude in a *Journal of Modern Literature* article (see Farrant 2019).

References

Attridge, D. (2018), 'Character and Counterfocalization: Coetzee and the Kafka Lineage'. In: Tim Mehigan and Christian Moser, eds, *The Intellectual Landscape in the Works of J.M. Coetzee*. New York: Camden House, 254–73.

Benjamin, W. (1998), *The Origin of German Tragic Drama*, trans. John Osborne. London: Verso.

Benjamin, W. (1999), 'The Work of Art in the Age of Mechanical Reproduction', trans. Harry Zorn, in *Illuminations*. London: Pimlico, 211–44.

Clarkson, Carrol (2009), *J. M. Coetzee: Countervoices*. Basingstoke: Palgrave Macmillan.

Coetzee, J. M. 'J.M. Coetzee Papers'. Austin, TX: Harry Ransom Center.

Coetzee, J. M. (1969), 'The English Fiction of Samuel Beckett: An Essay in Stylistic Analysis'. PhD thesis, University of Texas.

Coetzee, J. M. (1988), 'The Novel Today', *Upstream*, 6 (1): 2–5.

Coetzee, J. M. ([1990] 2010), *Age of Iron*. London: Penguin.

Coetzee, J. M. (1992), *Doubling the Point: Essays and Interviews*, ed. David Attwell. Cambridge, MA: Harvard University Press.

Coetzee, J. M. (1993), 'Thematizing'. In: W. Sollors, ed., *The Return of Thematic Criticism*. Cambridge, MA: Harvard University Press, 289.
Coetzee, J. M. (2002a), *Youth*. London: Vintage.
Coetzee, J. M. (2002b), 'What Is a Classic? A Lecture'. In: *Stranger Shores: Essays 1986-1999*. London: Vintage, 1-19.
Coetzee, J. M. ([2003] 2004), *Elizabeth Costello*. London: Vintage.
Coetzee, J. M. (2007), *Diary of a Bad Year*. London: Harvill Secker.
Coetzee, J. M. (2008), *Inner Workings: Essays 2000-2005*. London: Vintage.
Coetzee, J. M. (2009), *Summertime*. London: Harvill Secker.
Coetzee, J. M. (2013), *The Childhood of Jesus*. London: Harvill Secker.
Coetzee, J. M. (2016), 'On Literary Thinking', *Textual Practice*, 30 (7): 1151-2.
Coetzee, J. M., and Paul Auster (2013), *Here and Now: Letters 2008-2011*. London: Harvill Secker.
Coetzee, J. M., and Arabella Kurtz (2015), *The Good Story: Exchanges on Truth, Fiction and Psychotherapy*. London: Harvill Secker.
Currie, Mark (2010), *Postmodern Narrative Theory*, 2nd edn. Basingstoke: Palgrave Macmillan.
Dowd, Gavin (2008), 'Prolegomena to a Critique of Excavatory Reason: Reply to Matthew Feldman', *Samuel Beckett Today/Aujourd'hui*, 20: 375-88.
Effe, Alexandra (2017), *J.M. Coetzee and the Ethics of Narrative Transgression: A Reconsideration of Metalepsis*. London: Palgrave Macmillan.
Eyers, Tom (2017), *Speculative Formalism: Literature, Theory, and the Critical Present*. Evanston, IL: Northwestern University Press.
Farrant, Marc (2019), 'Finitizing Life: Between Reason and Religion in J.M. Coetzee's Jesus Novels', *Journal of Modern Literature*, 42 (4): 165-82.
Feldman, M. (2010), 'Beckett and Philosophy, 1928-1938', *Samuel Beckett Today / Aujourd'hui*, 22 (1): 163-80.
Felski, R. (2008), *Uses of Literature*. Oxford: Blackwell.
Foucault, M. (1997), 'What Is Critique?' In: Sylvere Lotringer and Lysa Hochroth, eds and trans, *The Politics of Truth*. New York: Semiotext(e), 23-82.
Gontarski, S. E. (2006), 'Greying the Canon: Beckett in Performance'. In: S. E. Gontarski and Anthony Uhlmann, eds, *Beckett after Beckett*. Gainesville, FL: University Press of Florida, 141-57.
Mulhall, Stephen (2017), 'Health and Deviance, Irony and Incarnation: Embedding and Embodying Philosophy in Literature and Theology in *The Childhood of Jesus*'. In: Patrick Hayes and Jan Wilm, eds, *Beyond the Ancient Quarrel: Literature, Philosophy, and J.M. Coetzee*. Oxford: Oxford University Press, 17-34.
Nietzsche, Friedrich (1968), *The Will to Power*, trans. W. Kauffmann. New York: Vintage.
Nietzsche, Friedrich (1974), *The Gay Science*, trans. W. Kauffmann. New York: Vintage.
Wilmer, S. E. (2012), 'Introduction: Negotiating the Archival Turn in Beckett Studies', *Deleuze Studies*, 6 (4): 585-8.
Woessner, Martin (2017), 'Beyond Realism: Coetzee's Post-Secular Imagination'. In: Patrick Hayes and Jan Wilm, eds, *Beyond the Ancient Quarrel: Literature, Philosophy, and J.M. Coetzee*. Oxford: Oxford University Press, 143-59.

11

Coetzee, biopolitics and the archive of impersonality

Richard A. Barney

The intimate connection between the work of J. M. Coetzee and the eighteenth century was no better signalled – we might even say inaugurated – than in the publication of his first novel, *Dusklands* (1974), whose second half contains a section titled 'The Narrative of Jacobus Coetzee', which recounts events set in 1760 regarding a Boer frontiersman's obsession with revenge on a group of natives apparently of Nama ethnic extraction.[1] The raw materials for the story also register the importance of the eighteenth-century archive, since as novelist, Coetzee based the 'Narrative' on research he did at the British Library and the University of Texas regarding early accounts of travellers in southern Africa, particularly a text titled the 'Relaas' of Jacobus Coetsé. Coetzee's reshaping of that material indicates that from the very beginning of his career as novelist, he has found the eighteenth century to be fertile terrain for exploring personal, ethical and political elements in both the European metropole and its periphery or in both the global north and south. Taken as a whole, in fact, Coetzee's fiction and expository prose reveal a remarkable prominence of eighteenth-century writers, who include Daniel Defoe, Jonathan Swift, Samuel Richardson, Jean-Jacques Rousseau, Johann Goethe, Friedrich Hölderlin and (stretching the century just a bit) Heinrich von Kleist.[2] These names are not merely an incidental part of Coetzee's favourite list of 'great authors'. Instead, they exemplify his preoccupation with a number of topics that issue from the impetus of early modernity, including the contours of individual human subjectivity, the status of the animal and the machinations of colonial empire and its aftermath.

All three of those topics converge on the eighteenth-century archive that this essay will investigate, and the first item, human subjectivity, serves as a launching point for considering how, despite its reputation as the era that founded the modern category of 'the person', the Enlightenment also provides an important context for examining Coetzee's interest in impersonality. With regard to the link between identity and authorship, Coetzee is well known for his remark in *Doubling the Point* that 'in a larger sense all writing is autobiography', and elsewhere, he has also noted that his literary commentary has often been a matter of 'the deep semantics of person' (1992: 17, 197).

An index of the impersonal becomes apparent, however, in the recognition that autobiography can also become *autre*-biography: as Coetzee has discussed with David Attwell, the gesture of recording the self's history can produce another narrative, one registering oneself as other or even an-Other (2006: 213–18). In these terms, Coetzee has been equally compelled by the requisites of impersonality, as evidenced, for instance, by his lecture 'What is a Classic?' and the novel *Youth*. In both cases, T. S. Eliot's declarations on the importance of surpassing the confines of the personal become the fulcrum for Coetzee's critical and fictionalized portrayal of authorship, the result, according to J. C. Kannemeyer, of several decades of having been influenced by Eliot's poetics.[3] In *Youth*, for instance, we find John, the protagonist, wrestling with the prospect of becoming an author while being daunted by the quandary that Eliot's views create about individual talent. '"Poetry"', we read, about one-third of the way into the story, '"is not an expression of personality but an escape from personality"'. This line, which is a quote from Eliot's famous essay, is followed by this passage: 'Then as a bitter afterthought Eliot adds: "But only those who have personality and emotions know what it means to want to escape from these things"' (2002: 61; see also 2001: 3–4).

As Coetzee notes in 'What is a Classic?', however, the escape from personality would be no simple matter since, he remarks, 'Eliot's poetry is astonishingly personal, not to say autobiographical' (2001: 3). In tracking that difficulty further in one of the few explorations of impersonality in Coetzee's work, David Attwell observes that 'there is always more to impersonality than it seems. … Impersonality is not an a priori quality inherent in a work of art, nor is it simply a function of the aesthetic. It is an *achievement*, an effect of labour in which the self is partially but not wholly buried beneath the superstructure' (2015: 8–9). That partial interment means, furthermore, that the author whose commitments are impersonal is perpetually confronted by a task that is never done. As Eliot himself observes, what happens to the author should be 'a continual surrender of himself as he is at the moment to something which is more valuable. The progress of an artist is a continual self-sacrifice, a continual extinction of personality' (1975: 40).

In ways similar to Eliot's description, for Coetzee the author's ongoing, perpetual challenge is to negotiate the competing – and ultimately irreconcilable – demands of the personal and the non-personal at the same time. This means occupying what Mike Piero calls a literary 'middle ground' between personality and its erasure, a scenario described alternately by Attwell as one constituted by vacillation (Piero 2014: 80; Attwell 2015: 3). While both critics acknowledge the importance of Eliot to Coetzee's fiction, they trace distinct trajectories of authors whose work has contributed to Coetzee's impersonal ethos: Attwell traces a historical line that goes back through Roland Barthes to Modernists such as Eliot and Pound before arriving at Gustave Flaubert, whose emphasis on style provides Attwell's earliest instance; for his part, Piero tracks impersonal precedents for Coetzee via Kafka, Joyce, Beckett and Stein, while emphasizing the work of Maurice Blanchot.

A more extended account of the history of impersonality would need to push earlier still in order to include John Keats's notion of 'negative capability', for example, despite Coetzee's apparent discounting of Keats's poetic, at least if we give credit to John's dismissive comments in *Youth* that 'Keats is like watermelon, soft and sweet and crimson, whereas poetry should be hard and clear like a flame. Reading half a dozen pages of Keats is like yielding to seduction' (2002: 21). Keats's legacy seems unpromising here, a potentially misleading detour in tracing the precedents for Coetzee's perspective. Hence this essay's point of departure will be to turn to an even earlier era in arguing first, that the imperatives of impersonality have roots much earlier than the nineteenth and twentieth centuries, going back at least to the Enlightenment; and second, that the stakes of impersonality have from the beginning extended beyond the literary – the primary concerns for Kannemeyer, Attwell and Piero – to encompass broader ethical and political issues as well.

In order to unpack those broader issues, this essay draws on the biopolitical perspective of the Italian philosophers Giorgio Agamben and Roberto Esposito, since their work, along with that of Michel Foucault, has made the Enlightenment a central part of their arguments. It is the Enlightenment, in fact, where in several ways the interests of these biopolitical theorists and Coetzee have converged, since they both consider it a crux for understanding just where modernity has taken us for the past three hundred years. Although both parties have different emphases, they consider the Enlightenment a crucial historical watershed of 'the personal' in the way that the period articulated foundational modern categories that include psychological interiority, personal privacy and individual rights. For Foucault, the emerging notion of the modern individual – presumably free, rational and self-determining – was in fact produced during the eighteenth and nineteenth centuries by a complex network of new medical regimens, improved statistical calculations and innovative educational institutions (see 1979; 1980; 2007). By his account, the concept of the person thus emerges precisely as one of the primary effects of the Enlightenment's new apparatus of the person, rather than as a natural outgrowth of organic individuality in isolation. In these terms, without having focused on impersonality per se, Foucault can be described as having articulated the person as a two-sided biopolitical entity: an a-personal construct par excellence.

Drawing particularly on Foucault's description of modern biopower, Agamben takes aim at what he calls the 'anthropological machine' – an entire sociopolitical regime whose design is to distinguish human personhood from nonpersonhood, as well as human beings from animals, with deleterious results for all those who fall outside the purview of 'the person'. As Agamben puts it, the persistently ambiguous result is that, in the West, *'man is the animal that must recognize itself as human to be human'* (2004: 26). For his part, Esposito agrees that the primary operation of that machine is to separate the human from its constitution by biological, 'animal' function, an operation that includes the nineteenth-century's institutionalization of human rights. As Esposito explains in *Third Person: Politics of Life and Philosophy of the Impersonal*, the conceptual hinge by which such a separation can be accomplished is what he calls the 'ideology of the person', whereby a mere living being can be distinguished from genuine personhood (2012: 5). The historical fallout of that scenario since the Enlightenment, however, has been a legacy of conceptual and institutional mechanisms by which the merely biological or 'animal' could supposedly be cordoned off from the person, often couched, Esposito demonstrates, in the vocabulary of immunization, whose medical authorization by proxy has produced the sociopolitical disenfranchisement of groups across a range of economic, gendered and racial applications.[4] While that exclusionary logic may have receded in more recent decades, Esposito argues that the biopolitics of the person will always have inimical implications given its inherently binary structure.

As an alternative, Esposito proposes the concept of 'the impersonal', which poses the prospect not of the *anti*personal, but instead the ability to bypass the dualist terms of the personal and its opposite. As Esposito comments:

> Of course the impersonal lies outside the horizon of the person, but not in a place that is unrelated to it: the impersonal is situated, rather, at the confines of the personal; on the lines of resistance, to be exact, which cut through its territory, thus preventing, or at least opposing, the functioning of its exclusionary dispositif. The impersonal is a shifting border: that critical margin ... that separates the semantics of the person from its natural effect of separation; that blocks its reifying outcome.
> (2012: 14)

Esposito elaborates further by examining the grammatical category of the third person, remarking that as a form of impersonal address, it is 'situated precisely at the point of intersection between no one and anyone: either it is not a person at all, or it is every person. In reality, it is both at the same time' (2012: 107). This articulation of the third person demarcates significant common ground between Esposito's and Coetzee's perspectives on impersonality, since Coetzee has also employed linguistic terminology in his discussion, for instance, of Gerrit Achterberg's poetry (1992: 71–2) with an eye towards tracing the fluctuating registers of 'I' among the first, second and third person. As Carrol Clarkson has demonstrated, this sort of focus has also served as the linguistic backdrop for Coetzee's formulation of a narrative 'middle voice' in his fiction, including his signature use of free indirect discourse.[5]

Within the broader framework of recent biopolitical commentary, Esposito's description of the impersonal can shed light on several political ramifications of Coetzee's fiction, particularly the way he has revisited – and even redeployed – several eighteenth-century texts, most prominently Jonathan Swift's *Gulliver's Travels* in *The Lives of Animals* (and in turn *Elizabeth Costello*) and Daniel Defoe's *Robinson Crusoe* in *Foe* and then in the Nobel prize lecture, 'He and His Man'. In each of these cases, Coetzee finds various means by which to displace the conventions of first-person narration and its association with self-contained (often masculine) authority, in some cases by introducing the perspective of a female narrator or protagonist and in others by submitting that convention to the rigors of free indirect discourse – all in the context of indicating the significance of this move with respect to colonial empire. In *Foe*, for instance, Susan Barton's first-person narrative instantiates her self-described voice as 'a free woman', while it also proves to produce an unrelenting sense of her own insubstantiality, a ghosting that induces her to ask 'Who is speaking me?' at one point, as she contemplates the implications of Friday's silence as colonized subject (1987: 123, 125). In the example of *The Lives of Animals*, delivered in free indirect discourse, Costello identifies the political stakes for the Houyhnhnms' island that would usually apply to what she calls Swift's 'somewhat too disembodied, somewhat too unhistorical fable' (1999a: 57): rather than the arrival of Gulliver as lone figure, she points out, there would have been the intrusion of a full cohort of European settlers, entrepreneurs and military men whose repeated visits would ultimately establish a full-fledged colonial stronghold.[6] What could be called the techne of impersonality thus varies from case to case, but nonetheless profoundly shapes these stories' depiction of embodiment, substantiality and their related politics.

While the novels of authors such as Defoe, Swift and others constitute an important part of Coetzee's Enlightenment archive, this essay aims to take the notion of the archive somewhat more literal-mindedly – that is, it proposes to dig down into its lesser-known corners in order to excavate not a counter-tradition, exactly, but a counter-current of the impersonal that pertains specifically to the eighteenth century. In other words, rather than consider eighteenth-century texts as merely the occasion for Coetzee to swerve or refract the period's presumed ideology of the person, I aim to explore an early, nascent strand in the eighteenth-century archive with tangible elements of impersonality already in play.[7] The point here is not to claim that Coetzee has been aware of this counter-current or explicitly drawn on it; instead, the goal is to sketch one small part of a genealogy of the impersonal that, if fleshed out in more detail, could describe the biopolitical stakes of impersonality as they have developed historically, ultimately setting the stage approximately two hundred years later for Coetzee's own contribution during the past four decades. This essay's brief genealogical account does not, moreover, aim to discover the impersonal's modern origins, any more than it will claim Coetzee as its ultimate endpoint in a projected temporal arc from the Enlightenment to the present. Instead, it offers what Foucault called 'a history of the present' (1979: 31) as the means for shedding historical light on the dynamics of Coetzee's singular version of impersonality that is both embodied and political.

The case in point for delving further into the archive will be John Thelwall, a late-eighteenth-century British novelist, poet and political radical, whose long-overlooked oeuvre has slowly begun to emerge 'out' of the archive in the form of recent modern editions and a substantial body of new scholarship during the past two decades.[8] Since Thelwall's story is likely unfamiliar to those outside eighteenth- and nineteenth-century studies, it should be helpful to offer a brief overview of his life and work. John Thelwall was a Jacobin activist, a powerful public speaker, and a prolific author of essays, poetry and fiction, which over the course of his career became increasingly focused on his ambitions for socioeconomic and political reform in Britain. Born to a family of silk merchants in 1764, Thelwall considered entering the trade but turned it down in favour of divinity studies, which he then abandoned for an interest in studying the law, the third vocation he left behind in deciding ultimately to become an author. During his time, he became a well-known figure in literary circles and periodically corresponded with the Romantic poets Samuel Coleridge and William Wordsworth.

After the outbreak of the French Revolution in 1789, Thelwall declared himself nothing less than 'intoxicated with the French doctrines of the day' (Seccombe 1898: 111); that turning point would transform his public profile into that of a dedicated reformer and activist. Over the course of the next five years, Thelwall would also become an amateur student of medical science, studying informally at Guy's and St. Thomas Hospitals before articulating a vitalist-inspired theory of animal physiology that would come to inform his arguments regarding Britain's ailing body politic. His increasing impact on public opinion led to his being jailed and tried for treason in 1794, a charge which he successfully defeated, but with the cost of being unable to return to public speaking. For a time, Thelwall withdrew from public life, aiming to find relief in writing his poetry. In the early 1800s, however, he re-emerged with familiar public animation, this time with new projects that included establishing institutions that provided children of the working poor with treatment for speech defects and programs in literacy. Until the end of his life, Thelwall became once more a frequent lecturer to English audiences, but he has remained best known for his staunch dedication to socioeconomic reform of the entire British system, which shaped his fiction and poetry as much as it did his journalism and public speaking.

As this brief sketch suggests, Thelwall was in many ways dramatically different from Coetzee in style and content. Unlike Coetzee, he cultivated a stalwart public persona of the committed radical, whose fiery rhetoric proposed new public policies that would, he believed, substantially overhaul the treatment of the working poor at home and colonial subjects overseas. To be sure, these traits contrast sharply with Coetzee's art of understatement, including his reluctance to proclaim solutions to political problems on the public stage, even given his advocacy regarding the better treatment of animals.[9] That said, there is also a general parallel to draw between Thelwall and Coetzee, particularly with regard to the impersonal. Taken as a whole, Thelwall's frequent invocation of a kind of personalized politics, articulated in the vocabulary of individual rights and powerful feeling, is countered in his work, as we will see, by a powerful move outside the confines of the person, just as in Coetzee's case, his conviction that all writing entails an autobiographical element is offset by an array of textual devices – including indirect free discourse, generically hybrid narration, and quasi-biographical character development – that displaces the prospect of consolidating the identity of his stories' narrating 'I'. To put it another way, Thelwall contends in proximity with what Coetzee rejects at a distance: the terms of the romantic, whether in the case of a small or a capital R.[10] If at times, Thelwall's claims for the importance of sincerity and fellow-feeling sound unsurprisingly similar to those made by his Romantic contemporaries, then it is also true that his most experimental fiction, which can be found in *The Peripatetic*, repeatedly challenges the prospect of contained, self-present subjectivity. In effect, *The Peripatetic* pursues a progressive political agenda whose formal experimentalism counters – and sometimes thoroughly undermines – its own investment in the individual's imagination or sentiment. Similarly, Coetzee's affinity for Eliot's ethos of the impersonal tracks a shared Modernist aim to critique, if not set aside, Romanticism's literary and intellectual legacy.

Within the broader framework of Thelwall and Coetzee's shared perspectives, then, there are three specific areas that deserve particular attention regarding the impersonal: first, both authors share an emphasis on human beings as inextricably *embodied* beings, a condition of physical vulnerability that is explicitly tied to the state of animals; second, in both authors we find that the shared precarity of embodiment corresponds to a pronounced variability or even permeability of human subjectivity, whose features can ultimately become more refracted than consolidated; and third, in both cases, the deflation of traditionally defined human ascendancy is tied to an interest in articulating human–animal commonality, which in turn is linked to a broader, revisionist sense of the political. Given the complexity of each of these topics, we can sketch only briefly these points of contact in Thelwall's and Coetzee's work. What follows is a contrapuntal reading of their fiction with the aim of tracing the outlines of those connections by focusing particularly on Thelwall's *Peripatetic*, the novel he published in 1793, whose daring formal and thematic features in many ways anticipate those in Coetzee's fiction.

Beginning with Coetzee: when it comes to Coetzee's take on the nature of human embodiment, there are a number of moments when duress or extremity produces his protagonists' new awareness of the biopolitical stakes of their bodies *as* bodies. After the Magistrate, for instance, has been imprisoned and tortured in *Waiting for the Barbarians*, he remarks that he has learned 'what it meant to live in a body, as a body, a body which can entertain notions of justice only as long as it is whole and well'. His tormenters, he tells us, 'came to my cell to show me the meaning of humanity' (1982: 113). If the Magistrate's suffering produces his new outlook on the inevitable violence that attaches to his role of administering the colony, a rather different perspective is created for David Lurie in *Disgrace*. There, in the aftermath of the attack on himself, his daughter and the dogs under her care, Lurie grapples with the travail of physical recovery, looking 'like a mummy', he says, in his wrapped bandages (1999b: 106). In the meantime, he also gains a new sense of the connections among several things, namely, the vulnerability of animals, the ethics of their human handlers and the general conditions of post-apartheid South Africa.

In the case of Thelwall, he is equally ready to link human physicality to the ethics of how to treat animals and one's fellow human beings, although by contrast, he turns to medical science in order to articulate a general theory of mammalian life. Drawing on his informal medical training, Thelwall produces *Essay, Towards a Definition of Animal Vitality* in the same year as *The Peripatetic*, a treatise that outlines a vitalist take on the basic conditions necessary for an entity's being alive. Thelwall writes: 'Wherever there is a perfect organization of the animal substance there, I conceive, we have the *susceptibility* (or … the PRE-DISPOSING CAUSE) of Life' (2002: 104). For Thelwall, moreover, this condition of susceptibility requires a certain kind of stimulus to bring life into full bloom. In the case of human or animal physiology, he argues, that stimulus is an element in the air absorbed by the lungs and distributed by the blood to the entire corpus: it is what he calls 'a fine and subtile, or aëriform essence' or an 'electrical fluid' (2002: 117, 119). In these terms, the respiratory organs, including the lungs, serve as the most important bodily aperture, thereby constituting the human being as a radically *open* system – both physiologically and sociopolitically. That is why, in an intriguing chapter of *The Peripatetic* called 'A Digression for the Anatomists', Thelwall identifies an anatomical triad of the brain, heart and lungs, in which the brain's function of rationality and the heart's dynamics of feeling are matched by the lungs' essential feature of vital receptivity. This move nearly equalizes the relation between human and animal life, and the novel repeatedly affirms this disposition, as when the narrator approvingly describes 'the feelings of the susceptible mind' (2001: 113).

That narrator is also the novel's protagonist, named Sylvanus Theophrastus, who in episodic fashion tells the story of his travels in the countryside surrounding London as he accumulates an appreciation for the landscape, while also gathering information about the local agriculture, industry and everyday life of common people – all with an eye towards a reformist agenda. If Theophrastus' susceptible body suggests a model inclined towards the impersonal, then it must also be acknowledged that in many ways, he exemplifies the figure of late-eighteenth-century personality, that is, none other than the sentimental man. As he frequently tells us, he is a valetudinarian, a man whose imagination frequently 'engrosses' him and one whose heart is continually moved by what he calls the 'Powers of sympathy' (2001: 94, 91). That said, however, given Thelwall's persistent aim to articulate the conditions of radical sociopolitical change and a new sense of collectivity – and it should be stressed, a collectivity among both human and animal populations – the arc of Theophrastus' experiences repeatedly exceeds and disrupts the confines of a narrowly personal definition.

The extra-personal dimension of Theophrastus' character and experience is tangible on a number of registers. First, there is the text's pronounced generic multiplicity, since it is an eclectic mix that includes travelogue, pastoral poetry, socioeconomic analysis, political satire and biomedical commentary, whose combined facets refract the presentation of Theophrastus' perspective.[11] Thus while Theophrastus is the putative author of all these portions of the novel, the diverse, often incompatible, discursive arcs created by this textual medley produces his persona more as a distribution, rather than a reliable consolidation, of narrative subjectivity. That formal multifariousness is matched thematically by a kind of double vision that appears early in the story with the introduction of a character named the Ambulator, in every sense a second version of Theophrastus. This is a man who, like Theophrastus, is 'a steady and determined advocate for *the genuine principles of* LIBERTY *and* EQUALITY' (2001: 113), yet his frequent disagreements with Theophrastus often suggest a displacement, rather than a mere duplication, of his social and political commitments. Furthermore, the men's 'mental attraction' to one another seems as much as anything a case of what Theophrastus calls 'the correspondent particles of matter' having 'a tendency to adhere' (2001: 112). The sheer materiality of human motivation is further complicated by frequent sequences in which Theophrastus' convictions completely collapse in the face of 'a thousand doubts which my system could never explain' (2001: 108), before he reassembles a new version whose standards are then submitted to further cycles of demise and self-revival. Under these conditions, the features of Theophrastus' personality are subject to constant forces of dissemination and deflection, all in the service of Thelwall's commitment to exploring newly equitable relations for both British citizens at home and colonial subjects abroad.

Ultimately, Esposito's image of the impersonal as traversing the conceptual borderline between the personal and its opposite proves particularly useful in measuring both the similarities and the differences in the topography of Thelwall's and Coetzee's respective biopolitical projects. To put it one way, the trajectory of the impersonal for Thelwall tracks the arc of a recurring swerve – first heading powerfully in the direction of individual sentiment, imagination and rationality, before then returning just as powerfully back towards the spheres of material embodiment, human–animal solidarity and political mutuality. It is thus no mere coincidence that as narrator, Theophrastus repeatedly stresses that his storytelling has 'so digressive a nature' that its 'straying' and 'eccentric' patterns perpetually veer away from any fixed centre (2001: 71, 72, 127, 141). Coetzee's version, by contrast, marks a more direct line of impersonal movement, as if its path were formed by maintaining a greater equilibrium between the non/personal's contending forces. In many ways, of course, this difference marks the historical gap between Thelwall, experimenting against the grain of personhood's cultural ascendancy during the Enlightenment, and Coetzee, who comes after both Modernist and postmodernist challenges to human subjectivity. For Coetzee, moreover, following Eliot's lead, since the work of impersonality in writing is never fully done, that means that an author must relentlessly concentrate his or her efforts on producing impersonal effects, while simultaneously drawing on personal or autobiographical elements: described this way, it is a task that suggests the relatively stable vector of a line of flight (to use Gilles Deleuze and Félix Guattari's well-known phrase), rather than the sinuosity of something like a sine wave. Recalling Attwell's remark about the impersonal as vacillation, we could also say that in Coetzee's case, the attendant textual fluctuations remain far less exorbitant or pronounced.

The graphic differences between Thelwall's and Coetzee's approaches to impersonality can be traced in more detail by considering briefly their contrasting portrayal of animals, including the political significance of human interaction with them. For Thelwall, it is often a matter of countering gestures – one towards anthropomorphic projection, the other towards a politics that exceeds bourgeois subjectivity. In a chapter of *The Peripatetic* called 'The Bird Catchers', for instance, when Theophrastus observes the plight of some skylarks that are being trapped for sale as pets to the women of England's upper classes, he begins with a highly sentimentalized rendition of their suffering, complete with personifying the birds as husbands, wives and family members who will 'taste the joys of liberty no more' (2001: 90–1). That rendition, moreover, includes what at first seems an overblown comparison when Theophrastus remarks that the captured skylarks must endure 'all the woes of cruel slavery'. It soon becomes evident, however, that he aims to issue a political indictment of Britain's colonial enterprise abroad, which produces a plethora of new luxuries – including sugar, coffee and tea – and which Britons consume with as little regard for their devastating human cost as they do in acknowledging the ethics of keeping wild birds as pets. Ultimately, the skylarks' symbolic imprisonment opens out to a description of far more ruinous *foreign* woes', as he puts it, which produce the 'Afric's sighs' and the 'negro's tear' (2001: 91). What began as personified meditation thus enlarges to suggest the visionary prospect of a radically transformed future, in which the collectivities typically divided along the lines of nationality, geography, race or species might become not equivalent, perhaps, but at least affiliated in more egalitarian terms both ecological and political. This gesture, however, also relies on a complex discursive move, since the personification of skylarks runs parallel to the need to humanize African slaves, who in eighteenth-century descriptions were frequently characterized as either a kind of animal (the familiar beast of burden) or as mere objects (a form of property). For Theophrastus, then, there is political urgency in the act of jointly personifying animals and slaves, while at the same time he aims to articulate a materialist form of human–animal relations, based in part on shared physiological susceptibilities, which can move beyond individualist notions of motive or community.

For Coetzee, by contrast, the challenge of examining the significance of animals, both ethically and politically, rests on the prospect of tracking a more measured – one could even say more disciplined – version of impersonality.[12] In many ways, his distinct approach comes down to refurbishing the eighteenth-century term *sympathy*, the word that Elizabeth Costello uses, for instance, in advocating for compassionate human engagement with animal life, rather than relying on its more recent equivalent, *empathy*.[13] In her exploration of sympathy's imaginative prospects, in other words, Costello adds *feeling with* to our contemporary sense of sympathy as merely *feeling for*. But despite all her passion in denouncing the abattoir and championing the work of empathic poets, Costello also proves to be an example of a crucial principle in Coetzee's impersonal approach to human–animal relations in general: that they be engaged *with sympathy but without sentimentality*. In this regard, Coetzee departs from the conventions of eighteenth-century literary sentiment, even while redeploying familiar tropes such as the human heart (see, for instance, 1999a: 34), by tracing a more restrained, even cautious, examination of animals' social, ethical and political importance.

Over the years, there have been various ways by which Coetzee has aimed to apply that sympathetic restraint in his fiction. One strategy is to limit a protagonist's or narrator's emotional proximity to specific animals: in Costello's case, for instance, despite her intense focus on animals' lives and deaths, she demonstrates no identifiable interest in particular domestic, wild or companion animals that she has encountered. The Magistrate in *Waiting for the Barbarians* poses a slight variation on this pattern when he hunts and then decides not to kill a ram outside the imperial outpost. While this incident involves a very specific animal whose death, the Magistrate realizes, he does not actually desire, it is also an encounter that he renders abstract almost immediately: it is a 'frozen moment', he says, when 'the stars are locked in a configuration in which events are not themselves but stand for other things' (1982: 40). The case of David Lurie in *Disgrace* offers another configuration, in which Lurie spends increasingly greater time with a scruffy dog at the animal clinic run by Bev Shaw, while maintaining a stalwart affective imperviousness – at least consciously – regarding his ultimate decision to euthanize the dog by the end of the story.

The most pervasive pattern in Coetzee's portrayal of human responsiveness to the animals they meet or imagine, however, regards the impersonal as a measure of the margins or outlying boundaries of what Lurie or other characters do not know – what lies beyond the full grasp of cognition or consciousness. In his decision about the ram, for example, the Magistrate finds only 'an obscure sentiment lurking at the edge of my consciousness' (1982: 39), although the ensuing events of the story indicate that it prompts his revaluation of both his relationship to the barbarian 'girl', whom he has previously described as having animal-like features, and to the Empire at large. For his part, Lurie's increasing concern for the well-being of animals in *Disgrace* comes to him almost unwillingly, as though he cannot understand his own motivations regarding two sheep destined for slaughter at a farm near his daughter's homestead. He considers the impending fate of the 'black-faced Persians' to be 'hardhearted', although he also admits, 'I am disturbed. I can't say why' (1999b: 123, 125, 127). His reflections become further elaborated as a tenuous fault line that runs between feeling and unknowing:

> A bond seems to have come into existence between himself and the two Persians, he does not know how. The bond is not one of affection. It is not even a bond with these two in particular, whom he could not pick out from a mob in a field. Nevertheless, suddenly and without reason, their lot has become important to him.
>
> (1999b: 126)

This description contains several hallmarks of the impersonal as an initially inchoate reflex containing the prospect of an emerging ethics – and ultimately, perhaps also a politics – regarding the treatment of animals. Delivered in free indirect discourse, it represents Lurie's feelings for animals at a remove from what he himself can identify or articulate. Furthermore, it circumambulates a specific and an abstract human relation to the plight of these two animals, as though that indeterminacy can modulate successfully between excess feeling and detached moral principle.

The scenario in this passage also indicates something further: that Coetzee's ethos regarding animals involves not only sympathy without sentimentality and sympathy without sentiment, but also a trajectory toward *sympathy as impersonal affect*. In these terms, the ability to move or be moved encompasses a graduated scale that is larger in scope than typically conceived, since at one end of the spectrum there is full-blown emotion, while at the other there is something like the register of 'influence' broadly conceived. In the context of the Enlightenment's legacy in Coetzee's work, it is particularly striking that this latter sense of affect has both eighteenth-century and more recent derivations. In the case of the eighteenth century, for instance, the vocabulary of literary sensibility was frequently tied to a medical discourse in which 'sympathy' described how the body's various parts could mutually index, relay and organize specific stimuli or physical states, particularly via the nerves as involuntary reflex. In many ways, Thelwall assumes precisely those sorts of bio-literary connections in *The Peripatetic*. More recently, theorists like Patricia Clough have offered a very different approach to affect by tracking Gilles Deleuze's ontology of versatile assemblages that can engage both human and non-human entities. Hence Clough defines affect as the 'bodily capacities to affect and be affected or the augmentation or diminution of a body's capacity to act' (2007: 2).[14] While Coetzee's fiction, by contrast, does not specifically follow either of these lines of thinking, it explores similar ground by illustrating what lies beyond personalized, conscious human response – including a perplexing sensitivity based on shared physical susceptibility, as in the case of the Magistrate and the ram, and the dynamics of bonding without affection, as with Lurie and the dog. In both instances, impersonal sympathy poses a puzzle and a challenge for both the characters and Coetzee's readers: namely, how to navigate the ethical or political choices once the disturbingly non-personal becomes palpable.

* * *

Taken as a whole, Coetzee's fiction registers nothing like what we have in Thelwall's *Peripatetic*: a powerfully utopian impulse in the way Thelwall imagines new political possibilities. As fictioneers, these two authors also have markedly different perspectives on the relation of writing to both readers and sociopolitical change: while Thelwall has genuine faith in persuading his readers that his specific proposals will improve the economic or political status quo, Coetzee aims instead to confront his readers with the inevitable responsibility of discovering such changes, but without offering them any kind of ready-made solutions. We can – and should – make these and other distinctions between these authors' respective dispositions. But by way of conclusion, I want to turn back to the topic at hand, the archive, since I think that taken together, these authors' contributions to thinking the impersonal also have significant implications for how we approach archival work. My final thoughts, then, are about how we archivists may well need to reimagine the job of being just that – archivists. It seems to me that one of the most powerful and often subterranean tropes that organizes how current archives are excavated, utilized and described has been precisely the trope of prosopopeia or personification. That is to say that in the process of sifting through the archive's sundry materials – including manuscripts, notebooks, photographs, receipts, ticket stubs and other ephemera – the need to give such disparate items character becomes a case of making them *into* character. In other words, particularly in the case of the study of individual authors, the tendency has been not just to create a portrait, but to reach for what the alchemy of personification claims for itself: the ability to bring the inert to life; to flesh out, literally, those sullen materials into the corresponding parts of the author's body in question – her brain, her heart, her hands and perhaps – following Thelwall – perhaps even the inspiration provided by her lungs. This is no doubt an inevitable professional hazard of archival labour, one we probably should not imagine can ever be completely done away with, just as Coetzee reminds us that writing is never far from the autobiographical impulse. But we should also remember that, historically, this trope gained particular potency during the period we have been considering, in which Enlightenment notions of 'the great man' or Romantic notions of 'genius' provided even more fuel for the rhetorical engines of archival personification. Given the profound challenge that both Thelwall's and Coetzee's fiction has posed for those literary legacies, then, I think we owe it to their work – as well as to our own as archivists – to consider what prospects the impersonal might offer for reimagining what remains important intellectual and cultural work. Might there be an archival analogue for specific literary devices, particularly those deployed by Coetzee, that can effectively deflect or reshape the ethical or sociopolitical implications of personality? Could writing about the archive, inspired in part by Thelwall's eclectic example, benefit by deploying an imaginative panoply of generic modes or conventions with the aim of refracting the personal? These and other questions, admittedly, will have to await another occasion for considering their answers, but if nothing else, we archivists-as-writers should consider the impersonal explorations of Coetzee and his Enlightenment counterparts as potential launching points for our own collective efforts and invention.

Notes

1 Jacobus Coetzee refers to these natives at some points as 'the Namaqua', at others as 'the Namaqua Hottentots', and at still others simply as 'Hottentots'; see, e.g., Coetzee (1996: 81, 116, 117). While Jacobus employs the pejorative term *Hottentot* to reference the people in what are now the regions of both the northern and southern Cape,

Dr. S. J. Coetzee, the novel's fictional mid-twentieth-century historian, distinguishes in his afterword what he calls 'the Namaquas' from 'Cape Hottentots' (1996: 140–1).

2 Overall, the scholarly attention to this list of authors – or to the relevance of the Enlightenment in general – has been relatively slight, with the major exception of Defoe, given *Foe*'s recasting of *Robinson Crusoe*. Some of the best commentary on Defoe includes Attridge (2005: 69–83, 196), Attwell (1993: 104–10; 2015: 124–36), England (2008), Lamb (2010), Poyner (2009: 91–109) and Spivak (1990). For discussion of Goethe, see: Attridge (2005: 156 n. 22), Sutcliffe (2009) and Wright (2010: 148, 152–7); on Richardson: Attridge (2005: 91) and Hayes (2009: 116–18; 2010: 138–43); on Rousseau: Attridge (2005: 141, 145, 153–5), Bell (2006: 175, 186), Iddiols (2009: 190), Moses (1994) and Poyner (2009: 69, 83–4, 152, 154, 167); on Swift: Attwell (1993: 74), Barney (2004), Dooley and Phiddian (2016) and Lamb (2010: 181–2); on the Enlightenment: Hallemeier (2013: 47–9, 69), Poyner (2009: 10, 22, 30, 63, 82, 83, 92, 150, 160), and Woessner (2010: 232–6).

3 See Kannemeyer's account (2012: 72, 81, 120, 498–9) of Eliot's impact on Coetzee's aim to be a poet during his years in high school, university and London, leading up to his lecture on the classics in 1991 and its later publication in 1993.

4 For Esposito's analysis of what he calls the 'immunitary paradigm', see especially *Bios* (2008: 45–77) and *Immunitas* (2011).

5 On the importance of linguistics for Coetzee's work, see Clarkson's discussions in *Countervoices* (2013: 25–6, 34–6, 52–4, 63–4); regarding Coetzee's commentary on Achterberg, pages 48–54, 56–8. I discuss in more detail the linguistic implications for the impersonal in Coetzee's work in 'On (Not) Giving Up' (2016: 514–15). For another discussion of the thematic inflections of middle voice in Coetzee's work, see Macaskill (1994); and on the third person, see Attridge (2005: 138–61).

6 In the case of *Elizabeth Costello*, there is a slight variation from the delivery in *Lives*, since the novel opens with the enigmatic, unidentified narrative voice of 'we' and 'us' (2003: 1–2, 15, 16), before deploying free indirect discourse consistently for the rest of the story.

7 In this regard, the argument of this essay departs from Attwell's emphasis on parody as the primary relation between Coetzee's work and eighteenth-century texts, whereby it produces either corrosive 'parodic effect[s]' of scientific discourse in *Dusklands* or 'respectful parody' of Defoe's storytelling in *Foe* (1993: 39–40, 74).

8 The first signs of contemporary recovery of Thelwall's work included Gregory Claeys' edition, *The Politics of English Jacobinism* (1995), followed by the publication of Thelwall's physiological theory edited by Nicholas Roe (2002) and two of his novels, *The Peripatetic* (2001) and *The Daughter of Adoption* (2013). My own work on these and other Thelwall texts over the years has focused initially on archives at sites such as the British and the Huntington libraries, before benefitting from more recent digital archives and scholarly editions.

9 One example of Coetzee's cautious approach to political activism would be the address titled 'Voiceless: I Feel Therefore I Am', which he wrote for an art exhibit event in 2007 sponsored by Voiceless, an Australian organization advocating the protection of animals. Coetzee asked the actor Hugo Weaving to read the address on his behalf, and it can be found at Weaving's website called 'Random Scribblings'. More recently, however, in a book review titled 'Australia's Shame', Coetzee has taken a more assertive political position regarding the issue of Australia's immigration policy.

10 On Thelwall's relation to literary Romanticism, see Murphy (2002), Roe (1990) and Thompson (2010; 2012).

11 On *The Peripatetic*'s multifarious generic form, see particularly Judith Thompson's discussion (Thelwall 2001: 37–41).
12 The ensuing discussion of animals in Coetzee's work has benefited a great deal from other arguments on the topic that have taken a specifically biopolitical perspective, including Peterson (2018: 43–63), Seshadri (2012: 53–62) and Wolfe (2008; 2010: 68–71, 82, 84, 87).
13 See, e.g., Costello's invocation of sympathy in *The Lives of Animals* (1999a: 34).
14 Clough's edited volume *The Affective Turn* (2007) offers a representative collation of the transdisciplinary reformulations of affect that have emerged during the past decade via perspectives that include systems theory, cybernetics, trauma studies and Deleuzian philosophy. For analyses of Coetzee's work from a more general Deleuzian framework, see, e.g., Bourassa (2015), Buelens and Hoens (2007), Hamilton (2005; 2011) and Patton (2010).

References

Agamben, Giorgio (2004), *The Open: Man and Animal*, trans. K. Attell. Stanford: Stanford University Press.
Attridge, Derek (2005), *J. M. Coetzee and the Ethics of Reading: Literature in the Event*. Chicago: University of Chicago Press.
Attwell, David (1993), *J. M. Coetzee: South Africa and the Politics of Writing*. Berkeley: University of California Press.
Attwell, David (2015), *J. M. Coetzee and the Life of Writing: Face to Face with Time*. New York: Penguin Books.
Barney, Richard A. (2004), 'Between Swift and Kafka: Animals and the Politics of Coetzee's Elusive Fiction', *World Literature Today*, 78(1): 17–23.
Barney, Richard A. (2016), 'On (Not) Giving Up: Animals, Biopolitics, and the Impersonal in J. M. Coetzee's *Disgrace*', *Textual Practice*, 30(3): 509–30.
Bell, Michael (2006), 'What Is It Like to Be a Nonracist? *Elizabeth Costello* and J. M. Coetzee on the Lives of Animals and Men'. In: J. Poyner, ed., *J. M. Coetzee and the Idea of the Public Intellectual*. Athens, OH: Ohio University Press, 172–92.
Bourassa, Alan (2015), 'The Analyst and the Nomad: Lacan, Deleuze and Coetzee's *Life and Times of Michael K*', In I. Buchanan, T. Matts and A. Tynan, eds, *Deleuze and the Schizoanalysis of Literature*. London: Bloomsbury, 137–53.
Buelens, Gert, and Dominiek Hoens (2007), ' "Above and Beneath Classification": Bartleby, *Life and Times of Michael K*, and Syntagmatic Participation', *Diacritics*, 37(2–3): 157–70.
Clarkson, Carrol (2013), *J. M. Coetzee: Countervoices*. Basingstoke: Palgrave Macmillan.
Clough, Patricia Ticineto (2007), 'Introduction'. In: P. Clough, ed., *The Affective Turn: Theorizing the Social*. Durham, NC: Duke University Press, 1–33.
Coetzee, J. M. (1982), *Waiting for the Barbarians*. New York: Penguin Books.
Coetzee, J. M. (1987), *Foe*. New York: Penguin Books.
Coetzee, J. M. (1992), *Doubling the Point: Essays and Interviews*, ed. D. Attwell. Cambridge, MA: Harvard University Press.
Coetzee, J. M.(1996), *Dusklands*. New York: Penguin Books.
Coetzee, J. M. (1999a), *The Lives of Animals*, ed. A. Guttman. Princeton: Princeton University Press.

Coetzee, J. M. (1999b), *Disgrace*. New York: Penguin Books.
Coetzee, J. M. (2001), 'What Is a Classic?: A Lecture'. In: *Stranger Shores: Literary Essays, 1986–1999*. New York: Penguin Books, 2–16.
Coetzee, J. M. (2002), *Youth*. New York: Penguin Books.
Coetzee, J. M. (2003), *Elizabeth Costello*. New York: Viking.
Coetzee, J. M. (2007), 'Voiceless: I Feel Therefore I Am'. Available online: at Hugo Weaving's website, 'Random Scribblings', http://hugo.random-scribblings.net/voiceless-i-feel-therefore-i-am-22feb07-sp-348963490/#.XiTQwlNKg6g (accessed 2 December 2019).
Coetzee, J. M. (2019), 'Australia's Shame', *New York Review of Books*, 26 September. Available online: https://www.nybooks.com/articles/2019/09/26/australias-shame/ (accessed 19 January 2020).
Coetzee, J. M., and David Attwell (2006), "All Autobiography Is *Autre*-biography': J. M. Coetzee Interviewed by David Attwell'. In: J. L. Coullie, S. Meyer, T. H. Ngwenya and T. Olver, eds, *Selves in Question: Interviews on Southern African Auto/Biography*. Honolulu: University of Hawai'i Press, 213–18.
Dooley, Gillian, and Robert Phiddian (2016), '"A Face without Personality": Coetzee's Swiftian Narrators', *Ariel*, 47(3): 1–22.
Eliot, T. S. (1975), 'Tradition and the Individual Talent'. In: *Selected Prose of T. S. Eliot*. New York: Harcourt Brace Jovanovich, 37–44.
England, Frank (2008), 'Foes: Plato, Derrida, and Coetzee: Rereading J. M. Coetzee's *Foe*', *Journal of Literary Studies*, 24(4): 44–62.
Esposito, Roberto (2008), *Bios: Biopolitics and Philosophy*, trans. T. Campbell. Minneapolis: University of Minnesota Press.
Esposito, Roberto (2011), *Immunitas: The Protection and Negation of Life*, trans. Z. Hanafi. Cambridge, England: Polity Press.
Esposito, Roberto (2012), *Third Person: Politics of Life and Philosophy of the Impersonal*, trans. Z. Hanafi. Cambridge, England: Polity Press.
Foucault, Michel (1979), *Discipline and Punish: The Birth of the Prison*, trans. A. Sheridan. New York: Vintage Books.
Foucault, Michel (1980), *The History of Sexuality, Volume I: An Introduction*, trans. R. Hurley. New York: Vintage Books.
Foucault, Michel (2007), *Security, Territory, Population: Lectures at the Collège de France, 1977–1978*, ed. M. Senellart, trans. G. Burchell. New York: Picador.
Foucault, Michel (2008), *The Birth of Biopolitics: Lectures at the Collège de France, 1978–1979*, ed. M. Senellart, trans. G. Burchell. Basingstoke: Palgrave Macmillan.
Hallemeir, Katherine (2013), *J. M. Coetzee and the Limits of Cosmopolitanism*. New York: Palgrave Macmillan.
Hamilton, Grant (2005), 'J. M. Coetzee's *Dusklands*: The Meaning of Suffering', *Journal of Literary Studies/Tydskrif vir Literatuurwetenskap*, 21(3–4): 296–314.
Hamilton, Grant (2011), *On Representation: Deleuze and Coetzee on the Colonized Subject*. Amsterdam: Rodopi.
Hayes, Patrick (2009), 'Literature, History, and Folly'. In: E. Boehmer, R. Eagleston and K. Iddiols, eds, *J. M. Coetzee in Context and Theory*. London: Continuum, 112–22.
Hayes, Patrick (2010), *J. M. Coetzee and the Novel: Writing and Politics after Beckett*. Oxford: Oxford University Press.
Iddiols, Kay (2009), 'Disrupting Inauthentic Readings: Coetzee's Strategies'. In: E. Boehmer, R. Eaglestone and K. Iddiols, eds, *J. M. Coetzee in Context and Theory*. London: Continuum, 184–97.

Kannemeyer, J. C. (2012), *J. M. Coetzee: A Life in Writing*, trans. M. Heyns. Melbourne: Scribe.

Lamb, Jonathan (2010), '"The True Words at Last from the Mind in Ruins": J. M. Coetzee and Realism'. In: G. Bradshaw and M. Neill, eds, *J. M. Coetzee's Austerities*. Surrey: Ashgate, 177–89.

Macaskill, Brian (1994), 'Charting J. M. Coetzee's Middle Voice', *Contemporary Literature*, 35(3): 441–75.

Moses, Michael Valdez (1994), 'Solitary Walkers: Rousseau and Coetzee's *Life and Times of Michael K*', *South Atlantic Quarterly*, 93(1): 131–56.

Murphy, Michael (2002), 'John Thelwall, Coleridge, and *The Ancient Mariner*', *Romanticism*, 8(1): 62–74.

Patton, Paul (2010), *Deleuzian Concepts: Philosophy, Colonization, Politics*. Stanford: Stanford University Press.

Peterson, Christopher (2018), *Monkey Trouble: The Scandal of Posthumanism*. New York: Fordham University Press.

Piero, Mike (2014), 'Coetzee, Blanchot, and the Work of Writing: The Impersonality of Childhood', *Media Tropes*, 4(2): 79–97.

Poyner, Jane (2009), *J. M. Coetzee and the Paradox of Postcolonial Authorship*. Surrey: Ashgate.

Roe, Nicholas (1990), 'Coleridge and John Thelwall: The Road to Nether Stowey'. In: R. Gravil and M. Lefebure, eds, *The Coleridge Connection: Essays for Thomas McFarland*. New York: St. Martin's Press, 60–80.

Seccombe, Thomas (1898), 'John Thelwall', *Dictionary of National Biography*, 56, 110–13. Available online: https://en.wikisource.org/wiki/Thelwall,_John_(DNB00) (accessed 23 September 2019).

Seshadri, Kalpana Rahita (2012), *HumAnimal: Race, Law, Language*. Minneapolis: University of Minnesota Press.

Spivak, Gayatri (1990), 'Theory in the Margin: Coetzee's *Foe* Reading Defoe's *Crusoe/Roxana*', *English in Africa*, 17(2): 1–23.

Sutcliffe, Patricia Casey (2009), 'Saying It Right in *Disgrace*: David Lurie, *Faust*, and the Romantic Conception of Language'. In: B. McDonald, ed., *Encountering Disgrace: Reading and Teaching Coetzee's Novel*. Rochester: Camden House, 173–201.

Thelwall, John (1995), *The Politics of English Jacobinism: Writings of John Thelwall*, ed. G. Claeys. University Park: Pennsylvania State University Press.

Thelwall, John (2001), *The Peripatetic*, ed. J. Thompson. Detroit, MI: Wayne State University Press.

Thelwall, John (2002), '*Essay, Towards a Definition of Animal Vitality*'. In: Nicholas Roe, *The Politics of Nature: William Wordsworth and Some Contemporaries*. New York: Palgrave, 87–119.

Thelwall, John (2013), *The Daughter of Adoption: A Tale of Modern Times*, ed. M. Scrivener, Y. Solomonescu and J. Thompson. Peterborough, ON: Broadview Press.

Thompson, Judith (2010) '"Thy Power to Declare": Thelwall, Coleridge and the Politics of Collaboration', *Romanticism*, 16(2): 164–83.

Thompson, Judith (2012), *John Thelwall in the Wordsworth Circle: The Silenced Partner*. New York: Palgrave Macmillan.

Woessner, Martin (2010), 'Coetzee's Critique of Reason'. In: A. Leist and P. Singer, eds, *J. M. Coetzee and Ethics: Philosophical Perspectives on Literature*. New York: Columbia University Press, 223–47.

Wolfe, Cary (2008), 'Introduction: Exposures'. In Stanley Cavell, Cora Diamond, John McDowell, Ian Hacking and Cary Wolfe, *Philosophy and Animal Life*. New York: Columbia University Press, 1-41.

Wolfe, Cary (2010), *What Is Posthumanism?* Minneapolis: University of Minnesota Press.

Wright, Laurence (2010), 'David Lurie's Learning and the Meaning of J. M. Coetzee's *Disgrace*'. In: G. Bradshaw and M. Neill, eds, *J. M. Coetzee's Austerities*. Surrey: Ashgate, 147-62.

12

Shades of the archive: J. M. Coetzee, the paradox of poetic sovereignty and the lives of literary beings

Russell Samolsky

1.

At a remarkable point in the 'Oxen of the Sun' chapter of James Joyce's *Ulysses*, an episode much given to the braided birth of life and language, a brash Stephen Dedalus boasts of the power of his art to summon the ancient dead: 'You have spoken of the past and its phantoms. ...Why think of them? If I call them into life across the waters of Lethe will not the poor ghosts troop to my call?' (Joyce 1986: 14.1112–14). Dedalus's assertion alludes both to Odysseus calling up the shades as well as to Hotspur's riposte in William Shakespeare's *Henry IV* to Glendower's claim, 'I can call spirits from the vasty deep': 'Why, so can I, or so can any man. But will they come when you do call for them?' (3.1:52–4). Averring that he is indeed 'lord and giver of their life' before whom even the great figures of the past must beck to his call, Dedalus invokes his sovereign power as a poet not only to call back the dead but also to give poetic life itself. The reader will quickly remark that Dedalus's invocation of his poetic sovereignty appears to both confirm and contradict his younger self's now famous proclamation: 'The artist, like the God of the creation, remains within or behind or beyond or above his handiwork, invisible, refined out of existence, indifferent, paring his fingernails' (Joyce 2007: 189). Like the God of creation, the artist is sovereign over his poetic creation, but whereas Dedalus in *Ulysses* proclaims his personal poetic sovereignty, in *A Portrait of the Artist as a Young Man*, he proclaims an aesthetic of godlike impersonality. Thought together, however, Dedalus's poetic theology draws a compelling analogy with Carl Schmitt's political theology.

Published in 1922, the same year as *Ulysses*, Schmitt's *Political Theology* argues that 'all significant concepts of the modern theory of the state are secularized theological concepts ... in which they were transferred from theology to the theory of the state, whereby, for example, the omnipotent God became the omnipotent lawgiver' (1985: 36). Likewise, Dedalus's poetic theology involves a similar transfer from Catholic theology to his secularized theory of art, and indeed to his art of the quotidian itself.

The comparison that I am most concerned in pursuing, however, is with Schmitt's celebrated pronouncement that 'sovereign is he who decides on the exception' (1985: 5). As opposed to the impersonal powers of the law of the state, the sovereign for Schmitt is possessed of a personal power precisely to decide the exception. Indeed, it can be said that the decision on the exception is what calls the sovereign into being, both in terms of his or her office, and also because the sovereign occupies a paradoxical position in that even though he 'stands outside the normally valid legal system, he nevertheless belongs to it' (1985: 7). As with the paradoxical position of the sovereign, the artist, for Dedalus, is like God, both within and beyond his art, and on yet another level, so too is Joyce himself with regard to his own poetic creations. Moreover, like the political sovereign, the poetical sovereign is endowed with the power of deciding the exception, which amounts to the decisionist power over characters to give or take life.

The relation of the artist sovereign to his literary subjects or characters is not simply an issue of Joycean or modernist poetics but retains a contemporary relevance. Offering a counterargument to the trope of artist as god of the story, Amos Oz asserts the independent lives of the characters who speak through him. Addressing his critics and their thought of the malleable lives of his characters before his sovereign fingertips, Oz remarks: 'To them, you are a little god, sitting at your desk writing. ... But the author has less latitude than they imagine. ... I am much less free than people assume. ... I can only say, "That's enough!" but I cannot change the characters, nor can I decide who will live and who will die or who will do what to whom' (Mazor 2002: 163–4). And in response to the question: 'They dictate to you what to write?' Oz answers: 'There is a certain point where if they don't start to lead an independent life, I discard the manuscript; it is not alive. ... The characters are alive only when they tell me, "You keep quiet now, sit down and write, don't interfere!"' (2002: 164).

In contrast to Oz, in his recent *The Good Story*, J. M. Coetzee argues for the antithetical notion of poetic sovereignty:

> Stories are written (dictated) by one person. ... I am rowing against a certain tide here, and I am aware of that. Let me note two currents in the tide. The first is the claim (by certain critics) that there is such a thing as the dialogical novel. The second is the claim (by many writers) that writing, at its most intense moments, is a matter of being dictated to rather than of dictating – there have to be two persons or two souls in the room for a poem (in the widest sense) to get composed.
> (Coetzee and Kurtz 2015: 52–3)

Coetzee's insistence on the singular author would seem to place him alongside, if not Joyce, then Dedalus at least, situating him as an authorial sovereign who 'dictates', in the double sense, the lives of his characters. It would appear that for Coetzee the matter is settled; however, as we recall, in something of a counterposition, he also rather famously argues in *Doubling the Point*:

> Writers are used to being in control of the text and don't resign it easily. But my resistance is not only a matter of protecting a phantasmatic omnipotence. Writing is not free expression. There is a true sense in which writing is dialogic: a matter

of awakening the countervoices in oneself and embarking upon speech with them. It is some measure of a writer's seriousness whether he does evoke/invoke those countervoices in himself, that is, step down from the position of what Lacan calls 'the subject supposed to know'.

(1992: 65)

Coetzee's two claims are not quite contradictory. In both he maintains the writer is one person, and in both he holds to a measure of authorial control, but there is considerable tension between them in that in *Doubling the Point*, Coetzee insists on good writing as decidedly dialogical and on puncturing the fantasy of the author's omnipotence, whereas in *The Good Story*, Coetzee insists on the singular author and appears to disavow the dialogical novel.

In what follows, I explore this divergence by contrasting a moment drawn from Coetzee's archive, a moment when he decides to kill off one of his characters, with Coetzee's display of David Lurie's dialogical composition of his libretto in *Disgrace*. I analyse the first moment in terms of Coetzee's avowal of the singular or sovereign author and the second as Coetzee's meditation on the limits of authorial sovereignty. Towards this end, I focus on various instances in his archive when Coetzee addresses himself in order to go on writing and consider what this reveals about his relation to his own author-figures. What I hope to draw out is the paradoxical nature of poetic sovereignty with regard to the lives of literary beings as revealed by the shades of Coetzee's archive.

2.

Glad for the shade of the Ransom Center and respite from the torch of the mid-summer Texas sun, a range of thoughts and impressions on Coetzee's archive came to me as I read through a set of his notebooks and manuscripts on my visits in 2016 and 2017. To record just a pertinent few: I was certainly struck by Coetzee's meticulous organization and saving of his daily drafts as if the archive of his texts was always being prepared for scholarly analysis from the beginning, the future archive already prepared for in advance. Even more so, I was taken by the steady accumulation of a handwritten page a day and Coetzee's immense will to revision – not only the mechanical secrets to the great puzzle of how writing gets done, I remember musing; but also evidence of that paradoxical feedback loop whereby the writing itself patiently guides Coetzee, revealing to him the contours of the story. What Coetzee's archive also reveals, however, is not the indifferent artist above his handiwork, paring his fingernails, but rather a maze of mostly handwritten drafts and notebooks that chart the decidedly personal and steely struggle of Coetzee writing his way through many great obstacles. After years of applying himself to the project that would become *Foe*, for example, Coetzee, despairing, finds that the book is blocked, refusing to come to life, but still he exhorts himself: 'Reached my lowest point yet, yesterday. Thought I would give it all up. Headache, depression. … Yet I don't want to let go. There is something in the book that engages me – perhaps not in the book as it is but in the book as it could be, in the future of the book' (HRC, CP,

33.6: 5-4-84). And months later, after much drafting, he again confides to himself: 'The only interesting thing about the project thus far is that I cannot give it up: there is something, somewhere that holds my interest' (HRC, CP, 33.6: 31-5-84). What these confessional moments intimately disclose is not only Coetzee's great determination in holding to his project but the uncanny way in which Coetzee himself becomes a character in his own archive, becomes, that is, conflated with his artist-figures that we know so well from his novels. I do not only mean the moments when Coetzee introduces himself as an 'I' into his writing, crucial as these are, but also those moments when he addresses himself about the practice of writing in the same way that his artist-figures do to characters in his novels: counselling the art of patience, to keep writing, to see what will come of it, to allow the work unexpectedly to reveal itself.

Working his way through an early version of *Life & Times of Michael K*, for example, Coetzee proposes turning an embittered K whose grandmother dies on the journey to her burial place into a killer. He tells himself: 'The problem is that this is just naturalism. ... Anyhow, let us pursue the idea for a while' (HRC, CP, 33.5: 16-12-80). And a few sentences on, he remarks: 'For much of the journey he is carrying only the corpse of his grandmother (shades of Faulkner!).' Some nine months later, we find Coetzee advising himself: 'There is a strong temptation to begin rewriting the book from scratch. But I suppose the thing to do is to plough on, perhaps going as fast as I can, and forgetting about quality, just to get the narrative line and to allow ideas to spring up/in' (HRC, CP, 33.5: 11-4-81). The counsel Coetzee gives himself about the writing of *Michael K* – the way that he speaks to himself about his own process of composition – becomes a source for the advice that David Lurie will later offer himself: 'Working as swiftly as he can, holding tight to Teresa, he tries to sketch out the opening pages of a libretto. Get the words down on paper, he tells himself. Once that is done it will all be easier' (1999: 183).

What led me, however, to the primary questions of this piece was my coming across a further entry in the notebook devoted to *Michael K*. Here Coetzee admonishes himself: 'There is no feeling between Michael and his mother, and I can't induce it. The longer she is around, the duller + heavier the narrative. Kill her off in Stellenbosch' (HRC, CP, 33.5: 26-5-81). The note refers, of course, to Anna K, and after numerous drafts Coetzee finds that she is belabouring the narrative, and decides that she must die by the time they come to Stellenbosch. What I found startling in Coetzee's directive to himself is the cool resolve of his poetic sovereignty – he cannot go on with her, and after giving her a bit more decrepit life he will kill her off so as to release Michael K. On the one hand, his directive might not seem anything out of the ordinary; characters die in literature all the time; authors sometimes have no choice but to kill them off. This is Coetzee deploying the decisionist act of the authorial sovereign. But at the same time, Coetzee also abjures claims of utter authority over his characters; indeed, he tells himself, 'I can't induce it,' as if there is something not entirely in his control about Anna K and her blocking the narrative. As Coetzee's doppelgänger JC proclaims: 'Stories tell themselves, they don't get told. ... That much I know after a lifetime of working with stories. Never try to impose yourself' (2007: 55). And yet, Coetzee's directive, 'Kill her off,' and his execution of his directive, is certainly a sovereign gesture, a most sovereign imposition. How then to begin accounting for this discrepancy?

Perhaps the first thing to note is that the question behind Coetzee's sovereign act would not so forcefully impose itself were it not for our looking into his archive. The second would be to remark that what Coetzee's assertion in *The Good Story* teaches us is that it is a mistake to conflate Coetzee's authors in his novels with Coetzee himself, and that in JC Coetzee presents a romanticized figure of the author, and of how stories get told. This is surely true, but the issue is more complicated, as JC's claim also partially accords with Coetzee's own analysis of storytelling and the ontological status of what he calls 'fictional beings'. In his short piece 'Fictional Beings', Coetzee gives an account of his reading the part of *The Sound and the Fury* devoted to Benjy. He begins with his perplexed failure to grasp or understand the logic behind Benjy's broken syntax but he perseveres with reading and gradually he finds he is 'better and better able to "do" Benjy' (2003b: 134). What Coetzee means by this is that his growing understanding of Benjy's linguistic gestures allows him to better enter or inhabit his mind. Switching to Faulkner's perspective, Coetzee tells us that although in one sense Faulkner knows that he has no true ingress into the minds of the Compsons and is merely constructing representations of their thoughts, 'nevertheless he finds it convenient to think that the Compsons are "real" and that somehow, magically, he is inhabiting each of them in turn for a while' (2003b: 134). It is this strange magic, Coetzee tells us, that subtends the very phylum of literary beings:

> In the account preferred by storytellers ... an account that we willingly entertain when we read or listen to stories, storytellers (a) inhabit real beings and represent them from the inside, and also (b) by this process create them out of nothing and turn them into real beings. It is a paradoxical position, but it does appear to be a position of some importance to human societies, which, in a paradoxical movement of their own, both (a) entertain it, and (b) dismiss it as nonsense.
> (2003b: 134)

We readily detect how Coetzee's paradox of the storyteller now meets up with the poetical sovereign. Coetzee remarks the power of the storyteller to create fictional beings from nothing or, as Dedalus puts it, to call up shades from across Lethe, the 'vasty deep' or the void. But this conjuration of literary beings from nothing rests on the temporal paradox of first inhabiting them from the inside as real beings, which, in turn, replicates the paradoxical topology of the political sovereign (to say nothing of God the sovereign creating this world itself ex nihilo). As Giorgio Agamben fittingly formulates it: '*Being-outside, and yet belonging*: this is the topological structure of the state of exception, and only because the sovereign, who decides on the exception, is, in truth, logically defined in his being by the exception, can he too be defined by the oxymoron *ecstasy-belonging*' (2005: 35). And, like the political sovereign deciding the exception, the poetical sovereign, who has by means both of the temporal and topological paradox of the exception called up a literary being from the void, might equally deploy her decisionist power to return this being to the void.

But is there not another way of considering this? Is it perhaps not equally true that Coetzee finds that he cannot 'do' Anna K? That he finds he cannot fully write his way into her literary being, and despite deploying his full artistic powers she stubbornly resists his full conjuration? That she, in effect, withdraws her characterlogical or literary being? She remains, in a sense, a shade of the archive, living her half-life in the various drafts of the archival underworld, accompanied there by other even less-realized fictional beings or shades. The question arises then as to how this sovereign decision gets made. After all, if we are to take seriously the real being of a literary character for author and reader, as Coetzee, in one sense claims we should, killing her off is no inconsequential matter.

We are offered some insight into this by another of Coetzee's author-figures, Elizabeth Costello. In the afterlife herself, Costello paradoxically conjures a scene of Odysseus having descended into the underworld, fending off pallid shades that clamour to drink the blood of a ram whose throat he has cut, in order to prove to herself that what she truly believes in is a body that can die. Costello, spokesperson for authors, but not one through whom Coetzee himself speaks, claims: 'I am a writer, and what I write is what I hear. ... That is my calling: dictation secretary. It is not for me to interrogate, to judge what is given me. I merely write down the words and then test them, test their soundness, to make sure I have heard right' (2003a: 199). In contrast to the sovereign author who calls up and banishes shades at will, Costello describes her calling rather as a medium or conduit through whom shades or literary beings elect to manifest themselves. Her choice is not which shade to call up but only in deciding if that shade is speaking clearly enough through her, if she has heard the proper words. Her role is only in being open to those shades that call upon her, even those from whom she would prefer not to hear, even those with whom she would decidedly not break bread in life. In this strange sense, paradoxically, the shade that unremittingly calls on her is a poetical sovereign of sorts.

Costello's art, then, is one of auscultation, of a deep sounding, or sounding of the 'vasty deep'. Trying to determine if she has properly heard a story of river frogs, 'she tries a test that seems to work when she is writing: to send out a word into the darkness and listen for what kind of sound comes back. Like a foundryman tapping a bell: is it cracked or healthy?' (2003a: 219). She listens for a tone but hears none, none at all, 'but she is too canny, knows the business too well, to be disappointed just yet' (2003a: 219). And then, sounding very much like Coetzee conferring with himself in his private notebooks, she encourages herself to have the patience to allow the shades of her frogs to emerge from their tombs: 'Give them time: they might yet be made to ring true. For there is something about them that obscurely engages her, something about their mud tombs' (2003a: 219). She finds that as she continues to trust in these river frogs and their cycle of death and life and their calling to her from within their tombs, the story begins to ring true:

> Yes, that she can believe in: the dissolution, the return to the elements; and the converse moment she can believe in too, when the first quiver of returning life runs through the body and the limbs contract, the hands flex. She can believe in that, if she concentrates closely enough, word by word.
>
> (2003a: 220)

Costello believes in that which undeniably has an existence outside of hers, and yet it is, paradoxically, only because this existence is set apart from hers that it can profoundly give life to her fictional beings, or, put, another way, her fictional beings depend precisely on that which is not her. If, as Coetzee contends in *The Good Story*, he does not believe in Costello's fiction of dictation, he does believe in her emergence as an independent fictional being. In a recent interview, he tells of a friend on a lecture tour who is asked by a member of the audience to say more about the Australian writer Elizabeth Costello. Coetzee remarks: 'I mention this story because it shows how a fictional being, Elizabeth Costello, can take up residence in the real world, and also how a fictional creation can escape the control of her creator' (2018).

Not all shades, Costello tells us, will elect her secretary of the invisible, or call on her for their manifestation, but I want now to examine *Disgrace* as Coetzee's meditation on the writer who calls up a shade only to find that he lacks the poetic power to give her, who he has called back to life, more life. I shall try, that is, to read Lurie's libretto as a meditation on the limits of poetic sovereignty and, in so doing, analyse the novel itself as an archive of shades.

3.

Drawing, no doubt, on his own experience of coming face to face with the despair of poetic failure, Coetzee interfuses David Lurie with this same despair as he confronts the composition of his opera: 'Sometimes he fears that the characters in the story, who for more than a year have been his ghostly companions, are beginning to fade away. … Their loss fills him with despair, despair as grey and even and unimportant, in the larger scheme, as a headache' (1999: 141–2). But even as he feels the characters fade, Lurie tries the gambit of shifting the period of the opera, and, remarkably, an older Teresa emerges who herself calls to the shade of Byron in the underworld, bringing him breath by breath back to life. Reflecting on this emergence, Lurie says: 'That is how it must be from here on: Teresa giving voice to her lover, and he, the man in the ransacked house, giving voice to Teresa' (1999: 183). The poignant metalepsis of Lurie's libretto echoes the paradox of poetic creation, and it is thus not only in the sense of the gratefully unexpected that the re-emergence of the fading shade of Teresa is extraordinary. As he delves deeper into their underworld he is blessed with the coming to light of their words and music:

> And, astonishingly, in dribs and drabs, the music comes. Sometimes the contour of a phrase occurs to him before he has a hint of what the words themselves will be; sometimes the words call forth the cadence; sometimes the shade of a melody, having hovered for days on the edge of hearing, unfolds and blessedly reveals itself.
> (1999: 183)

Despite his claim that Teresa 'has immortal longings, and sings her longings. She will not be dead', in the end Lurie finds that he lacks the poetic power to sustain the shade of Teresa (1999: 209). He cannot wholly call her back to life as she cannot wholly call Byron back to life. Sadly, he remarks to himself: 'Poor Teresa! Poor aching girl! He has brought her back from the grave, promised her another life, and now he is failing her. He hopes she will find it in her heart to forgive him' (1999: 214). In sombre contrast to Dedalus and his asseveration of his sovereign power of calling shades across the waters of the Lethe into life, Lurie learns the limits of his powers of conjuration and giving poetic life. If the words and music that brought Teresa and her Byron to life were blessedly revealed to him, he finds now that he cannot grant her what Harold Bloom terms the 'blessings of more life' (1987: 160). If, in his poetic struggle, he cannot win for her the blessing of more life, if he cannot hold her from going back down under, he does hope for her forgiveness. His stance, then, is not one of denying the life of this withdrawn shade (even as Byron withdrew from Teresa back into stony sleep). If he cannot quite ask for her blessing, he does hope for her forgiveness, something he cannot compel, and only she can grant, even as he will never know if she does or does not. It is in this sense that the libretto and the scene of its composition marks a meditation on the limits of poetic sovereignty, which in contrast to sovereign poetics holds itself open to the dialogical alterity of poetic life. While Lurie's composition of the libretto contrasts with Coetzee's claim that there are not 'two souls in the room' when a poem is composed, it does both evoke and display the dialogism of 'awakening the countervoices in oneself and embarking upon speech with them' (Coetzee and Kurtz 2015: 53; Coetzee 1992: 65). It invokes too a step down from claims of poetic mastery.

In the wake of his faded shade, what Lurie wishes to leave behind in the place of the immortal song of Teresa is now only a 'note of immortal longing'. In an opera that he knows will never be realized, all he might still hope for is 'that somewhere from amidst the welter of sound there will dart up, like a bird, a single authentic note of immortal longing. As for recognizing it, he will leave that to the scholars of the future, if there are still scholars by then. For he will not hear the note himself, when it comes, if it comes' (1999: 214). What Lurie wishes to leave behind is, in effect, an archive – an archive that will house his immortal note, that, paradoxically, he will not live to hear. He imagines this note, like a darting bird, almost calling itself up, but, dialogically, this note is also a shade that awaits its future hearing, and scholarly calling up. Lurie has after all just spoken of the 'shade of a melody', that having hovered at the verge of hearing reveals itself, and like Costello sending out a word, which she likens to a foundryman testing the tone of a bell, he hopes to have sent out a note to the future that will ring as true – a shade, therefore, that hovers at the verge of the hearing of the scholars of the future before it discloses itself to them.

This gesture, however, is paradoxical in that on the one hand it marks a limit to the legibility of the archive, and on the other, it opens the archive to the promise of the future to come. If, for Lurie, this note remains forever other to himself, forever a shade, in truth, what he has bequeathed us is also, in part, a secret archive, an archive that holds its secret because it is a note that we scholars, even we scholars of the future, will properly never hear. In this sense, this immortal note of which Lurie notes, 'when it comes, if it comes', Coetzee knows, will never come, will always be a shade, hovering at the verge of hearing, in the underworld of an archive – that is, a shade of the archive itself, the shadow or spectre of an archive that *Disgrace* archives.

What then is the significance of this spectral archive, and what is the effect of our being placed in the same position as Lurie with regard to the immortal note we will never hear? One lesson, I think, that this note performs without performing, so to speak, is that we can never be sovereign scholars of Coetzee's archive, calling up all its shades, for some of its secrets will always be shaded by interpretability, and others forever undisclosed. Yet, Lurie has learned too from the fading of Teresa that if a note of this opera is to live on it will do so only by virtue of his giving it up to something beyond himself, to the possibility of the *arrivant* of the future to come.

In addressing this note to the scholars of the future, Lurie's project resonates with Jacques Derrida's analysis of the archive in *Archive Fever*. We recall that Derrida also invokes the scholar of the future, whom he sees as possibly anticipated in Marcellus's entreating: 'Thou art a Scholler, speake to it, Horatio' (1995: 39). Derrida differentiates this scholar of the future from the classical scholar precisely in her willingness to address the phantom: 'A scholar who would dare to admit that he knows how to speak *to* the phantom, even claiming that this not only neither contradicts nor limits his scholarship but will in truth have conditioned it' (1995: 39). It is perhaps on such a scholar that Lurie's hopes rest for the recognition of his immortal note that might fly up from the underworld of his archive. Although he proclaims that the archive is always shadowed by the death drive, for Derrida it is necessarily conditioned as well by all that is contained in the promise of the future:

> The archive: if we want to know what that will have meant, we will only know in times to come. Perhaps. Not tomorrow but in times to come, later on or perhaps never. A spectral messianicity is at work in the concept of the archive and ties it, like religion, like history, like science itself, to a very singular experience of the promise.
> (1995: 36)

It is to this promise that Lurie offers his note, the promise that it will in its future recognition constitute the archive of his opera.

There is, however, one last shade that unexpectedly calls to Lurie from the shore of Lethe. He does not know how this voice cries out from within himself but he knows it is Allegra, the daughter Byron has forsaken, and who, burning up with malaria, calls to her father, '*Come and fetch me!*' (1999: 186). Although he feels for this child, as with Teresa, he can give her no more life. And, while he cannot know it at this time, it will be Allegra and not Teresa who foreshadows and perhaps helps prepare him to accept and affirm Lucy's child to come.

In his early drafting of *Disgrace*, Coetzee places the focus precisely on the question of the future and how to live on when confronted by visions of looming death and thinks of himself as embroiled in his protagonist's existential block:

> The moral centre of the book: this man consistently takes the line, Nothing matters, soon I will be dead anyway. In other words, he cannot see beyond his death. Somehow he (I too!) must get beyond that. Hence, of course, the daughter, the only way in which he (I too!) can conceive of the future. (Think of James Joyce on the girls in Shakespeare's late plays.).
> (HRC, CP, 35.2: 21-4-96)

With the loss of his son (a correlation with Shakespeare that Coetzee notes with his parenthetical, 'I too!'), he looks to his daughter as the one who will allow him to conceive of his future.¹ He remarks how this thought is further conditioned by Dedalus's theory of Shakespeare composing *Hamlet* out of the loss of his son Hamnet and working through the bleak tragedies to his later romances by means of his consideration of daughters (prompted by the birth of his granddaughter). Joyce's Shakespeare chapter has much to do with authorial power, privacy and paradox, but its reference in Coetzee's archive as a source for *Disgrace* also provides material context for the opening of this chapter. Contending with the pressure of realism that was moulding the composition of *Disgrace*, Coetzee questions whether there is 'something in the South African material that drives one toward this dull realism? A respect for this material that is essentially fearful?' (HRC, CP, 35.2: 24-10-96). Remarking on this, David Attwell asserts:

> It is a bitter reflection, confirmed by similar frank expressions of resentment in the novel's preparatory papers. Even if it is the case, which it is, that the published novel manages to transform its raw material into an aesthetically detached achievement … the resentments are not far beneath the surface.
>
> (2015: 193)

Oddly, the effect of this purgation would appear to have *Disgrace* confirm Dedalus's aesthetic of detachment in *Portrait* and return us to the question of the sovereign powers of the artist.²

4.

Unlike Franz Kafka, for example, Coetzee, it appears, had no thought of burning his archive but it is with the burning up of one of his literary beings that I will conclude this piece.³ I also return to the theme of Coetzee speaking to himself in order to speak to, and sometimes through, his author-figures but with a curious twist. It is likely because of his struggle with the constrictions of realism that Coetzee noted this quotation from Y. H. Yerushalmi's *Freud's Moses* as applying equally to artistic creativity: 'Freud on scientific creativity: the "succession of daringly playful fantasy and relentlessly realistic criticism!["]' (HRC, CP, 35.3: 26-12-97). It is partly by means of his critique of Yerushalmi's theatrical 'Monologue with Freud' that Derrida takes up his theorizing of the archive, and he does so by deploying his own coup de théâtre. Taking up a story through which Freud means to talk of himself, Derrida claims: 'Here is the *coup de théâtre*, the dramatic twist. Freud pretended to speak of someone else, of a colleague. (If I were to be immodest to such a point, doubly immodest, I would say that he did what I am doing in speaking of a colleague, Yerushalmi, while I am speaking of myself)' (1995: 89). What I am particularly interested in following here is the way in which the coup de théâtre, defined not only as a dramatic twist but also as an addressing of oneself while apparently addressing another, aligns with the coup de grâce in *Disgrace*.

We recall that it is while he is witnessing the killing of the caged dogs Lurie sees a dog, 'with a gaping throat-wound … flattens its ears, following with its gaze the movements of this being who does not even bother to administer a *coup de grâce*' (1999: 95). In 'Fictional Beings', Coetzee speaks not only of the writer entering the fictional being of the human but of animals too, and here we see Lurie passing through the uncomprehending mind of the dying dog as both he and the dog regard this unconscionable being. What Coetzee's notebook reveals, however, is one of the reasons why this massacre takes place: 'The robbers have to kill all the dogs (bar the bulldog). The plotting problems if there are dogs left alive in the cages are too great' (HRC, CP, 35.2: 4-10-96). We are immediately reminded of Anna K, and presented with another instance of Coetzee's decision to kill off literary beings whose lives he cannot sustain. In this way the exigency of killing off the dogs guides the plot but it also opens a comparison with Lurie's *Lösung*. Although he warns himself against sentimentalizing, he thinks, finally, of his guiding the dogs to their deaths in the theatre as an act of love, an elevating, bestowing of grace on those whose 'period of grace is almost over' (1999: 215). This marks a sheer contrast with that being who will not even administer the coup de grâce. In some respects, this is certainly true but the notebooks and drafts also reveal a more suspicious backstory that leaves its trace in *Disgrace* as we know it. For a considerable portion of his drafting of the novel, Coetzee had Lurie committing suicide; to his surprise, however, he comes to find Lurie resistant to this end. Coetzee notes: 'This man has no sense of having been caught out, of his friends turning on him, of shock, of desire for suicide' (HRC, CP, 35.2: 1-11-96). Lurie will not be sent to the far shore of Lethe, but that Coetzee considered having him take his life with Lethal, the drug used to euthanize the dogs, divulges a displacement that leaves its trace in *Disgrace*.[4]

There is moreover another footprint that remains, which is Lurie's musing on the three-footed dog's incomprehension before its death:

> What the dog will not be able to work out ... what his nose will not tell him, is how one can enter what seems to be an ordinary room and never come out again. ... It will be beyond him, this room that is not a room but a hole where one leaks out of existence.
> (1999: 219)

Lurie again places himself in the uncomprehending mind of the dog in the face of death, which brings together the hole in the dying dog's throat and the hole where one leaks out of existence. In a subtle sense this conflation requires us to think this correlation between the refusal to administer the coup de grâce and the bestowing of a dying grace as one of interlinked power, for in grasping, and indulging, in the dog's utter incomprehension, does Lurie not himself attain a godlike power over the dog that would unconditionally die for him? I do not mean to force a full equivalence here, but rather to claim Lurie's dispatching and burning up of the dog is not indissociable from his indulging a godlike power.

Indeed, Coetzee's late notes find Lurie considering his godlike power, and this brings us finally back to poetical sovereignty and shades. We know the dog will go on to become the three-footed dog that Lurie will consider entering into the opera but before this, in his notes, Coetzee has Lurie naming the lame dog Byron, linking the lameness of the dog to Byron's clubfoot, perhaps, but, more importantly, linking the dog both to Byron as poet but also Byron in his opera who is sunk on the distant shores of Lethe.[5] Moreover, thinking of the dogs he both loves and submits to death, Lurie proclaims, 'If

I am to be God ... I must learn to kill impartially' (HRC, CP, 35.3: 24-1-98). The note ends with, 'The dog Byron, before it goes in to be killed, behaves guiltily, creeping on the floor, flattening its ears. The shame of dying' (HRC, CP, 35.3: 24-1-98). This clearly conflates the dog with Kafka's K, who dies uncomprehendingly in *The Trial* – 'Like a dog ... as though the shame was to outlive him' (1998: 231). I want, however, to close with an earlier entry devoted to the interleaved *Disgrace–Lives of Animals* notebooks:

> The whole of Kafka can be read out of the phenomena of the laboratory animal. Our contempt for animals who will never understand what we are doing with them, despite the fact that what we are doing is quite banal. The gap is not between human and divine, simply between one order of signification (metonymic: smells) and another (symbolic: language), a gap which will never be crossed.
> (HRC, CP, 35.3: 22-8-97)

This note deflates Lurie's fascination with the power he has over the dog's incomprehension in the face of its expiration. He is correct that the dog's nose will not explain this moment of extinction that leaves lingering only the residue or smell of being, but what he takes to be a divide between orders of power, even divine power, in the face of death is no more than a difference between orders of signification, between body and language that recalls the paradox of Costello and the frogs.

There is, however, one further coup de théâtre of the archive, of those moments where Coetzee addresses himself. That is, might I not also be accused of acting like a sovereign critic, a critical sovereign who exploits the paradoxical topology of the presence of Coetzee as author in his archive? For, in my analysis, it is not simply that Coetzee's addressing himself with regard to his artistic practice echoes that of his artist figures addressing themselves with regard to their artistic practices, thereby conferring a certain reality upon them. (I do not wish to claim the opposite, that this confers a certain fictitiousness on Coetzee, although it is easy to fall into the trap of wholly conflating the claims of Coetzee's authors with those of Coetzee himself.) It is also that my analysis deploys the paradox, not unlike the paradox of authorship itself, that Coetzee himself becomes split into author and archived author – the inscribed 'I' that is somehow both Coetzee in and out of the archive, the 'I' in the archive that will outlive the 'I' who wrote the texts housed in the archive. If this is so, however, it is only because of Coetzee's refusal of the sovereign act of consigning his archive to oblivion; it is only by virtue of Coetzee holding open his archive to scholars of the present and future, which is why, even as he kills off characters, Coetzee would not burn his archive, for it houses those shades from which underworld half-life they may still call and be called up.

Notes

1 For more on Coetzee's loss of his son, see Kannemeyer (2012: 455–7).

2 Although writing for Coetzee might be a means of working through his fixations, I do not believe Dedalus's position of aesthetic detachment is one with which Coetzee would agree, nor do I wish to suggest that Attwell believes he would.
3 On the contrary, addressing the conservation of his archive, Coetzee remarks: 'I write these words from my home … an area prone to destructive bushfires. It is a secondary source of satisfaction to me that, even if this house itself goes up in flames, the work of my hands will have been whisked away to a place of safety in the vaults of the Ransom Center' (Tisdale 2013; n.p.).
4 For astute commentary on this displacement see Attwell (2015: 207–8).
5 I have examined the ethical issues involved in entering the dog into the opera in Samolsky (2009).

References

Agamben, G. (2005), *State of Exception*, trans. K. Attell. Chicago: University of Chicago Press.
Attwell, D. (2015), *J.M. Coetzee and the Life of Writing*. New York: Penguin.
Bloom, H. (1987), *Ruin the Sacred Truths: Poetry and Belief from the Bible to the Present*. Cambridge, MA: Harvard University Press.
Coetzee, J. M. 'J.M. Coetzee Papers'. Austin, TX: Harry Ransom Center.
Coetzee, J. M. (1992), *Doubling the Point: Essays and Interviews*, ed. D. Attwell. Cambridge, MA: Harvard University Press.
Coetzee, J. M. (1999), *Disgrace*. New York: Penguin.
Coetzee, J. M. (2003a), *Elizabeth Costello*. New York: Viking.
Coetzee, J. M. (2003b), 'Fictional Beings', *Philosophy, Psychiatry, & Psychology*, 10 (2): 133–4.
Coetzee, J. M. (2007), *Diary of a Bad Year*. New York: Penguin.
Coetzee, J. M. (2018) (video), 'In Conversation: J.M. Coetzee with Soledad Constantini'. Available online: https://www.youtube.com/watch?v=4VNk52t-YPM&t=16m30s.
Coetzee, J. M., and A. Kurtz (2015), *The Good Story*. New York: Penguin.
Derrida, J. (1995), *Archive Fever*, trans. E. Prenowitz. Chicago: University of Chicago Press.
Joyce, J. (1986), *Ulysses*. New York: Random House.
Joyce, J. (2007), *A Portrait of the Artist as a Young Man*, ed. J. P. Riquelme. New York: W. W. Norton.
Kafka, F. (1998), *The Trial*, trans. B. Mitchell. New York: Schocken Books.
Kannemeyer, J. C. (2012), *J.M. Coetzee: A Life in Writing*. London: Scribe.
Mazor, Y. (2002), *Somber Lust: The Art of Amos Oz*. Albany, NY: SUNY Press.
Samolsky, R. (2009), 'Acts of Mourning: Art and the Lives of Animals in J.M. Coetzee's *Disgrace* and *Elizabeth Costello*'. In: E. Boehmer, K. Iddiols and R. Eaglestone, eds, *J.M. Coetzee in Context and Theory*. , London: Continuum, 147–58.
Schmitt, C. (1985), *Political Theology: Four Chapters on the Concept of Sovereignty*, trans. G. Schwab. Chicago: University of Chicago Press.
Tisdale, J. (2013), 'J.M. Coetzee's Association with the University of Texas at Austin', *Ransom Center Magazine*, 21 March. Available online: https://sites.utexas.edu/ransomcentermagazine/2013/03/21/coetzeeopen (accessed 30 July 2018).

Part Six

Conversations with Coetzee

13

Waiting for the Barbarians and the origins of *Incoming*

Richard Mosse

In 2014, I became aware of a powerful new type of thermographic military surveillance camera that can image human body heat, day or night, from a distance of 30.3 km (about 18 miles). This military tool was designed and built by a multinational weapons company here in Europe, to be sold to military and police forces for the purpose of battlefield situational awareness, long-range border enforcement for detecting and tracking insurgents, and for search and rescue. Too large and unwieldy for aerial surveillance, the camera was designed to sit on a remotely operated sentry or gimbal on border fences or on isolated military outposts or on naval ships. This military tool was never intended for storytelling. Yet it possesses a remarkably expressive aesthetic quality, with a subtle tonality and jagged, blown-out highlights, rendering the world in a heat signature of relative temperature difference. By imaging medium-wave infrared, it is able to perceive heat radiation, depicting the human body not as we see it, but as a glowing organism, revealing the most intimate human processes such as respiration, circulation and perspiration.

Around this time, a friend named Marta Giaccone gave me the gift of John Coetzee's powerful and discomfiting novel *Waiting for the Barbarians*. This difficult story struck me to the heart. Though it was written in an undisclosed landscape in an unspecified historical era, describing a remote imperial outpost of an unnamed Empire, the novel seemed entirely contemporary, speaking powerfully to some pressing issues of our day, such as fear of the other, torture, racial objectification and empire. Anyone who has read the novel will remember Colonel Joll's tinted sunglasses at the start of the novel, and of course the Girl's blindness, a result of being tortured with a hot iron. Vision and blindness are important motifs within the book, and I feel this translates as the vision of surveillance and the entanglement of the political and the visual, especially in relation to ideas of empire: charting, surveilling, mapping, controlling. The book left me with an uneasy new awareness of complicity in evil – the Magistrate's, but also my own.

These issues swirled around inside me, coalescing with many of the questions raised by this sinister new camera technology. The more I thought about it, the more these two incongruous things, the novel and the surveillance camera, seemed to speak to each other. They converged in my imagination, and I began to dream of using this camera to create a film of the story of *Waiting for the Barbarians*, shooting scenes from a great distance, perhaps 2 or 3 km. This tool of long-range border enforcement and insurgent detection technology seemed an appropriate tool for this tale set on the distant remotest edge of the Empire, on a vast plain, a town populated by people gazing out at the horizon, waiting in fear for the barbarians. Indeed, the camera's name is actually Horizon. The scenes in which the Magistrate and the Girl are tracked at far distance by barbarian scouts seemed apposite. But then, when I began to dig a little deeper into some of the camera's intended purposes, it became clear to me that the two, the story and the medium, would create many sparks of meaning when brought into dialogue with each other. The intimate scenes in which the Magistrate massages the wounded legs of the Girl, or the graphic scenes of torture – I imagined how the camera would amplify that intimacy and that violence to a nearly monstrous level.

With great excitement, I began to read around the subject. To write *Waiting for the Barbarians*, Coetzee is said to have borrowed from the strange Italian novel *The Tartar Steppe* by Dino Buzzati. I read this book also. It is a very different book, a beautiful and haunting novel also set in a remote imperial military outpost, also about watching and waiting for the barbarian enemy. Both books seemed to describe the brittle moment of calm experienced just prior to imperial collapse, a moment, perhaps, in which some of us in the West currently live. Buzzati is said to have borrowed from or based his story on Franz Kafka's *The Castle*, a novel which seems utterly relevant to the current state of Europe. With these three texts in mind, I began to dream of making *Waiting for the Barbarians* into a film. With a little research I found that there had already been several failed attempts in the past by other film-makers. These attempts are discussed in Hermann Wittenberg's excellent introduction to the book *Two Screenplays*, which also contains Coetzee's own screenplay adaptation of his novel *Waiting for the Barbarians*.

I began to speak to friends about the idea of making a film of this novel with the powerful thermographic camera. I wanted somehow to reach out to Coetzee to ask him for his permission. Perhaps he would decline, or have specific ideas, I wasn't sure. A good friend, the Irish artist Helen O'Leary, who teaches at Pennsylvania State University, said that John Coetzee had recently visited to give a lecture, and she had hosted a dinner for him and various students and faculty in her home. John, she explained, liked what she had cooked and had asked for her email address, so she could send him the recipe. Helen gave me John's email and said to say that she had given it to me and that she says hello. With great trepidation, because for some reason I am terribly scared of my heroes, I composed a short nervous email explaining how I wanted to remake his novel as a work of video art and asking for his permission. At this stage, I had conducted various tests with the thermal camera in and around London, and I explained to John that I would be happy to send him this short clip to show him how the medium represents the world, and help him understand my visual strategy. John responded, asking to see the clip. I sent it to him. And the next day, John wrote a short email granting me permission.

You have to understand that I have been a documentarian for as long as I can remember. I have never made a work involving actors, costumes and sets. I have no concept of how to go about such a task. But I was willing to take a leap in the dark.

And so I flew out to the volcanic island of Lanzarote with the cinematographer Trevor Tweeten and the thermal camera, in the hopes of trying to shoot a few scenes from the novel, to get an idea of how it would look. We met a woman named Lucy on the plane down. Lucy was working as our flight attendant. I asked if she would like to spend her weekend acting out a few scenes from this novel, and she agreed. I would be the Magistrate, and Lucy would play the Girl. Somehow we managed to find some medieval-style costumes. And we managed to procure a horse. And these are some of the scenes that we shot. I feel I make a very convincing lecherous old Magistrate, and Lucy a very beautiful Girl, so I feel the scenes are well cast. However, beyond that, it was clear I had not yet hit gold, creatively speaking.

I guess our takeaway from this short trip to Lanzarote was that I lacked the experience to construct a convincing fictional narrative. And *Waiting for the Barbarians* is very much a psychological drama, about the passions and emotions simmering away inside the Magistrate's heart, and as such would require a director of great subtlety – and an actor of great talent – to tease out on screen. But I feel we learned a great deal about the camera, how it depicts nature in a rather unsurprising and conventional way, but it really comes into its own when it portrays the human body and other sources of heat. Such as images of the bowl of warm water that I massaged Lucy's foot with. The currents of water in the bowl evoked a swirling galaxy, unlike anything we had ever seen, and the warm water that I washed her leg with looked like blood.

I returned to New York to try to meditate on this short experiment, and work out which direction to take the project in. I felt more than a little underqualified to begin the task of adequately conveying such a complex tale. One thing I wanted to do was to do the job right. I spoke to one or two movie producers, to ask for advice on creating a proper feature film with a budget, and there were questions of who owns the rights. Evidently the rights had been bought, and the first thing to do would be to find out who owned them and see if they would be willing to sell them. It all began to seem incredibly expensive, so I quickly abandoned the idea. I did play with the idea of a more Brechtian approach, to re-enact the story in my studio with more expressive costumes and a more stylized approach. But I abandoned this also, as I did not want to take liberties with the novel, which is so sparely written and perfectly formed. In any case, Philip Glass had already gone down this route and I had no wish to tread on his turf.

This was a critical moment for me. I was still extremely inspired by the novel and how it correlated with the camera technology I had begun to experiment with, but I was at a point of giving up. Giving up, I find, is actually a very important stage in the artistic process. It can lead to failure, but it can also lead to breakthrough. Sometimes both. 'Try again, fail again, fail better.'

It was around this time, in 2015, that Europe was in the grip of an exponential mass-migration crisis the likes of which we had not seen since the Second World War. In 2014 alone, more than a million refugees had landed on European shores seeking asylum, and those numbers showed no sign of abating. It was a crisis of extraordinary proportions. Our inability to manage and share the world's resources, to prevent the loss of arable lands resulting from global warming, and the endless series of wars resulting from and contributing to climate change – this constellation of factors had produced a perfect storm of human displacement. But unlike what happened in the wake of the Second World War, when we enshrined the human rights of the refugee in the 1951 UN Refugee Convention, our response to this crisis of human displacement has been woefully inadequate. Instead of recognizing those rights, European nations have found ways to erode them. Certain nations shirk their asylum duties or have found ways to refoule refugees to other countries, a human rights violation in itself, while others, such as Hungary and Croatia, like Thailand and Australia, have simply closed their borders to refugees. Indeed, the European Union's (EU's) response has been termed Fortress Europe, and we have created border-enforcement agencies such as Frontex to keep these refugees out. Think of the Magistrate's Castle, or the fortress in *The Tartar Steppe*. And the special Horizon camera that I was exploring is indeed an integral part of this Fortress Europe response, a technology of discipline employed by the military-humanitarian complex formed by our governments, in response to the refugee crisis, to enforce EU borders and keep these people (read barbarians) out.

Without thinking too hard about it, but keeping *Waiting for the Barbarians* very firmly in mind, I launched myself into documenting the refugee crisis, trying to intuitively unpack some of these issues for myself, bringing them to bear on what we encountered, while creating primary testimonial documentary material of these historical events as they were unfolding. I had abandoned the ambition to create a variation of Coetzee's novels with actors and sets, and instead returned to what I knew best. As my grandfather always said, 'Cobbler, stick to your last.' So I was returning to an approach that I knew best, returning to my discipline, but was folding into it many of the themes and questions that had arisen through my initial experiments, attempting to smash the thermal surveillance medium against Coetzee's text. And of course, the refugee crisis was deeply related to that novel, and I hoped that each viewer, in their own way, would feel the same uneasy sense of complicity that I felt while reading *Waiting for the Barbarians*. That was my ambition, to remind and confront the viewer that this camera technology exists and shows how our governments perceive the refugee – so that form of objectification and depersonalization is inbuilt and is very much a part of what my project attempts to reveal. In a way, this is an attempt to get viewers to think through and engage with how the refugee is portrayed and represented by our governments and societies, and to make them feel discomfited by and uneasy with their own complicity.

The erosion of human rights is at the heart of *Incoming*. It is, in its own peculiar way, an attempt to visualize Giorgio Agamben's idea of 'bare life' – the crisis that the figure of the refugee creates in the modern nation state, the rights of the citizen versus the rights of the dispossessed and stateless refugee, and how that crisis has pushed our liberal democracies towards authoritarianism through the various states of emergencies called by certain unscrupulous politicians and their politics of fear. The way that the camera sees, the way it dehumanizes its subject, portraying the individual as a mere biological trace – alludes to, at least to me, this idea of bare life. These are some of the themes that emerged through the process of making *Incoming*.

We were actively trying to work against this camera's original purpose, to reveal the way in which this technology, and our societies, objectify the refugee. But we were also attempting to subvert that objectification by pushing the medium from dehumanization towards a kind of re-humanization, by embracing the camera's potential for very intimate, corporeal portrayal of the body's sweat, breath and blood circulation – to evoke a sense that we are all simply pools of heat, whether refugee or citizen, we are all the same living, breathing humans in spite of where we come from or how we may look. By exploring the camera medium, we found it possesses terrific potential to create an extremely tender new form of portraiture, the likes of which we had never seen before, and which we hoped would more adequately communicate some of these difficult journeys made by refugees that we had witnessed.

Privacy is also a central theme in *Incoming*, as the camera shows heat rather than visible light, making it impossible to identify an individual. Remaining anonymous is often important to refugees for numerous reasons, including the Dublin Convention on EU asylum law, which states that a refugee must claim asylum in the first EU country in which they initially land – meaning that, if you had made it to Germany and German asylum authorities had found documentary evidence of you landing on a Greek island some months before, you would then be sent back to Greece and forced to claim asylum there. *Incoming*'s depersonalized and anonymous visual strategy addresses and attempts to resolve this narrative dilemma.

Last, but not least, we soon realized that the simple metaphor of heat, imaging heat, which we hoped would speak sideways about climate change and global warming – also spoke more practically, even indexically, about the struggle of the refugee. To lose one's home is to lose many things, but primarily one loses warmth. In the Irish language we have a well-known proverb, *Níl aon tinteán mar do thinteán féin*. This is our way of saying 'There's no place like home', but it translates as 'There's no hearth like your own hearth'. The hearth, the floor of the fireplace – the hottest part of the home – is at the centre of the very idea of home.

Refugees leave everything behind, especially the home. They literally leave the heat behind them. And they expose themselves to the elements, the cold sea waves, the winter rain and the snow. Homes are replaced with tents and shelters. People die of exposure.

One night, on the coast of Lesbos, we witnessed hundreds of refugees whose boat had broken into pieces, drowning, hypothermic, struggling for survival under cover of darkness, some of them children, many dying. While we recorded this terrible disaster, our thermal camera was able to portray the index of hypothermia, to accurately read the body heat of these victims of drowning, and reveal the vigorous transferral of life-giving warmth literally rubbed into their bodies from the hands of emergency workers and volunteers under cover of darkness, at a time of night when a normal video camera would have difficulty seeing. The metaphor had been sublimed – the camera had become a thermometer scientifically revealing these individuals' bodily struggle to stay alive, to cling to what James Joyce once called 'good warm life'. I cannot think of a more adequate and effective way of representing and communicating these tragic and very urgent narratives.

So, in the same way that Coetzee borrowed from Buzzati to create something completely new, and Buzzati borrowed from Kafka in the same way, and I am sure Kafka stole from someone else, I was also inspired by, learned from, and borrowed from Coetzee's important novel *Waiting for the Barbarians*, and – through a journey of my own – turned it into something really quite far removed from the original, but which, I feel at least, is deeply related to *Waiting for the Barbarians*. And so I would like to thank you, John, for inspiring and motivating me, and so many of us, to continue to create, and continue to stimulate discussions that allow us to understand the world we live in.

14

Curating Coetzee: From Austin to Adelaide

Jennifer Rutherford

Traverses, a *Festschrift* organized in honour of J. M. Coetzee's seventy-fifth birthday in Adelaide in 2014, was a literary undertaking of a magnitude rarely attempted in Australia: thirty-five keynote speakers drawn from around the globe, public lectures, musical performances, film screenings and an exhibition of archival manuscripts, related artworks and adaptations. The thematic intention was to explore the way Coetzee's works have travelled beyond the literary domain to influence social and political theory, philosophy, ethics, animal rights advocacy, and to explore creative responses to the work (see Figure 14.1).

My role in *Traverses* was principally to curate an exhibition of documents from the newly opened J. M. Coetzee archive. The first exhibition of its kind, we wanted to make available insights from the archive only recently accessible to a small band of Coetzee scholars. During the curatorial process the project grew to include the production of a mobile app featuring twenty filmed interviews, selected manuscripts from the archive, and related critical and contextual materials.

In this chapter I focus on the processes that led from that first intention to curate an exhibition of archival manuscripts to the final production of the *Traverses: J. M. Coetzee and the World Mobile App*. Logistical and materially driven as much as creative or scholarly, this undertaking negotiated the difficult terrain of cultural hierarchies, institutional conflicts and funding pitfalls; in short, everything one might expect of a project that left the generic protocols of traditional literary scholarship behind. The contemporary university is wordy with the rhetoric of 'engagement and impact' but has little understanding of what such translations may entail. My main focus here, however, is the practical and creative insights that arose as we navigated the process of creating an exhibition from the archive and then transformed the exhibition into a virtual platform.

In the early stages of discussing *Traverses*, Nicholas Jose suggested that the Harry Ransom Center at the University of Texas at Austin might be prepared to loan documents from the newly opened Coetzee archives they had acquired in 2011. David Attwell had begun working on these materials and was able to provide a catalogue annotated with suggestions of what items he considered of most interest. Embarking on the project, I set off to Austin with only a few days to navigate my way through the

Figure 14.1 Installing *Traverses: J. M. Coetzee in the World*.
Source: Exhibition – Kerry Packer Civic Gallery, Adelaide, 2014.

collection. I found the archive instantly intriguing. Relying on extensive photographing of materials for later review in Australia and working at great speed with the limited time frame I had available, I caught glimpses of Coetzee's writing in formation, from nascent ideas being worked through in notebooks, to drafts recording meticulous revisions, to first sightings of the literary influences that intrigued the young Coetzee.

Sifting through the many documents meant contending with questions about the purpose of archival research. In prior archival research, I had been engaged with the more traditionally scholarly matters of interpretation and evaluation, testing the veracity of documents, tracing evidence, reading for innuendo, gaps, distortions and so on. Here, the questions facing us were very different. We wanted to provide archival insights to a reading public that would otherwise have no access to this material, and to provide an insight into Coetzee's processes of textual production without contriving overly simple stories. How should we negotiate, for example, the relationship between the complex literary games Coetzee plays with authorship and the way an exhibition of his archive might appear to promise an authentic author? As David Attwell writes of Coetzee:

> Coetzee is always deliberately present and not present in his work. The desire for self-actualisation is a function of needing to bear witness to one's existence in a situation in which one is in danger of culturally disappearing; but the culture in whose terms one wants to be recognised also regards such acts of self-testimony as crude, gauche. The solution is to vacillate: knowing that one can't simply return,

and embrace with conviction the fate of being provincial …, one has to remind the dominant culture that its representations *are* representations. Self consciousness about language is often related to the problem of not-belonging.

(Attwell 2015: 27)

Was it possible to create an exhibition without falling into a crude representational logic? The archive was vast, ranging from the very early notebooks, which were incredibly enticing in the glimpses they gave of a younger apparently less-defended author, and later manuscripts which were suggestive of a tight authorial hand. As Michael Cawood Green suggests in this volume, the archive is 'an actively produced site of creation and reflection rather than a passive source of information' (126–7). How could we avoid constructing the *semblant* of an essential author and at the same time make a compelling exhibition providing insight into that same authorship?

Rita Horanyi and I spent an extended time sifting and selecting the photographed manuscripts in order to develop a curatorial direction able to provide multiple pathways through the archive. After much ado, a request list was finally dispatched to the Harry Ransom Center; in response we received a very different and much truncated list of what they were prepared to loan. We had to begin again, examining the documents the Ransom Center was prepared to make available and pondering how we might build an exhibition without any direct curatorial input into manuscript selection. The ensuing exhibition ended I think, more in the spirit of *Traverses* than our original intention in that it shifted the exhibition's focus to the creation of pathways from the exhibited manuscripts to their contexts and the myriad works they had inspired.

Our decision to exhibit the original documents rather than facsimiles created enormous difficulties from beginning to end, but the auratic quality of the manuscripts and notebooks would have been lost in facsimile. The manuscripts were displayed in magnificent colonial cabinetry on loan from Adelaide's Botanical Museum, selected to visually reference the weight of the colonial history of Australia and South Africa. This decision entailed its own logistical difficulties. The cabinets had been held in storage in a dusty warehouse for many decades and turned out to be as heavy as their intended historical reference. Finally on display, the drafts, notebooks and diaries provided tantalizing glimpses into Coetzee's creative processes as his literature evolved from early works forged in the crucible of apartheid South Africa to the most recent novels written in the very different context of Adelaide. Many visitors were fascinated to see Coetzee the craftsmen at work in these manuscripts, tuning and tightening each sentence till it resonated like timpani. Equally fascinating were the insights into the structural crafting of the works as Coetzee's notebooks and diaries morphed into literary drafts and as the writer hit upon ideas that would be foundational in his literary evolution.

One of the aspects of curating the *Traverses* exhibition that made our persistence worthwhile was the number of school students who came to the exhibition and were enthralled by our story cabinet of J. M. Coetzee reading in a continuous loop.[1] Passages were selected for their likely familiarity to the reading public, enabling audiences to explore the manuscripts and hear Coetzee reading simultaneously. This was one of the few elements of the exhibition that was criticized. Shannon Burns, for example, wrote: 'The recordings of Coetzee reading passages from his novels are magnificent in themselves, but I found it hard to concentrate on the manuscript material with Coetzee's voice echoing around me. Headphones would have been a better option' (Burns 2014). I loved the way the story cabinet provided a rhythmic quality to the exhibition, allowing Coetzee's distinctive prosody to sound, bringing other worlds and other temporalities into continuous play. Such acoustic elements were a key component of the curation. Film adaptations of novels, artworks created in dialogue with Coetzee's oeuvre, and filmed critical discussions created a reverberating context allowing viewers to move between different performances, adaptations and responses to the works.

A sculpture by Berlinde de Bruyckere entitled *to J.M. Coetzee* hung in a central position in the gallery space.[2] We did not include an explanatory note in the exhibition notes to this work but allowed its ambiguity to remain unresolved. *To J.M. Coetzee* was exhibited next to a video interview with philosophers Raimond Gaita and Paul Patton discussing *The Lives of Animals*, creating an auditory drift between this discussion, De Bruyckere's painfully viscid hanging torso, and the many other traces throughout the gallery of Coetzee's interrogation of the denial of dignity and honour to the lives of animals. A cabinet focusing on indignity and shame included a handwritten early draft of *Disgrace*, a handwritten draft of *The Lives of Animals*, Elizabeth Costello's statement and an intriguing flow chart from the University of Cape Town's disciplinary proceedings. A collection of rare first-edition books was on display during the exhibition, culminating in their auction for animal rights organization *Voiceless*.

Another cabinet focused on the early colonial works. Manuscripts on display included early drafts of *Dusklands*, the handwritten first draft of *In the Heart of the Country*, and a related notebook and intriguing casebound notebooks including notes on the characters in *Life & Times of Michael K*. A third cabinet focused on the autobiographical works and included amongst the manuscripts on display, a handwritten draft of Coetzee's Nobel acceptance speech.

Other works throughout the gallery space illuminated the contexts of some of these works. Kai Easton's film *Karoo Country* captured the pared-down world of *In the Heart of the Country* and *Boyhood* through choreographed stills that rediscovered the landscapes of Coetzee's childhood.[3] Artist Lisa Harms created a photographic essay from images drawn from the archive providing evocative and moving snapshots into the visceral, bodily and emotional life of the young Coetzee. Lisa Harms and Adam Jenkins developed a functioning android app for the exhibition which gallery visitors could upload to their Android devices. This contained a bank of interviews with critics and philosophers responding to Coetzee's work, audio recordings of J. M. Coetzee reading key passages of his works and photographs drawn from the archive. Out of the decision to create this android app, the idea grew of creating a mobile digital application (the first of its kind on the work of J. M. Coetzee), in order to transform the exhibition into an enduring work accessible to larger global audiences.

A number of excellent literary apps have been produced that experiment with using digital modalities to extend the domain of literary scholarship. Faber and Faber's *The Waste Land and Other Poems* app is exemplary; a high-cost production with high-end production values well beyond our modest research funds. The opportunity provided by *Traverses* – many of the world's best Coetzee scholars, fellow writers, critical thinkers and activists were gathering in one place alongside a selection of never-before publicly viewed rare archival material, artworks and photographs – seemed too good an opportunity to miss. No doubt we had fallen prey to the kinds of desire archives inspire but we decided to use the occasion of the *Festschrift* to create an accessible multimedia platform that would generate a new form of Coetzee scholarship, extending the field of literary criticism by utilizing virtual modalities.

The logistics were again challenging in that this involved filming as the *Festschrift* unfolded, selecting many of the younger interviewees in medias res in response to the vitality of their presentations. We wanted the app to represent the great minds that have engaged with Coetzee's writing and the voices of young scholars bringing new insights to Coetzee scholarship. Writers, artists and political activists, drawn from around the globe were included and some of those scholars and artists in Adelaide who have been deeply engaged by Coetzee's presence amongst us. Significantly, we did not want to reproduce approaches to criticism that are better served by traditional forms of scholarship. In directing the interviews, I asked interviewees to speak directly to camera on the aspect of Coetzee's work that most engaged them. This form of address was difficult for some in that it required a lively and passionate address rather than the more carefully nuanced statements of written scholarship. In directing these short films my intention was to attempt to achieve footage with the directness and liveliness of good documentary footage; to create the energy that holds an audience to the speaker's word. Given the very careful nature of Coetzee scholarship I trusted the integrity and depth of interviewees' responses but wanted to liberate them from the de-energizing qualities of this same scholarly constraint. The films, each of approximately twenty minutes' duration, were later cut by Lisa Harms into short vignettes of a few minutes' duration and arranged in a continuous scroll to form an interconnecting web of ideas. This scrolling device, designed by Lisa Harms and engineered by Adam Jenkins, is signposted by topic headings which provide immediate shortcuts for the viewer enabling them to find illuminating discussions of key aspects of Coetzee's oeuvre, its contexts, and its philosophical, political and affective dimensions.

Each film vignette is linked in various ways to key critical commentaries, to Coetzee reading related passages, to related adaptations and photographs, and to archival manuscripts. The app includes archival material, a photographic museum, Kai Easton's beautiful stills of Karoo country and selected examples of Coetzee's early photography. Interconnected pathways enable users to make connections between place, autobiography, history, politics, style and memory. I hope that young students just starting to read J. M. Coetzee, or perhaps struggling with their first undergraduate essays, will find a new and very engaging way to encounter the work from hearing the author read, seeing the work in its nascent form, engaging with the scholarship it has inspired and hearing some of the world's great minds talk about the work. The app is designed to be very simple to access, to provide quick interconnecting pathways between topics and various contents. You can download a simple version on Google play or for a more elegant version go to iTunes: https://apps.apple.com/us/app/traverses/id1265691203.

Acknowledgements

The *Traverses: J. M. Coetzee and the World* exhibition and mobile app were a collective effort. I would like to acknowledge Dr Lisa Harms: digital designer, artist and editor, Dr Rita Horanyi: researcher, curatorial assistant and editor, and Adam Jenkins: IT engineer. I would also like to thank the faculty of Education, Arts and Social Sciences (EASS) at the University of South Australia (UniSA), the Harry Ransom Center at the University of Texas at Austin and the Arts Faculty, Adelaide University. Many individuals helped in the project (see *Traverses: J. M. Coetzee in the World a mobile app* for a full credit list). I would particularly like to acknowledge the assistance of J. M. Coetzee, Kai Easton and Hermann Wittenberg.

Notes

1. J.M. COETZEE READS, 2014, installation Lisa Harms and Jennifer Rutherford, recording Phil Van Hout speakers, cabinet, selected readings by J. M. Coetzee from: *Boyhood: Scenes from Provincial Life, Disgrace, Slow Man, Summertime, Elizabeth Costello.*
2. Berlinde de Bruyckere, 2013, *to J.M. Coetzee*, 2012–13, wax, epoxy, iron, cloth, polyester; on loan from Visual Art Collection, the University of Adelaide.
3. Kai Easton (director), 2014, *Karoo Country*, projected video loop (5.48 minutes duration). Music by Abdullah Ibrahim, 'Water from an Ancient Well', used with the kind permission of Abdullah Ibrahim and Sony for the duration of the exhibition.

References

Attwell, David (2015), *J.M. Coetzee and the Life of Writing: Face to Face with Time.* New York: Penguin.

Burns, Shannon (2014), 'Coetzee Colloquium', *Australian Book Review*, December 2014 (367). Available online: https://www.australianbookreview.com.au/abr-online/archive/2014/126-december-2014-no-367/2263-coetzee-colloquium.

Coetzee, J. M. 'J.M. Coetzee Papers'. Austin, TX: Harry Ransom Center.

15

34° South

Kai Easton

This project maps the coordinates brought together in the travelling exhibition, *Scenes from the South*, launched at the Amazwi South African Museum of Literature to mark J. M. Coetzee's eightieth birthday on 9 February 2020.

In this work, I mark the approximate latitudinal line of Coetzee's 'southern spaces'. It happens that in 2002 he emigrated from Cape Town, where he was born in 1940, to Adelaide, South Australia, going east across the Indian Ocean almost in a direct line; it happens that he then began to spend time in Buenos Aires (from about 2014) which, in navigational terms, takes him in the other direction, west across the Atlantic. All three cities are positioned along a latitudinal line that hovers at 34 degrees South.

This is the first series. The seven images were taken in February and March 2020 on the journey back from Makhanda to Cape Town after the exhibition launch, travelling west via Coetzee's maternal lines, and that borderline town of Avontuur which means, in Afrikaans and in Dutch, 'adventure'.

Figure 15.1 Welcome to the Western Cape, Route 62.
Photo Credit: Kai Easton.

Figure 15.2 Entrance to Avontuur.
Photo Credit: Kai Easton.

Figure 15.3 At the gate of Diepkloof.
Photo Credit: Kai Easton.

Figure 15.4 South Africa–Australia T20 International at Newlands.
Photo Credit: Kai Easton.

Figure 15.5 Cape Town Cycle Tour 2020.
Photo Credit: Kai Easton.

Figure 15.6 Kalk Bay fisherman with bicycle.
Photo Credit: Kai Easton.

Figure 15.7 Cape of Good Hope | expect delays.
Photo Credit: Kai Easton.

Index

24 Parker Ave, Buffalo, NY 31
34° South 225

Achterberg, G. 182
Ackerley, C. J. 149, 151, 154–5
Adelaide 12, 219–23, 225
Africa 25
Age of Iron (Coetzee) 11, 24, 59–60, 64–5, 67, 135
Albert, P. 10, 17, 24
Amazwi South African Museum of Literature 1, 12, 19
Amsterdam (McEwan) 103
Anker, E. S. 8
Archive Fever (Derrida) 5, 44, 47, 49, 52
archives 63
   ambivalence 47–50
   ancestral 10
   antecedent 4
   author 7
   conventional understanding of 8
   defined 1
   depth of 7
   extensive 4
   HRC 4
   impersonality of 179–90
   method in 8–9
   negation of 29–40
   as a place of consignation 6
   as place of origin 6
   practice research 117–28
   questions 2
   realism 133–47
   shades of 197–208
   Texas 4
   theory in 8–9
   unfinished status of 7
   Venn diagram 95
   volatile 6–8
   as a work 7
Archive Stories (Burton) 25

arkhē 6
Arts and Humanities Research Council (AHRC) 117–18
Attridge, D. 43–4, 77, 141
Attwell, D. 2–3, 5, 11–12, 19, 31, 43–5, 52, 59–61, 69, 98, 120–8, 126, 134–5, 156, 180–1
Atwood, M. 103
Austerlitz (Sebald) 169
Austin 18, 29, 61, 124–5, 149, 219–23
Australia 117, 216, 219–21, 224
autobiographical-metafictional 5
autobiography 32
autre-biography 7–8
Avenue Road 24
average sentence length 101, 106

Ballard, J. G. 111
Banville, J. 103
Barnes, J. 103
Barney, R. 12
Barry, E. 151
Barthes, R. 32
Baxter Theatre 63
BBC 122
Beatty, P. 103
Beckett, S. 11–12, 18, 100, 149–54
Beckett's Dying Words (Ricks) 150
Ben Engeli, Cid Hamet 173
Biko, S. 11, 80, 84, 88–90
biography
   of Coetzee 19
   compositional 5
   Kannemeyer, J. 3
Black Consciousness 66–7, 80
Blanchot, M. 32, 180
Blind Assassin, The (Atwood) 103
Boehmer, E. 53n.1, 97
bondage 34
Booker Corpus 103
Booker Prize 4, 24, 97, 103

Book Fair 62–3
BOSS *see* Bureau of State Security (BOSS)
Boyhood (Coetzee) 4, 24, 34–5, 44, 47–8, 98, 169
Bragg, M. 122
Breede Valley Municipality 24
Breytenbach, B. 66
Brief History of Seven Killings, A (James) 103
Brink, A. 66
Bryant, J. 134
Bureau of State Security (BOSS) 80
Burton, A. 1, 9, 25
Buzzati, D. 214
Byzantium, C. 82

camera 22
Campground Road 24
Cape Librarian 19, 22
Cape Town 17, 19, 22, 35, 62–3, 81, 85–7
Castle, The (Kafka) 214
Catton, E. 103
Childhood of Jesus, The (Coetzee) 10, 43–6, 49–53, 98, 164
Children's Encyclopaedia (Mee) 22
Clarkson, C. 60, 152, 165, 182
Clingman, S. 61
Coetzee, J. M. 1–13, 17, 100
  academic career 4
  creative process 3
  family photo 23
  fictions 4, 6, 9
  interests 5
  personal life 3
  political commitments 4
  writing career 3, 4, 6–9
Coetzeean 95–7
Coetzee-Booker Corpus 105
Coetzee Bot 110–14
Coetzee Corpus 97–103
Coetzee scholarship 1–3, 8
Cold War 61
Congress of South African Writers (COSAW) 63–4
Conservationist, The (Gordimer) 59
Corpus data 99
Cowper, W. 35

Danta, C. 51, 53
Dean, A. 5, 25
Defoe, D. 179, 182
Derrida, J. 5–8, 43, 47, 50–3
desire 84–8
Diary of a Bad Year (Coetzee) 127
Dichtung (Goethe) 30
Disgrace (Coetzee) 11, 59, 133–47
Dooley, G. 97
Doubling the Point 7
Doyle, R. 103
dramatis personae 89
du Biel, B. 20, 25
Dusklands (Coetzee) 2, 4, 10, 20, 31–2, 43, 45, 78, 98, 134
Dutch East India Company 21
Dwelling in the Archive (Burton) 25

Easton, K. 4, 10, 12–13
Effe, A. 36
Eliot, T. S. 180
Elizabeth Costello (Coetzee) 11–12, 59, 70, 91, 101–5, 124, 133–47, 158, 171, 188, 202–3, 222
English 10–12, 22, 25, 27, 30, 103, 121, 125, 143, 151–3, 184
English Fiction of Samuel Beckett, The (Coetzee) 7, 149, 164
Esposito, R. 181–2, 186
Essential Gesture, The (Gordimer) 66
Evans, N. 9
Evremond Road 24
Exercise Book 22, 25–6
existential humanist 150

Farrant, M. 11–13
Farrell, J. G. 103
Fathers and Sons (Turgenev) 66
Fellowships in the Creative and Performing Arts (FCPA) 128n.2
Felski, R. 8
Fiela se Kind (Matthee) 19
Fitzgerald, P. 103
Fluid Text, The (Bryant) 134
Ford 98
Fordham, F. 134
For the Sake of Silence (Green) 124
France 12
Freud, S. 48–9, 52, 86

fundamentalism 63

Geertsema, J. 97
genetic criticism 9
Genette, G. 36
German 25
Ghosting of Anne Armstrong, The (Green) 127, 129n.7
Giving Offense (Coetzee) 5, 67
God of Small Things, The (Roy) 103
Goethe, J. 179
Gontarski, S. 166
Good Story, The (Coetzee) 5, 169, 199
Gordimer, N. 10–11, 59–64, 66–70
Gramsci, A. 60
Granta (magazine) 18
Green, M. C. 11
Gross, P. 126
Guadalupe Street 18
Guardian, The 97

Harper, G. 118–20, 123
Harry Ransom Center (HRC) 1, 3–5, 12, 13n.1, 18, 21, 25, 29, 61, 70–1n.1, 95, 98, 120–2, 124–5, 149, 164, 199
Harvard 4, 18, 121
Henry IV (Shakespeare) 197
historiography 8
history 2, 5, 10–11, 20, 22, 30, 32–3, 40, 46, 59, 62, 67, 77–8, 81, 126, 136, 180, 183
Hölderlin, F. 179
Hopkins, J. 172
Hornby, N. 98
Houghton Library 4, 18, 121
hypomnesis 51

Incoming (Mosse) 6
Indian Ocean 25
In the Heart of the Country (Coetzee) 2, 35, 78, 80, 135
'Into the Dark Chamber' 11
Irlam, S. 10

James, M. 103
Jerusalem 33
J.M. Coetzee and the Life of Writing (Attwell) 3, 5, 44–5, 78, 120, 122, 123, 134

J. M. Coetzee and the Politics of Style (Zimbler) 98
Johannesburg 11, 22, 62
Johnston, P. 11, 152
Jonker, M. 36
Jose, N. 219
July's People (Gordimer) 59, 61–2

Kafka, F. 214
Kannemeyer, J. 2–3, 19, 24, 121–2, 180
Keats, J. 32, 35, 180–1
Kgosana, P. 79
Kristoboulos, M. 81–2, 86

Langkloof 17–19, 21, 25
language 106–8
Last Orders (Swift) 103
Late Bourgeois World, The (Gordimer) 59
Late Essays (Coetzee) 5
Lawlor, L. 47
Leeu-Gamka 17
Lessness (Beckett) 100
Life & Times of Michael K (Coetzee) 12, 24, 60–2, 69–70, 103
literary authority 163–4
literary thinking 164
Lives and Archives (Dean) 25
Lives of Animals, The (Coetzee) 60, 127, 182
Loefke, S. 21
London 47
London Review of Books (Meaney) 7
Lorimer, H. 122
Luminaries, The (Catton) 103

Makhanda 1, 19
Malan, D. F. 22
mal d'archive 8
Manchester Guardian 35
Mandela, N. 81
marmoreal coldness 33
masterful images 126
Master of Petersburg, The (Coetzee) 32
Matthee, D. 19
Mbembe, A. 25
McEwan, I. 103
Meaney, T. 7
Mee, A. 22

Memory: The Question of Archives (Derrida) 47
'method wars' 8
Meyerskraal 17, 25, 27
Michener Center for Writers 18
Midnight's Children (Rushdie) 103
Milford Road 24
Mosca, V. 10
Moses (Freud) 48–9
Mosse, R. 6
Mowbray Nursing Home 17
Musil, R. 85
Muslim communities 63
Mutloatse, M. 66

Nachlass 6
Namaqualand 20
narrative 44
National English Literary Museum 19; *see also* Amazwi South African Museum of Literature
Nazi Germany 82
negative capability 32, 35
Neuman, J. 97
Newby, P. H. 103
New York 30–1
New York Review of Books (Gordimer) 60
New York Times 97
Ng, L. 97
Nobel Prize 4, 59, 98
None to Accompany Me (Gordimer) 59
Norway 156
Notebooks 44, 48

Offshore (Fitzgerald) 103
Outeniqua Mountains 19

Paddy Clarke Ha Ha Ha (Doyle) 103, 105
paternal authority 53
Peri Bathous 37
Peripatetic (Thelwall) 185
Philosophical Society 172
Photographs from Boyhood (Coetzee) 10
Poe, E. A. 30
poetic sovereignty 197–208
polymorphous perverse 86
Popper, K. 166
Press Council 88

Rand Daily Mail (Sparks) 88
Reading and Responsibility (Attridge) 43
realism 133–47, 170–4
Refiguring the Archive (Hamilton) 25
Research Grants Practice Led and Applied (RGPLA) 128n.2
revolution 78–80
Richardson, S. 179
Ricks, C. 150–1
Ricoeur, P. 8
Robben Island 81
Robinson Crusoe (Defoe) 22, 182
Rosebank Junior School 22
Rousseau, Jean-Jacques 179
Roy, A. 103
Rushdie, S. 63, 67, 103

Samolsky, R. 12
Satanic Verses, The (Rushdie) 63
Scenes from Provincial Life (Coetzee) 2, 17, 23–4, 29–30, 35, 38–9, 98, 133
Scenes from the South 19
School of Advanced Study 13
Sea, The (Banville) 103
Sebald, W. G. 169
Second World War 12, 156
self-archiving 120, 123
Sellout, The (Beatty) 103, 105
semantic contexts 108–9
Sense of an Ending, The (Barnes) 103
Shakespeare, W. 197
Sheehan, P. 97
Siege of Krishnapur, The (Farrell) 103
sketch difference
    for black/white 110
    for good/bad 110
    for woman/man 109
sketch engine's model, 115n.6
Smuts, J. 28
Snyman, H. 89
Something to Answer For (Newby) 103
South Africa 1–2, 11, 31, 33–6, 38–9, 45, 60–1, 63–4, 67, 77–80, 85, 119, 124, 135
South African National Archives 30
spareness 97–103
spare tradition 98
Sparks, A. 88

Staley, T. F. 98
State University in Buffalo 30
Stewart, P. 11–12
St John Street 18
Stoler, A. L. 9
Summertime (Coetzee) 1–2, 5, 7, 10–11, 29–40, 44–6, 48–53, 98, 169
Sunday Times 35
Swift, G. 103
Swift, J. 179, 182

Tartar Steppe, The (Buzzati) 214, 216
teleological reconstruction 134
Texas 2, 4, 7, 11, 18, 24, 29, 61, 121, 164
text length 100–3
Thelwall, J. 183–90
Third Person: Politics of Life and Philosophy of the Impersonal (Esposito) 181
Traverses 219–23
truer realism 170–4
Turgenev, I. 66–7
Two Screenplays (Wittenberg) 214

UK Research Excellence Framework (REF) 11, 117
United States 45
University of Cape Town (UCT) 18, 24, 63, 121, 149, 172
University of London 13
University of Texas 1, 3, 11, 18, 124
US Census Bureau 111

Van Beulen, A. J. 21
Van der Vlies, A. 10–11
Venn diagram 95
Victoria West 17
volatile archives 6–8
Von Kleist, H. 179
Vorlass 6

Wahrheit (Goethe) 30
Waiting for the Barbarians (Coetzee) 2, 6, 11, 77–92, 127, 135, 213–18
Weekly Mail 62–4
Wehmeyer, P. 19, 21
Wehmeyer, V. 17, 20
Wehmeyer Street 18
White Writing (Coetzee) 5
Willemse, H. 66
Willowmore 10, 17–19, 27
Wilm, J. 6, 51, 69
Wilmer, S. E. 166
Wittenberg, H. 10–11, 214

Yerushalmi, Y. 48–9
Youth (Coetzee) 12, 44, 47–8, 98, 169

Zille, H. 88–9
Zimbler, J. 98
Zipf-Mandelbrot law 100
Zondagh, J. 19

www.ingramcontent.com/pod-product-compliance
Lightning Source LLC
Chambersburg PA
CBHW072146290426
44111CB00012B/1989